Giggs
The Autobiography

RYAN GIGGS
with
JOE LOVEJOY

MICHAEL JOSEPH
an imprint of
PENGUIN BOOKS

MICHAEL JOSEPH

Published by the Penguin Group

Penguin Books Ltd, 80 Strand, London WC2R ORL, England

Penguin Group (USA) Inc., 375 Hudson Street, New York, New York 10014, USA

Penguin Group (Canada), 90 Eglinton Avenue East, Suite 700, Toronto, Ontario, Canada M4P 2Y3

(a division of Pearson Penguin Canada Inc.)

Penguin Ireland, 25 St Stephen's Green, Dublin 2, Ireland

(a division of Penguin Books Ltd)

Penguin Group (Australia), 250 Camberwell Road,

Camberwell, Victoria 3124, Australia (a division of Pearson Australia Group Pty Ltd)

Penguin Books India Pvt Ltd, 11 Community Centre,

Panchsheel Park, New Delhi – 110 017, India

Penguin Group (NZ), cnr Airborne and Rosedale Roads, Albany,

Auckland 1310, New Zealand (a division of Pearson New Zealand Ltd)

Penguin Books (South Africa) (Pty) Ltd, 24 Sturdee Avenue,

Rosebank 2196, South Africa

Penguin Books Ltd, Registered Offices: 80 Strand, London WC2R ORL, England

www.penguin.com

First published 2005

1

Set in 13.5/16 pt PostScript Monotype Garamond
Typeset by Rowland Phototypesetting Ltd, Bury St Edmunds, Suffolk
Printed in England by Clays Ltd, St Ives plc

A CIP catalogue record for this book is available from the British Library

Hardback ISBN 0–718–14843–6
Trade paperback ISBN 0–718–14870–3

To Stacey and Libby

Contents

List of Illustrations   ix

Acknowledgements   xv

Punchdrunk!   1

Cardiff Born   4

Opportunity Knocks   16

Early Days   26

Lift-off   38

Paradise   55

The Family   67

Double Bubble   74

The George Best Treatment   93

Welsh Wails   100

Fergie's Fledglings   107

'You Don't Win Anything
with Kids'   122

New Faces   132

Gunned Down   146

Wales Captain   155

History Is Made   173

'Easy, Easy'   199

Fergie's Finest?   210

Arsenal at the Double   220

That's More Like It   235

Fatherhood   249

Not Our Year   254

Russian Revolution   272

The Future   305

List of Illustrations

First Section

Me as a baby

And as a toddler with my Aunt Hayley

At Bristol Zoo with my Nan, my mum's mother

With Hayley and Nan

And me sporting another classic T-shirt design

Growing up

Me and my brother Rhodri

My dad, Danny Wilson, playing rugby for Cardiff in 1976 (Empics/S&G/Alpha)

Playing for Deans, my schoolboy club side

For Salford Under-11s

And Salford Boys Under-15s at the English Schools Trophy final in 1989 (Empics/Neal Simpson)

With Nan in Cardiff, wearing an England Schoolboys blazer

The England captain

Playing for England Under-15s (Action Images)

My first start for United against Manchester City in 1991 (Action Images)

In the players' lounge at Old Trafford with my cousin Calum

The Rumbelows Cup Final against Nottingham Forest in

1992. The first time I made Roy Keane's acquaintance (Empics/Neal Simpson)

United win the league for the first time in twenty-six years in 1993 (Professional Sport)

The gaffer with the trophy (Empics/Neal Simpson)

Celebrating with Incey again

With Eric – the best player I've played with (Empics/PA/Malcolm Croft)

Second Section

My first big sponsorship deal with Reebok (Action Images)

Meeting Nelson Mandela in South Africa (Empics/Phil O'Brien)

Robbo bids us farewell in 1994 (Empics/Phil O'Brien)

Completing the double in 1994 (Empics/PA/John Stillwell)

With Neville Southall (Empics/Neal Simpson)

Celebrating the 1996 title with Roy Keane (Empics/PA/Rui Vieira)

With Dani Behr (Rex Features/News Group)

And Davinia Taylor (Mirrorpix)

Playing the role of roadside flower-seller for a Reebok ad campaign (Getty Images/Alex Livesey)

A Champions League classic. Celebrating a goal in United's 1998 3–3 thriller against Barca (Getty Images/Clive Brunskill)

My favourite goal – in the 1999 FA Cup final against Arsenal (Action Images/Darren Walsh; Empics/Michael Steele; Empics/PA/David Jones; Getty Images/Manchester United/John Peters; Action Images)

The treble is on. Celebrating the championship in 1999 (Action Images)

And afterwards in the dressing room with Teddy, Becks, my half-sister Bethany and Becks's son Brooklyn

Celebrating the double with the 1999 FA Cup win against Newcastle (Empics/PA/Owen Humphreys)

With Mum and the silverware so far

Harry Swales, my agent, and I hold the cup

The treble! (Empics/Michael Steele; Empics/Michael Steele; Empics/Phil O'Brien)

Third Section

The Welsh managers: Terry Yorath, Bobby Gould, John Toshack and Mark Hughes (Empics/Phil O'Brien; Action Images/Tony O'Brien; Empics/PA/Nick Potts; Wales News Service)

Playing for Wales in 1993 (Empics/Paul Marriott)

Beating Germany in 2002 (Action Images/Alex Morton)

Beating Italy in the Euro 2004 qualifiers (Action Images/Darren Walsh)

Celebrating our fourth goal against Azerbaijan in a Euro 2004 qualifier at the Millennium Stadium (Getty Images/David Cannon)

A rare run-in with the ref during a tense game against the Russians in Moscow (Getty Images/AFP/Mladen Antonov)

The Russians celebrate during the return leg (Empics/PA/Nick Potts)

Wales miss out again (Getty Images/Ross Kinnaird)

A strange feeling – playing against Nev and Becks at Old Trafford (Wales News Service)

Time off during the FIFA World Cup Championships in Rio, January 2000 (Empics/PA/Phil Noble)

In action against Southampton (Action Images/John Sibley)

25 February 2001 (Action Images/Darren Walsh)

United clinch their seventh title in nine seasons with a win against Coventry (Empics/Neil Simpson)

Thanking the supporters with my sister Bethany, at my testimonial against Celtic in 2001 (Action Images)

Testimonial team photo (*The Sun*/ Mark Robinson)

Fourth Section

My family. Aunt Stacey, Mum, Grandad, me, Nan and Aunt Hayley

With Rhodri and Bethany

With Mum, Rhodri and the Premiership trophy

With Stacey and our daughter Libby

With Libby

The Gaffer with his Number Two, Carlos Queiroz, in 2002 (Action Images/Darren Walsh)

Equalizing against Chelsea at Stamford Bridge in 2002 (Getty Images/Manchester United/Matthew Peters)

Eight titles, eight bottles (Professional Sport)

Winning the title for the eighth time in 2003 (Empics/Mike Egerton)

Tempers fray against Arsenal (Empics/Neal Simpson)

Playing Rangers at Ibrox in the 2003 Champions League (Empics/Neal Simpson)

In Red Square for Wales's Euro 2004 qualifier against Russia (Empics/PA/Rebecca Naden)

Battling against José Mourinho's FC Porto team in the 2003–4 Champions League (Empics/PA/Martin Rickett)

Winning the 2004 FA Cup final to finish the season on a high (Getty Images/Manchester United/John Peters)

Wayne Rooney scores his first goal for United (Action Images/Darren Walsh)

In full flight (Empics)

Front endpaper: Carling Cup semi-final, Chelsea v Manchester United, 26 January 2005 (Corbis/Ian Hodgson/Reuters)

Back endpaper: Ryan's best ever goal, FA Cup semi-final v Arsenal, 14 April 1999 (Getty Images/Sean Botterill)

Acknowledgements

I would like to thank everybody who has helped me to tell my story. The project was conceived by my 'ghost', Joe Lovejoy of the *Sunday Times*, and my agent, Harry Swales, without whom the tale would not have been told. My gratitude goes to both. Rowland White, at Penguin, was an enthusiastic, encouraging editor and a consummate professional. Much of the technical work was done by John Southall, in Wales, who ensured that the book was delivered on time. Finally, as ever, thanks to Stacey and Mum, for their love and support, and to Tony Camilleri, who reckons he taught me how to bend it like Beckham!

Punchdrunk!

Nobody could accuse me of not punching my weight the night Manchester United won the European Cup – the night really was a knockout. After what had been the most dramatic finale in the tournament's long history, the post-match party, like the game, went the distance and I ended up in a fight with the chairman's son.

After the final against Bayern Munich, which we won with two goals in added time, the players were on such a high that we seemed to linger outside the Nou Camp for hours, talking to anybody who wanted to listen. It was as if we didn't want to lose the moment – didn't want to leave the scene of our greatest triumph. We had to in the end, of course, and at the party afterwards, in the Grand Salon of the Hotel Arts in Barcelona, we were allowed three guests each. I took my mum, my auntie and my girlfriend, Emma. I should have had my brother, Rhodri – he would have been handy to have around, given what happened. It was already gone two o'clock in the morning by the time we finally got there, but the place was heaving. Everybody got stuck into the drink and was having a good time right away. I was soon the worse for wear. And that ended up in an argument that had fists flying.

It was getting very late, about six o'clock in the morning, and we were all bladdered, when one of the guests, a cabaret act from Manchester called Foo Foo Lamarr (his real name was Frank), came on. He was a friend of my mum's. He was well known in Manchester and used to drive a Rolls-Royce which everybody in town recognized. His funeral was huge and made all the papers when he died a couple of years ago. Anyway, the music had finished by this time, and he was encouraged with dramatic cheers to get up on stage and do a bit of his stand-up act. So he did a few gags, and suddenly we could hear this bloke behind us shouting and mocking, my mum wasn't having it and turned round and told him to behave, then Nicky Butt's mum also jumped to Frank's defence. The heckler wouldn't let it go and had a go back at my mum. I wasn't having that. Not someone abusing my mum. I'd had more than a few drinks, so I went berserk, but by now I was a little the worse for wear and I couldn't see straight, let alone fight, so when I waded in and tried to punch him, I hit a chair. He shot back and took a swing at me, and suddenly we were rolling on the floor, punching each other, with 'Butty' joining in. A crowd of blokes, teammates among them, came over and pulled us apart. There was a messy pause, then I went for him again. This time, though, when somebody grabbed me violently from behind, they got me around the face and my nose, which I'd broken playing against Inter Milan in March, went again. That ended it. The manager's son, Darren Ferguson, who played for Wrexham, threw out the loud-mouthed punter I'd been scrapping with. At least I *thought* he was an ordinary punter. He turned out to be James Edwards, son of United's chairman, Martin.

To make matters worse, I had a sore head and I wasn't going to be popular with the gaffer when I was late for the team coach in the morning. He'd heard about the incident, of course, and asked me what had happened. I was expecting the worst. Then I told him who I'd been fighting with and he seemed surprised: 'Oh it was him, was it?' he said. 'Don't worry, son.' No more was said, except that Martin Edwards himself apologized to my mum and to Frank for his son's behaviour!

I had a fight with the chairman's son, ended up with a broken nose, my clothes covered in blood and as bad a hangover as I've ever had. The night we won the European Cup is one I'm not likely to forget.

Cardiff Born

They tell me my arrival coincided with George Best walking out on Manchester United for the last time. I was born on 29 November 1973 at St David's hospital, Cardiff. The old building is no longer there but its name lives on in a new hospital which opened in 2002. Mum was seventeen when she had me, very young, so she had to go back to work afterwards while I stayed with her parents. She worked as a children's nurse and as a cook in a café in the docks. That part of Cardiff was very different then, before the Bay development. It was a rough area. A lot of my dad's family were from Butetown, in the docks, and the house we lived in was in Ely, which was on the wrong side of the tracks, too.

My earliest memories are of staying at my grandparents' house – my mum Lynne's parents, that is. I spent a lot of time with both sets of grandparents, but mostly with Mum's side of the family. My mum had a couple of jobs, to make ends meet, but my parents couldn't afford a house at first, so I grew up with my grandparents in an area of Cardiff called Pentrebane. The two sets of grandparents lived a twenty-minute walk away from each other, either side of the Ely river. My dad's parents, Danny and Winnie, were black, the children of merchant seamen who came from Sierra Leone and settled in Tiger Bay, where Shirley Bassey comes from, in the 1920s. Probably because it has been a major port in its time, Cardiff is a multi-racial city.

My dad, Danny Wilson, played rugby union for Cardiff and Newport. He played at half-back with Gareth Edwards before Gareth Davies, of Wales and British Lions fame, came along. Mum and Dad had me very young – they were both seventeen – and I'm sure that put an even greater strain on their relationship. They never married, and I'm not surprised. It was a fiery relationship which would occasionally spill over into real unpleasantness. No one should have to endure that and she deserved better. When I came along he was into his rugby and didn't have time for much else, so Mum managed to hold down two jobs and relied on her parents to babysit me all day. Three years later my brother, Rhodri, was born, so by the time they were twenty or twenty-one they had two kids. It was not the easiest of starts, and there often seemed to be an uneasy atmosphere in the home. There were many arguments, and too many of them became physical. Sometimes in front of me and Rhodri, and I hated it. After one particularly bad fight, when I was nearly three, my father was arrested, and my mum ordered him to leave the house. Obviously it was a bad time, but I grew up with it and accepted it as normal because I didn't know any different. It was a view of family life that can't have done me any good. It definitely had an effect on me. The trips I had to my grandparents were a relief from all the rows, and were like a little holiday. Despite his bullying, aggressive nature, I have to admit that at one time I did look up to my dad. Perhaps that's always the way. He was an impressive-looking man because of the way he carried himself. He had that chest-out Cantona strut and was naturally confident, both on the rugby pitch and off it, so I had respect for him, but I was always a 'mummy's boy'. It wasn't until we moved to Manchester that I realized the full extent of the rotten life my dad gave her. He was a real rogue, and a ladies' man.

Obviously I knew he was good at rugby, but I was so

young that I didn't take much notice. I remember going to see him play once, at the Arms Park – not the big ground where they played the internationals but the smaller club ground next to it. I can also remember watching a cousin of mine, on my dad's side, playing in an under-16s tournament on the main ground as a curtain-raiser to a big game. We sat right at the top of the stand, miles away from the action, and couldn't see much. It wasn't until we moved to Manchester, when I was seven, that I really grasped that my father was a top-flight rugby player, and by then he had switched to rugby league, with Swinton.

And while Dad may have been a rugby player, you don't play rugby in the street when you're five or six, not even in Cardiff. I suppose it must seem strange for a rugby player's son, but I don't recall having a rugby ball at home, and the replica kit I wore was the Welsh football team's yellow shirt, not the red rugby one. Later on I played rugby, but as a toddler it was all football. Of course, I wasn't living in the Valleys, which is the real rugby stronghold. Cardiff is more of a football city. And although Cardiff City haven't been in the top division for over forty years, they have always drawn bigger crowds than Cardiff RFC.

Cardiff City was the first football club I was interested in because my mum was a City fan. She used to go all the time, with my granddad. She was a big admirer of John Toshack, who played for Cardiff before going on to make his name with Liverpool. At one game she even ran on to the pitch at Ninian Park to give him a birthday present. I only found out about that recently, after he'd taken the Wales manager's job. He was massive in Cardiff at that time and Mum thought the sun shone out of his backside. I didn't have any real heroes. The only person I looked up to was my dad.

I went to Hwyell Dda primary school in Ely, just a short walk down the road from home – more or less at the bottom of our street. The one thing that sticks in my mind about that was singing the national anthem, 'Mae Hen Wlad Fy Nhadau' ('Land of My Fathers') before assembly every day. It didn't do much for my Welsh-language skills, but it was good practice for later!

I never played organized football back then when I was living in Cardiff, but my mum and her parents say I used to drive them mad just kicking a ball against the wall all day. The house next door was on a corner, and there was a largish grassy area at the side of it. Not much more than a scrap of waste ground, I used to play there all the time with the other kids from the area whenever I could. I knew I was better than everyone else. It never really struck me as unusual though – certainly not as a gift, or anything like that. I could just do things with the ball more easily than the others. And inevitably, when it came to picking teams, I was always the first to be chosen. Either that or they said it wasn't fair and stuck me in goal!

My dad played a bit with us when we were growing up, but it was more my mum's parents who encouraged my football. People tell me I inherited some of my dad's physical characteristics. He had pace, and he was obviously a good ball player, but balance was his main asset, as it is mine, so, if for nothing else, I'm grateful to him for passing that on, at least.

When I was seven, my dad came home one day and said he'd had this great offer to go and play rugby league for Swinton. There was a lot of money involved, he told us, and he couldn't say no. I know Mum didn't want to go, and leave the protective support she had from her parents, and I hated the idea. I didn't want to leave Cardiff and my mates. I was only a kid and I couldn't understand why we had to move so far from home. I knew I was going to miss my grandparents badly, especially on my mum's side. But we had no choice. Dad's mind was made up.

Racism tends not to be a major issue in Cardiff, and it was certainly not a problem for me. That came later, when we moved to Manchester. In Cardiff I tended to experience it in reverse! Down in the docks my dad had four sisters, so I had a lot of black cousins, and they used to take the piss out of me for being the only one who was white. Even my brother, Rhodri, is darker-skinned than me. I can remember one of my cousins saying, 'We can tell he's got black in him because he's got big lips and a big nose.' 'Thank you very much,' I thought. 'That's lovely!' She was only having a laugh, but at the age of six or seven, you want to blend in, not be regarded as different in any way. I got it from both sides. But stick from my own family for looking white is one thing, proper racial abuse when I came to Manchester for having a black dad was quite another.

It didn't happen straight away though and, despite the piss-taking we still made friends locally, me and my brother, nearly as soon as we got there.

The club house Swinton had got for my dad was on the corner, with an apple tree in the garden. The kids from the area were all riding around on their bikes in the road outside and we started throwing apples at them – this was on our first day. They threw them back and it turned into something like a snowball fight. There were squashed apples all over the road outside, where they'd run over them with their bikes. We got a right battering off my dad when he came home and saw the mess. He hit the roof – it was our first day! He made us scrape it all up, but we'd made some friends out of it, so we figured it was worth it.

I went to Grosvenor Road school, in Swinton. I got the micky taken at first but I lost my accent so quickly that I started to feel at home there soon.

It helped, of course, that I had a father who was a big celebrity locally. As soon as we got up there a press photographer came to take a family photo, which was in the local papers. We had the picture, framed, on the wall. Me and my brother were in waistcoats, collars and ties. We were usually a right pair of scruffs. It barely looked like us!

We used to go and watch my dad play for Swinton, home and away. He was some player, a real local hero. After a while, though, having a famous father who was black proved to be a double-edged sword. I was doing well at sport, too, and I think jealousy was behind the racism I encountered. To look at me, you wouldn't think of calling me black, but because he played rugby, and had his picture in the papers all the time, the kids at school knew my dad was black, and they would wind me up and call me all sorts. It came from the older boys, not the lads in my class, where I was pretty popular. But kids two years older would give it 'nigger' and stuff like that. My dad was famous locally and I was good at sport, and some of the nonentities who didn't have those advantages got stuck into me out of envy. With Rhodri, you can tell he comes from a mixed race background, but in my case there's no way anyone could have known, but for the pictures of my dad that appeared in the papers. Experiencing racism for the first time did come as a bit of a shock. There was none of it when I was growing up in Cardiff. In the part of Manchester we moved to, there were two black kids in the whole school, and not even that at certain stages. They weren't used to it, and kids always pick on anybody who is different from the rest. Obviously I didn't like being called a 'nigger', but I wasn't like Rhodri, I didn't get into fights over it. I thought the best way to handle it was to treat it with contempt and ignore it.

Before long I was also encouraged to play rugby league, as well as football. For quite a while nobody could tell which I'd be better at. I played rugby all the way through high school, from ten to fourteen, by which time I was playing for Lancashire Boys. They more or less told me I'd play for Great Britain if I stuck at it. For Salford Boys and a local team called Langworthy at weekends I played stand-off, like Dad. But for Lancashire, who had top young players from Wigan and St Helens, I was out on the wing and also the goal kicker. It's hard to believe now, but for a year I played four games every weekend: Salford Boys football on Saturday mornings, Salford Boys rugby in the afternoon, Langworthy rugby league on Sunday morning and football for a Sunday League team called Dean's FC in the afternoon.

Strangely enough, I found rugby much easier, and at the time I was probably better at that than I was at football. I'd watched my dad for four or five years and absorbed a lot. I knew everything about the game and especially about playing stand-off. When I played for Salford, we'd always get hammered by the top teams, the Wigans and St Helens! But I was usually satisfied that I was making an impact personally. It was something at least. Salford was my district, Langworthy my club. And with Langworthy, a semi-professional outfit, it was very different. We were the best team in the area and we'd beat everyone, and it was an addictive feeling.

At school they played football and rugby. The PE teacher, Robert Mason – I still see him today – was keener on rugby, even though all the lads at the school preferred to play football. He encouraged me to play rugby more than my dad. There was a pitch called Rabbit Hills, at the bottom of our street in Swinton. But while Dad would come to some of the games, he'd never really say much. There was no 'I liked that,' or 'You should have done this.' He kept his opinions to himself. Although, as I said, I found rugby easier, that was really only true until I was thirteen. The year after that, size came into it. The other players were getting bigger and better, and I was no longer even the best in my own team. Despite that, in my trial for Lancashire I was the only player from Salford to get picked. The others were the cream of the crop from the top clubs though, a lot of them from St Helens and Wigan, which is where we had the trial. We were in the changing room, getting ready, and all the other lads knew each other – born rugby players from big rugby backgrounds. You could tell they were big-time from the gear they all had. I had none of that. I was there playing in my football kit. As I got changed, I looked around and thought to myself, 'I don't really belong here.' Then when we got out on the pitch this giant of a lad steamed in with a textbook tackle that nearly broke me in half. It told me in no uncertain terms that I was in with the big boys now.

I held my own well enough, and I was still the quickest, but they were all so much stronger. From the way they spoke, you could tell they were in it for real, not just playing at it, as I felt I was. Rugby was their life. I went on to play one game for Lancashire, against Cumbria away, at Barrow I think it was, but that was it. I knew I was going to have to make a choice between rugby and football. While I had a big interest in rugby league – and still do – and even liked rugby union, enjoying the old Five Nations and following Jonathan Davies before (and after) he switched codes, it was clear to me that football was where my heart was.

At school I did well until I was about eleven, when football and girls took over. My first girlfriend was called Nadia; she was a year younger than me. Nadia Applegate. I was eleven and she was ten, she lived close by and I used to see her after school. It was all very innocent, and didn't last long, but after that schoolwork definitely took third place in my priorities. I'd been in the top set at primary school and again in my first year at high school, but then it was all downhill. I was quite good at history and geography, but hated English and maths. I never learned Welsh because they didn't teach it at primary school in those days, and I'd moved to Manchester by the time I would have started it. Coming from Cardiff, where it has never been that popular, my family didn't speak Welsh, and much as I'd love to be able to speak my country's language, I've never found the time and motivation to give it a go. The national anthem is my limit!

It was playing for Dean's, one of the two big Sunday League teams in the Salford area, that first got me noticed as a footballer. It was a football club and a youth club combined, and they shared our school field. The manager was a guy called Dennis Schofield, a great bloke – a real football man who is still going strong now. He looked to be about 100 when I was ten, but if you see him today he's still as fit as a fiddle.

Dennis was a milkman, but how he ever got his round done is a mystery. He couldn't pass any sort of football game without stopping to watch. Anyway, the school had a match, I was on the left wing, and Dennis, who was passing, parked his milk float next to the pitch to have a look. I must have played well that day because at the end he walked across to talk to me. I was waiting for my mum to pick me up when he introduced himself. 'I'm Dennis. I run a good football team called Dean's and I want you to join us.' He gave us the details and I gave him our address. 'Right,' he said, 'we'll pick you up before the game and drop you off at home afterwards. There's a game on Sunday, do you want to play?', and I did. There was no messing. He must have been sure too, because I didn't even have to train with them first.

When I turned up for that first game I knew none of the other lads. As I was getting changed, one of them said: 'You're Danny Wilson's son, aren't you?' I told him I was and he said, 'I go and watch Swinton, he's a great player.' That lad, Simon Platt, became one of my closest friends. He was my best mate for five or six years. On the other side of me in the changing room was Stuart Grimshaw, who is my best friend now. That was the first time I met him as well. Simon, who was a nutter, played at left-back and Stuart was centre midfield. They already knew each other as they went to the same school. Stuart was the lad who had everything: the best shinpads, the best boots, a perm in his hair, the lot. He says he did a milk round to pay for it all, but I think his parents had a bit more money than the other mums and dads.

In my first game we played Stretford Victoria, the top team in the area, and got hammered 9–0, but somehow I was still named man of the match! It was no compensation. I came off gutted, I'd only played for the school before and we never lost, let alone got a stuffing like that. I'm going, 'Nine-nil, I don't believe it,' and everybody is saying, 'Can you come next week? Please, you've got to.' I said, 'I'll come if you want, but do you really think it's worth it?' All the parents were coming up to Mum, telling her how well I'd done. I didn't dare say what I really thought. I spent the whole game stood on the left wing, waiting for the ball which never seemed to come, but I must have done something, I suppose, otherwise they wouldn't have made such a fuss. It was hard to believe after the result that day, but we finished second in the league, behind the Vics. We won most of our games, did get better, and eventually we won the league. In the end I played for Dean's right through the age groups, from ten until I was fourteen.

Dennis, who managed our team, and a few others as well, was a scout for Manchester City, and he took three of us to train with them. There was me, my mate Stuart Grimshaw and a lad called Darren Walsh, whose dad used to give us a lift. We had to be at City's old Platt Lane training ground for five o'clock and train for an hour on the astroturf. Right from day one I hated it, absolutely hated it. Even though I was with a couple of my mates I never enjoyed myself, and it got so bad that I used to dread Thursdays, which was our training night. City did their best, to be fair. One of their top scouts, Eric Mullender, was very good to me. He would get me boots and tracksuits, and he treated me a little bit differently to everybody else, really looked after me, but it was no good. Right from the off I didn't take to City. I'd rather have gone out with my mates than train with them. Darren Walsh's dad would give me a lift, and it was a five-minute walk from my house to the pick-up point on the main road. I used to wait at the bus stop for him hoping that he wouldn't show up, but he always did.

It wasn't that City were hard on me, or not nice people. I just didn't take to them, I'm not sure why. The other kids there were fine, good lads, and there were some decent players there too. I remember Adie Mike, who went on to play for the England youth team with me, and John Foster, who played for City a couple of times.

But there was no getting round it. By that stage I was a United supporter, and that was one of the reasons I didn't like it with the other lot. My mum's mum was a mad United fan, she loved George Best, and it was her who first insisted that I become a Red. At City I used to wear a red top for training sometimes and they'd make me take it off. I wasn't trying to wind them up or show my true colours. I only had a couple of tops and one of them was red, but they wouldn't have it. It wasn't a United one, just red, but maybe I knew where my future lay even then.

Opportunity Knocks

The first Manchester United player I idolized was Mickey Thomas, who was at Old Trafford from 1978 to 1981. That was basically because Mickey was Welsh and left-footed, like me. He was playing when my dad took me to Old Trafford for the first time, when I was eight. I was lucky to catch him because the trip was a rarity. It was another five years before I started going with any regularity. I was thirteen. And by then, I was smitten.

It's strange sometimes how your breaks happen in football. I was playing for Dean's and training with City and everybody just assumed that I'd be joining them when I left school. Everybody but me, that is. I never saw it that way. United were my team, and it was a local newsagent who helped to shape my life. Until you were fourteen, you couldn't commit yourself to any club, so City never had a proper claim on me, and I was lucky that this newsagent, Harold Wood, who was a steward at Old Trafford, came to watch Dean's every week, with his daughter, Gaynor. He'd been telling United about me, but they never sent anyone down to have a look. He wasn't to be put off, though. Finally, God bless him, Harold went straight to the top and managed to speak to Alex Ferguson himself. 'He's with City at the moment,' Harold told him, 'and if you lose him you'll regret it.' The 'gaffer' sent someone to watch me play for Dean's. Things happened quickly after that and United offered me a trial over Christmas.

People make this big thing now about how I was going

to join City, but it's not the case. I played only one game for them, when I was thirteen. I was never committed to them in any way. To be perfectly honest I knew I was never going to join them. The schoolboy system was very different then, nowhere near as organized as it is now. Everything was quite vague – at least it seemed like that at the time. It wasn't just City who'd shown an interest either. I'd played at Anfield for Salford Boys and Liverpool were interested, but that was never going to happen, they were the last club a United fan wanted to join, and Preston were keen, too. When I went there for a trial on the astroturf, I enjoyed it much more than I had ever done at City. In the end, it came down to a choice between four clubs: United, Preston, City and Bury, who were also in the frame. That was my order of preference, and if I had anything to do with it it was always going to be United.

My trial with United was for a week over Christmas 1986, when I was thirteen, but by the time I got there, I think Alex Ferguson had already made up his mind. Before that, Salford Boys had played a United eleven, and I was captain. Nick Barmby was playing for United along with a lad called Raphael Burke, who was the best player in the area at that age. I was an apprentice with him at United later, and I was surprised that he never made it. He was a right-winger, one of those kids who is unbelievable at fourteen, but doesn't train on. As we played, Alex Ferguson was watching from an office window. I scored a hat-trick, and after that, there was no real need for a trial, I just went straight to the halls of residence, at the university, with the United lads I'd just played against, and there was no looking back. I loved the training under Brian Kidd, who was in charge of youth development. The chief scout was Joe Brown, so they were the people I was dealing with. I still went for the trial but I think my performance for Salford Boys probably made up their minds about me there and then. On my fourteenth birthday, Alex Ferguson and Joe Brown came to my mum's house (Dad had gone by then) and knocked on the door. I'd been playing for them as a schoolboy, and there was never much doubt that I was going to sign. They were exciting times for the family. Money was being offered for me to sign for other clubs, and I was told that one club were talking about £50,000, which was a fortune to us at the time. It wasn't just money either. I was amazed at the incentives being bandied about to tempt me to sign. Another club offered me a supply of boots and trainers, and were also prepared to promise me an apprenticeship and one year as a fully fledged professional, which was quite a big deal to a fourteen-year-old schoolboy. I did *think* about that, but deep down I was always going to sign for United, come what may. All they offered was two years on associate schoolboy forms. It didn't matter. It was enough for me.

I make it sound easy, but at that time I was never that confident. I honestly didn't think I was going to make it. I looked at players like Nick Barmby and Raphael Burke, who were fantastic at that age, and thought I wasn't in the same class.

When the gaffer came to the house to sign me, I'd forgotten that he was coming and I wasn't there, I was out playing with my mates. Back then he had a big, gold Mercedes, a massive car, and I remember running down the East Lancs Road, coming round the corner and seeing it parked. It was on double yellow lines, but that sort of thing has never bothered him. My heart sank. 'Oh shit,' I thought, 'Alex Ferguson was coming and I forgot. I'll get it in the neck now.'

I took a deep breath and went inside. Mum had made him a cup of tea and he hadn't been waiting too long. I signed there and then – quickly.

I don't remember any wild celebrations as such, just everyone being happy for me that I'd signed for United. If anything, it was played down. It wasn't mentioned at school, announced at assembly or anything like that. The PE staff were really good and complimentary about it, but the English and maths teachers – both women – had a very different attitude. 'You're not going to make it as a footballer,' they told me. 'Make sure you concentrate on your schoolwork.' That put a real damper on it. It definitely wasn't a cause for celebration as far as they were concerned.

It was at that stage, as a fourteen-year-old, that people started to take notice of me in the area. I was captain of the England schoolboys and had signed for United. It was quite a big deal locally, and a lot was made of it in the local press. I'm Welsh, but I qualified for England because I played for my school, Moorside High, and my district, which was Salford Boys, and a letter came, saying I'd been selected. They seemed to pick one player from each district in England – I know I was the only one from Salford anyway. I caught a train down to Nottingham Polytechnic, where the trials were, and spent four or five days there. There were 126 boys in all in that first pick. Some squad, eh? I think even Alex Ferguson would be happy with that! We had games and did different training drills, and when we came away I never thought I'd beat the first cut, let alone end up captain. Over a period of months, after different get-togethers, the 126 was whittled down to eighty, then forty, then twenty-five, and eventually to the final eighteen. Each time I was surprised to make the cut. I think they used Nottingham Poly originally because there was so many of us, but after that we went to the National Sports Centre, at Lilleshall. The whole process took about six months.

I genuinely didn't expect to get through. I'd experienced

trials before, from the under-11s at Salford Boys onwards, and I never thought I would get in the teams. Obviously I did, but I was never that confident. The worry was that, as a winger, it can be difficult to show what you're capable of. It's a one-off opportunity to shine, and if you're stuck out wide and nobody gives you the ball, what can you do? It's much easier for central midfield players, because they're constantly involved. At least that's how I felt about that first England Boys trial. I felt I hadn't done much – certainly not enough to catch the eye. But they must have seen something, although I never knew what! I certainly never expected to be coming back.

It was after the final cut that they made me captain for the 1988–9 season. Dave Bushall, who was manager of England Schoolboys, works at United now, looking after the young players who live in digs. Two or three years ago, still curious about the trials, I asked him, 'Why did you make me captain?' And he said, 'Because the other players all looked up to you.' I was amazed, I simply had no idea. Never realized. I was never a shouter or an organizer. I've never been that sort of player, and at fourteen I was even quieter and more reserved than I am now.

People now see it as strange that me, a Welsh lad, should captain the England Boys, and it certainly attracted a fair amount of comment, but I never thought of it that way at all. From my point of view, I went to an English school, so why not? That's the way it worked and it was a great honour, don't get me wrong. But I always knew, even as I was captaining England Schoolboys, that the next year I'd be playing for the Wales youth team and I looked forward to it. I never felt English, always Welsh. Every other weekend and every school holidays I went back to Cardiff, sometimes for the day – just for Gran's Sunday roast! England was just a bit of prestige that helped me get on in my career. Looking back, I have to admit it was weird singing 'God Save the Queen' before matches, when I'd spent so much time perfecting the Welsh anthem at junior school in Cardiff. I'm Welsh through and through, so I suppose I can understand people thinking the England thing was strange, but at the time it seemed to be a logical progression – playing for my school, Dean's, Salford Boys, Greater Manchester and then England.

In that one season as captain, I played nine times for England and we won seven and lost two. We were beaten 1–0 by Scotland at Old Trafford, which was one of the worst days of my life. You can just imagine what the gaffer was like after that. You couldn't get the smile off his face. He let me know all about that one for years afterwards. Christian Dailly, later of Blackburn and West Ham, was the Scottish captain. The other defeat was against Germany, 3–1 at Wembley, but we made amends for that when we beat them two days later at Birmingham. I scored, then missed a penalty. Then, when we got another penalty, Nick Barmby took it and scored. We won 2–0. That was our best result that season, because the German lads were huge. We couldn't believe it when we were lining up in the tunnel opposite six-footers with moustaches – at 14! They bullied us in the first game, they were brilliant, but we learned quickly and booted them off the pitch at Birmingham. And even for a Welshman playing for England, beating the Germans was sweet. We were a good side, we won away to Holland, 2–1, and France 1–0. We beat Wales 4–0 at Swansea and I scored. That was a weird day for me, I can tell you! And it didn't go down well with my family either. They had all travelled from Cardiff and had mixed feelings. The following season I was playing with those same Welsh players in the Wales youth team and, needless to say, I got a lot of stick for what happened at the Vetch. I don't regret playing for England in any way, though, not at all. The training facilities at Lilleshall were marvellous, the kit we had was fantastic and it was the first time I'd been in the national newspapers. The *Independent* did a big piece on me, which the family loved. They are all things I look back on with pride. No, there are definitely no regrets, I just think of the opportunities England gave me: playing and scoring at Wembley and winning in Holland and France. I played at Wembley twice, which was a massive experience, in every way. They were great occasions, there were 50,000 there, all screaming kids. When I played for the Welsh youth team against England at Wrexham, it was a hell of a contrast. Wales had a fairly ordinary side – I can't think of anybody else who made the grade – and the Welsh FA had no money, so the facilities and the kit were nothing like what I'd been used to with England. But even then, it never occurred to me that I should have stuck with England. The Welsh lads were so welcoming, they treated me so well that I felt at home immediately. The year before I captained the England Boys, my dad had taken me to Wembley to see them play Brazil. Lee Clark, who went on to make his name with Newcastle, was my predecessor as captain, but I never sat there thinking, 'I could be doing that next year,' that wasn't the point of the exercise. Because of their reputation in the game, it was Brazil we went to watch.

Dad was with us until I was nearly fourteen. It was very upsetting when he left, but I was happy that it happened in the end. There had been so many arguments – a lot of them violent – and me and my brother would get dragged into it. The last fight was a massive one, and it was all so sad, because once he'd been a hero to me. I admired the confident manner he had, the way fans loved him and his ability as a rugby player. So no matter how badly he treated us, his family, I still looked up to him. Even that last day, after Mum had thrown him out, I remember walking to the bus stop with him, carrying a big black sports bag with all his stuff in. Mum had kicked him out before, but we all knew this was it. He'd had his last chance. I sat at the bus stop with him, waiting for the bus, crying. My dad was going, I didn't know if I'd ever see him again. I didn't want him to go, but deep down I knew he had to after all that he'd done to Mum over the years. I didn't know where he was going, he wouldn't say. Presumably it was to another woman. He'd been caught at it a few times. In the end, his temper just became too much. He'd been out and had too much to drink once too often.

After he left us, he moved to Sale and played for a rugby team called Trafford Borough. He was coming to the end of his career and it was a newly formed club in the Second Division. After Swinton I've no real recollection of him playing, but I went though a stage when I would go to his house in Sale on a Sunday. He was living with a girlfriend. That didn't bother me too much, I was just happy to have him out of the picture at home. My brother, Rhodri, has always been closer to Dad than I have. Dad always treated him a little bit better, I felt. He was more caring towards him, I don't know why.

My attitude to my father has hardened, rather than softened, as time has gone by. A couple of years ago I bumped into him in a nightclub in Cardiff. I was out with the Welsh squad and he was there with his mates. He came over and asked me, 'Are you all right?' and I said, 'Yeah, OK.' Then he told me: 'Wait there and I'll have a chat with you when I come back.' I should have told him to piss off, or said we'd got nothing to talk about, but I just left. I suppose I could have told him what I really thought of him as a father, but there's a time and a place, and a nightclub isn't it. Since then, he has come to see me in the Welsh team hotel near Cardiff. We talk, but things will never be the same as they once were.

My mum deserves nothing but respect. She has worked hard all her life, and still does now. She is a firm believer in the work ethic, and has always impressed on me that if you work hard, you'll get your rewards. For as long as I can remember, she has believed in my ability and supported me all the way. In my Sunday League days, a lot of the mums would come and watch, and they became friends. No matter what the weather, they would be there. They took turns washing the kit. Mum has always been completely dedicated to my football, never missed a single game if she could possibly be there. She loves watching me play, and still comes to all the United games now.

She knows me better than anyone, and after a match she'll maybe say: 'Was your hamstring a bit tight today?' I'll tell her it was and she'll say, 'Yeah, I could tell from the way you were running.' Nobody else will have noticed, but she'll have spotted it. That comes from twenty years of watching me play football, which has given her a better insight than anyone else has about the way I play.

Obviously her life has changed over the years. It's no longer a case of scrimping and saving – she lives in a nice house, which I was able to give her, and drives a nice car. But she still does the same job she's had for the last twenty-five years, as an auxiliary nurse in a children's hospital. She still works nearly every day and her biggest enjoyment is still watching me play football, so I wouldn't say her life has changed dramatically. It's only the materialistic things, which don't matter to her as much as they do to some people.

I left school as soon as I could. For my last year I would bunk off to go and train with United. It wouldn't be allowed now, but everything was a bit more casual then and I didn't get into any real trouble for it. By that time I had long since lost interest in academic work. I still wasn't convinced that I was going to be good enough to make football my career, but I was determined to give it a go. All I was interested in was getting on at United and fitting in. I loved the place from day one, it was everything I'd hoped it would be.

Early Days

By the time I was fifteen I was an apprentice, but already playing for United's reserves, with and against men twice my age. Everybody at the club was aware of me then and most knew me. I didn't realize it at the time, but I've learned since that I'd been noticed when I played for them as a schoolboy. I had a few games in the reserves with the likes of Russell Beardsmore, Mark Robins and Lee Martin, who were all four or five years older than me, but were making their way at the same time.

As an apprentice, I never cleaned any of the senior players' boots, but I had to clean and look after our dressing room, which was the worst job of the lot. I did that and what was called balls and bibs. You had to stay out on the training ground until the first team finished and look for all the balls they'd booted everywhere and the bibs they'd dropped. After doing that, I'd have to clean our room. All the apprentices had to stay behind until the senior pros had finished. By this time the senior players knew me and they were all good to me, Steve Bruce especially so, as the club captain.

Brian Kidd was the youth development officer, and Kiddo was the biggest influence on all of us. He was the B-team manager as well, and from an early age he went out of his way to look after me. As a schoolboy he'd sort me out with boots because I was always the same size as him. I wouldn't say we were poor, but we certainly weren't well off as a single-parent family, and I couldn't buy the best boots, like all the others had, we just didn't have that sort of money, so Kiddo would get me the ones he used, from Adidas. Eric Harrison, who has had the credit for most of the good young players who have come through in the last decade, managed the A team. The way it worked, the B team was the next step up from the youth team, but the best players from the youth team would also play for the A team. It sounds confusing, but obviously it worked.

We can simplify it in my case, because I played for the youth team and the first team at the same time, more or less jumping the rungs on the ladder in between. I did play a few games for the reserves, but I can't remember them. Basically, it was a stage I missed out.

As a schoolboy and again as an apprentice, I remember the gaffer and his assistant, Archie Knox, coming to watch us train most Tuesdays and Thursdays. Archie would get involved with the apprentices' work, taking part of a session along with Eric. Sometimes they would split us into two groups and Archie would take one and Eric the other. The gaffer would stand and watch for the most part. Just occasionally he'd have his say, but as far as I was concerned there was not much point, because I couldn't understand a word he said. For ages I just couldn't penetrate that thick Glasgow accent. Archie was much the same. If either of them asked me how I was doing, I was more likely to say, 'Sorry?' and ask them to repeat themselves than tell them what they wanted to know. I still don't get half of what the gaffer says. Probably explains a lot!

Archie used to run us in pre-season, and boy could he run. He was a real long-distance man and his runs were killers. I was as scared of Archie as I was of Eric. He was a real man's man. When he shook your hand, you had to untangle your mangled fingers afterwards. 'Call that a handshake?'

he'd say as he crushed your hand in his. 'This is a real man's handshake.' 'OK,' I'd wince, 'yeah.'

Looking back, the whole thing was very 'old school'. When you become an apprentice now, it's a different world – one carefully structured to bring the best out of you, both as a footballer and as a person. There are no menial chores any more. If you're not training, you're doing schoolwork. Back then, it was more like joining the army and Eric Harrison was sergeant major. I had some real bollockings from him, and you couldn't answer back. I tried it a couple of times, but I soon learned not to. He was an intimidating man. As apprentices, sometimes we'd train in the morning and then do weights in the gym in the afternoon. Eric would come in and go to the bench-press machine. He'd make sure everyone had noticed him, and he'd lift not just the weight on the bar, but the whole machine. He'd do it just once, growling as he did so, then walk around checking on everyone. He just wanted to let us know that if anybody wanted to take him on, he was an awesomely strong man. A couple of times I saw different apprentices square up to him, big lads they were. Eric would stand there with a 'Come on, then' expression on his face, and they backed down. We never thought much of it at the time, it was just his way of keeping us under firm control. 'Don't mess with me,' it said. Simple as that.

He'd think nothing of sending a player off during training, then following him to the touchline, looking him in the eye and challenging him to disagree with the decision. Anyone who got that treatment would hold up his hands and say: 'You're right, sorry.'

Once I came in to train and it was snowing, there was a thick covering on the ground. 'There's no way we can play in this,' I thought. 'We'll probably do a bit of running.' Eric strode out on to the pitch with a rugby ball and made us play rugby for half an hour – real competitive stuff, too. There's no way it would happen today. And yet Eric was brilliant at what he did. He was tough, but he was also an excellent coach and tactician. He made the game so easy. He won the A-team league something like twelve times on the trot, against all the top sides, like Liverpool and Everton. He was that good, technically and tactically.

I first played for the United youth team when I was still at school. The big thing at that age is the FA Youth Cup; that's the competition all clubs use to groom lads for the first team. For the Youth Cup games, we prepared in much the same way as we do in the Premiership – we'd stay at the best hotels and the intensity of the build-up made it a special occasion. It was definitely a step up from the average A-team game. When I was a schoolboy, we got to the semi-finals, where we lost to Sheffield Wednesday, then in my first year as an apprentice we got to the last four again and got beaten by Tottenham.

Eventually, in my third season, we won it, but by that stage I was in the first team, so I didn't play in the early rounds of the Youth Cup, only the semi-final against Tottenham at Old Trafford and the second leg of the final, against Crystal Palace.

At fifteen my parents' split was brought home to me sharply when I had what I suppose you could call an identity crisis. United play in a prestigious youth tournament in Switzerland every year, and I was picked to go – I remember Sir Matt Busby came with us. Anyway, before each game the referee would inspect all the players' passports, to check that nobody was over the age limit. When he called out my name I blushed with embarrassment at the sound of the name 'Ryan Giggs'. Everybody at the club knew me as Ryan

Wilson. I was down on the teamsheet as Wilson. The rest of the team looked around, puzzled. I broke the silence: 'Yeah, that's me.' It was the first time any of my teammates knew about my change of name and my parents' difficulties, and I hated the fuss.

When I left school, with my dad gone, it seemed logical to go back to using my mum's name. I'd hated changing from Giggs to Wilson in the first place, but then I didn't want to change back to Giggs. Kids like stability in their lives, and having got used to one name, the last thing I wanted to do was to start all over again with another. It was all too complicated. It drew too much attention for the wrong reasons. I know a lot of people who had seen me play for Salford Boys and join United were left wondering whether Ryan Wilson and Ryan Giggs were one and the same.

As an apprentice I was on £29.50 a week plus £10 travelling expenses. Because I was living at home, not in digs, my mum got a cheque for £40 for my food and accommodation. That's what the landladies who put up lads in digs were paid. I wasn't exactly rich, but I wasn't on that basic money for long, so I survived. To be fair, it was more than any of my mates was getting. Especially as I'd get win bonuses for the A team or the reserves, which were £8 and £10, on top of my basic, so most weeks I was picking up £50 or £60. Not too bad!

I could afford to go out two or three times a week, usually to the pub, but never drinking alcohol, of course. I was only fifteen. And the girl I was seeing, Sue, was four years older than me. She was clever – she was at the Halifax Building Society, where she became manageress. I went out with her for four years, so it was a pretty serious relationship. I'd see her nearly every night, or I certainly wanted to. She was my first love, I suppose. There was a lot of kudos in having a girlfriend four years older. She was reckoned to be quite a catch. We met at school. I was on my first visit, having a look around, and I held the door open for this girl, who was beautiful. 'Thanks,' she said. 'No problem,' I replied as she sailed through. So our first words hardly had the makings of an epic romance! Obviously I'd never seen her before, but the lad who was showing me around said, 'That's Sue Rothwell, she's the fittest girl in the whole school.' My first year was her fifth year, so I didn't see much of her while we were at school, but four years later she'd left and I was going out with her. We met up and just hit it off straight away.

She had a car, a Mini Metro, to run us around in. Another advantage that came with her age. I didn't have to rely on Sue for ever, though. I passed my driving test when I was eighteen. The day I passed we had a night game at Old Trafford and I drove my stepfather's Sierra Estate in. I pulled up at Salford Quays and stalled at the lights, surrounded by fans, all laughing. 'Just passed your test, have you, son?' I parked in what used to be the players' car park, just opposite the ground, got out of the car, and a supporter asked me for my autograph. As I signed he said, 'Is that your car, over there? I think you've forgotten to put the handbrake on.' I turned and saw it rolling downhill, just about to hit one of the other players' cars. I had to run and jump in to put the handbrake on. Talk about embarrassed! It was a good job I was on my own.

I wanted a car of my own. By the time I passed my test I'd played twenty-five games for the first team, and there was an unwritten agreement that after twenty-five appearances you were a regular and qualified for a club car. At that stage I was getting £170 a week and giving £40 of that to Mum for my keep. So I went to Bryan Robson, the captain, and said, 'Listen, I can't really afford a decent car yet, I'm driving my stepdad's. D'you think the gaffer would let me have a club car?'

Bryan said, 'Of course he will, yeah. You deserve one, you're part of the team now, you're in the first-team changing room.' Steve Bruce walked in and Robbo called him over: 'Giggsy wants a club car, what d'you think?'

Steve looks at me and says, 'No problem at all, just go and tell the gaffer.'

Great, I thought, and went and knocked on the gaffer's door. 'What's up, son?' he said. I told him I'd just passed my test and wanted a club car. He went absolutely nuts. 'Who the fuck d'you think you are? You've played a handful of games and you're coming in here with your fucking demands. I wouldn't give you a club fucking bike!' Outside I could hear Robbo, Brucey, Incey and Choccy McClair all splitting their sides laughing. They'd done me. They ripped into me for weeks after that. I got the car in the end, though! Danny McGregor, the commercial manager, got me a deal with Ford and I had an Escort for a year.

These days, it's hard to imagine first-team players driving Escorts, but people forget that, when I first got into the side, Manchester United were a completely different club. The previous season, 1989–90, they had finished thirteenth in the old First Division, thirty-one points behind the champions, Liverpool.

That year, the gaffer was under a bit of pressure. I remember being in a pub, the Bull's Head in Swinton, where I shouldn't have been, because I was too young, watching us play Oldham in the semi-finals of the FA Cup. United won that one and went on to win the Cup. We went from strength to strength after that.

Back then, though, the team was changing and evolving

all the time as the gaffer looked for the perfect formula. The chance was there for good young players to come through, and I suppose you could say I was fast-tracked. The set-up at the old training ground, called The Cliff, had three dressing rooms, for the apprentices, the reserves and the first team. I was never in the reserves room. I can remember Lee Sharpe, for example, moving up through all three, but I was moved straight from the apprentices' to the first-team room, and at the time I didn't want to go. All my mates were apprentices, and I wanted to stay in with them. I'd go in with the first-teamers, get changed quickly and get out of there, I wouldn't hang around for the banter or anything like that. I was intimidated by the older players, and their sarcasm. There was only Sharpey who was anywhere near my age, and it was only with him I felt I had anything in common.

There were a lot of wind-up merchants in there. Les Sealey, the goalkeeper, was pretty bad like that, and Paul Ince and Steve Bruce would always take the piss. That said, they were the guys you took to straight away because by taking the mick they were involving you in their circle, not ignoring you, like some. Choccy McClair was hard work. I didn't get his jokes, they went straight over my head. I was just a kid, really, and he seemed too clever, too sharp.

Young players can usually tell when their chance is coming, and the previous week I'd travelled with the first team for the first time when they played Sheffield United away. We lost that one, 2–1. I was in the squad for the first time and shared a room with Darren Ferguson, the gaffer's son. It was between me and him for one of the substitutes' places – there were only two in those days – and Daz got the nod. So I was on the fringes of the squad, and then I heard a whisper, like you do, that I might be involved against

Everton. I didn't actually know for certain until an hour and a half before kick-off. I hadn't been playing particularly well for the youth team or the reserves, nothing like that, but it seemed to be a logical progression. I'd had a few training sessions with the first team, did all right, and now I was playing with them. The team was in the middle of a bad run of seven league games without a win when I got my first team debut against Everton on 2 March 1991. It should have been a celebration but it felt more like a wake: we had key players out injured, like Bryan Robson, Steve Bruce, Neil Webb and Mark Hughes, and it was widely described as our worst performance of the season. We lost 2–0 at home. We never looked like scoring. I got on when Denis Irwin joined the injured list, with hamstring trouble. There was me and Danny Wallace up front – two real heavyweights! Mike Newell and Dave Watson got the goals, but apart from that all I can really remember is getting kicked by Dave Watson. The ball was played up to me and he came straight through me from behind. He was a tough guy, Dave, and that was his way of saying 'Welcome to the big boys' league.'

It was a terrible match, played on a dreadful pitch. They were having trouble with the grass at Old Trafford at the time, and we played on a mixture of sand and ankle-deep mud – not my kind of surface at all. Afterwards, the gaffer said we were second to every ball and lacked imagination. And he did so pretty forcefully too. I can only say he was spot on: we were terrible.

At that stage I was playing up front a lot, not on the wing. I'd never played as a striker until I went to United, but Eric Harrison and the gaffer both saw me as a front player. Eric still thinks that's my best position, up front. Quite a few people have said that over the years – I remember Terry Yorath saying it when I first got into the Wales team.

I'm not sure that my technique as a finisher is up to that. In retrospect breaking into the first team so early might not have helped me in that respect. I missed out on a lot in the years when a young player should be learning his trade. Other people, who serve their full time in the apprentices and the reserves, benefit from training designed to improve the individual player and work on weaknesses as well as strengths. In the first team you're supposed to be the finished article, your basic technique is taken for granted, and you train replicating match situations more. I wasn't coached, as an individual, as much as the other young lads. I was never encouraged to work on my right foot, for example. I should have been but, as a seventeen- and eighteen-year-old, if you'd asked me whether I wanted to play in the first team or stay in the reserves and work on my technique, I know what I'd have said!

My first start in the first team was a lot more memorable than the Everton game. It was two months later, on 4 May 1991, in the derby at home to Manchester City. It was my full debut, and I was much more nervous than I'd been before the Everton game. I was starting, so it really was my big chance. I remember standing in the old changing rooms an hour and a half before kick-off and the gaffer having a board up, reading out the team in formation. The goalkeeper, Gary Walsh, first, then the back four: Irwin, Bruce, Pallister and Blackmore. Then the midfield: Phelan, Webb, Robson and Ryan, you'll start on the left.

When we first arrived at the ground, I didn't even think I'd be a substitute, but then Mark Bosnich, who had played the previous week, came up to me in the players' lounge, where we were all relaxing, and said, 'I've heard a whisper, I think you're playing you know.' I said, 'Nah, no chance,' but it was then that I got my head around the fact that I might be sub. When the gaffer said I was playing, the importance of the occasion hit me hard. Suddenly I had sweaty palms and I know I went very quiet. Normally, I'm never bothered by nerves before any game, but I was that day.

The gaffer has his own ideas about when to throw in certain players. He reckons some young lads – Darren Fletcher, for example – are better suited to away games. I've never asked him why he chose that particular day to start me. Maybe he had nobody else! At least I didn't let them down. I got the only goal – or so they said. It was an own-goal really, but it was credited to me. Choccy McClair put a cross in, I got the slightest of touches and it deflected in off Colin Hendry. I celebrated as if I'd scored, but at the back of my mind I knew I hadn't, and it didn't feel like my goal. But that night, in an interview on *Match of the Day*, Hendry said, 'I don't want the goal, give it to the young lad,' and the gaffer agreed with him and said I should claim it, so I did.

There were two other Welshmen in the team that day, Clayton Blackmore and Mark Hughes, and having them around always made me feel better. They were very different personalities, Clayton loud and outgoing, Sparky the quiet introvert. I remember Clayton announcing to everybody, 'There's three of us now, the Welsh are taking over this club.' If there was any banter about me, Clayton, or sometimes even Mark would say, 'Leave the Welsh lad alone,' which made me feel more welcome in the dressing room. I'd always looked up to Mark Hughes. He and Bryan Robson had been my heroes. Robbo and Brucey were the most helpful and encouraging of the senior players: Robbo always sprang to my defence on the pitch, telling defenders that if they tried to 'do' me, they'd have him to answer to. Viv Anderson, who was still there then, was the one who would take the piss out of me most. He was very loud, was Viv, but in a nice, bubbly way. I'd first met him when I was fifteen, when, as a schoolboy, I'd trained with him. I went past him a couple of times. Afer he'd taken some stick for it, he made a point of having a word. 'If you try that again,' he told me, 'the ball might go round me, but you won't!' Yeah, he would take the piss, but in a way that included you and made you feel part of the group.

At the end of 90–91 I'd played one full match and one as sub. The team had finished sixth in the old First Division, one place behind Man City and twenty-four points behind the champions, Arsenal. We'd lost the Rumbelows (League) Cup final to Ron Atkinson's Sheffield Wednesday and gone out of the FA Cup in the fifth round, losing 2–1 at Norwich. What saved the season for us, and made it a memorable one for the fans and players alike, was winning the old Cup-Winners' Cup – the club's first European trophy for twenty-three years. It was a marvellous night for all concerned, but especially for Mark Hughes. We played Barcelona in the final, in Rotterdam, and Sparky had not been a success in the spell he had there between 1986 and 1987, so he felt he had a point to prove. The occasion inspired him to produce possibly his best performance in a United shirt, scoring both goals in our 2–1 win.

The club celebrated in style, but I had played no part in any of the cup games that season, and didn't really feel part of it. All the same, there was a mood at the club that the team had turned a corner, that the gaffer's efforts were starting to gel. I knew I still had a lot to do to establish myself. All I was looking for in 91–2 was a few more games. I wasn't really at all prepared for what happened.

Lift-off

The summer of '91 was an exciting time for me. I made my first, and what turned out to be my only, appearance for the Wales under-21s in Poland at the end of May. Gary Speed, then at Leeds, was our captain, I roomed with Chris Coleman, now manager at Fulham, and we won 2–1. Mark Pembridge and Nathan Blake played and we got a great result against a strong Polish team that hadn't been beaten for twenty-odd games. At the same time as I strengthened my position in the Welsh international set-up, Manchester United was on the verge of becoming the dominant force we became throughout the nineties. Sir Alex Ferguson and the board were never going to settle for sixth place, which is where we had just finished, and the gaffer was now in a position to spend big to bring about the desired improvement. The club had been floated as a public company, which raised a lot of money, and we were now very active in the transfer market.

During the closed season, the gaffer brought in Andrei Kanchelskis, the Ukrainian winger, from Shakhtar Donetsk, for £650,000, paid Queens Park Rangers £2m for Paul Parker, their England defender, and made what he still considers to be his best value-for-money signing ever when he got the man who became the world's top goalkeeper, Peter Schmeichel, from Brondby for just £505,000. The arrival of the 'Great Dane' spelled the end for two of our 'keepers, Jim Leighton and Mark Bosnich, who eventually drifted off to Dundee and Aston Villa respectively. Jim had been out of the picture since he was dropped for the FA Cup final replay against Crystal Palace the previous year.

I still wasn't that confident about playing much, I certainly didn't feel as if I had 'arrived', so it was no surprise when I was left out of the starting line-up for the first two league games, at home to newly promoted Notts County and away to Villa. Andrei was picked ahead of me in the No. 11 shirt. Lee Sharpe was still very much in favour with the gaffer, so there were three wingers competing for two places, and quite often Lee and Andrei would play, and when I played with Lee, I'd be on the right. As it turned out, me and Andrei played most games together. It was healthy competition, and I particularly enjoyed the balance the team had with me and Andrei on the wings and Mark Hughes in the middle. Andrei was lightning fast – in the sprints in training I used to wear the baton out chasing him. He was not only quick, he looked it with that powerful, bustling running style. Over the first few yards I had the edge, but once he got going there was no catching him. It was a great combination. The three new signings – Andrei, Peter Schmeichel and Paul Parker – all played in the first two games and helped to get us off to the best of all starts: two clean sheets and maximum points. I was sub on the opening day, when there was tremendous excitement around the ground. There's nothing quite like big new signings to get the fans going, and the gates were shut an hour before kick-off, with thousands locked outside. I got on for Darren Ferguson with a quarter of an hour left in a comfortable 2–0 win against Neil Warnock's Notts County, Sparky Hughes and Bryan Robson getting the goals.

It was Kanchelskis who took Old Trafford by storm that day, destroying an experienced full-back called Alan Paris. Both goals came from his crosses, and we could have scored six from his service alone. Of course, the fans took to him at once; they had a new hero, which was a bit worrying for me and Sharpey, who had a serious injury at the time. Andrei was stuck in a hotel at first, waiting for his wife to come over, so the senior players took it in turns to invite him to their homes for a meal. Robbo took him under his wing, taking him to the races, which Andrei loved, and to a Paul Simon concert with the rest of the lads. I remember the first English phrase he mastered was 'no problem'. For a long time *everything* was 'no problem'.

I was sub again, and didn't get on, for the game at Villa, where a Steve Bruce penalty was the only goal, but then I had the bit of luck I needed. Andrei had arrived with Achilles tendon trouble, which now flared up and forced him out of the next four games, and with Sharpey also injured, I had my chance and was determined to seize it. I was in for the next two games, away to Everton and at home to Oldham. We drew 0–0 at Goodison and beat Oldham 1–0, but I was disappointed with my performance in both games. I knew I hadn't really got into them, and when I was dropped in favour of my Welsh mate Clayton Blackmore it came as frustrating but predictable news.

I was feeling low at that stage and needed a bit of encouragement. Fortunately Kiddo was always brilliant in those situations. The previous season he'd stepped up to assistant manager when Archie Knox left. It was definitely good for me. We'd always got on well, he'd really looked after me since I left school, and I felt much more comfortable with him than I had with Archie. He was much more approachable, not that you had to approach him. He had the ability to sense when something was wrong, or if you were worried about something, and he'd approach you. I'm sure that Kiddo moving up eased my progress in the first team, and he helped me a lot now, telling me not to lose heart, that the gaffer really fancied me as a player, and that if I just kept working at it, the big breakthrough would come. He was right, of course. I was back in the side when we played Norwich at home in early September, and that was the first in a run of thirteen starts.

Norwich had a good side in those days – they'd finished fourth in the league in '89 – but we took them apart inside half an hour. I was still only seventeen and a lot of people have said that was the game when I really arrived. I scored one goal, hit a post with another shot and was a bit unlucky when their goalkeeper, Bryan Gunn, made a brilliant save.

We weren't at full strength: Incey and Sharpey were injured, and Andrei, who had been out for four games, had to go off very early with a recurrence of the Achilles problem that had first let me in. But we absolutely bombed them. It was 3–0 and all over after just 28 minutes. We'd hit them with all three goals in an eight-minute spell, and that was that, game over. Denis Irwin got us up and running with his first goal for the club, from 20 yards, then Choccy McClair made it 2–0. I got the third, anticipating a backpass that was too short and rounding the 'keeper, who had come out, before rolling it into the net from a tight angle. It was my first 'proper' goal for the club – the first one I didn't feel embarrassed about celebrating. It was a great feeling and fed my confidence. I nearly scored again five minutes later, when Neil Webb put me through, but this time, after taking the ball round Bryan Gunn, I shot against the base of a post.

It was after this game that people further afield than Manchester started saying nice things about me. Dave Stringer, the Norwich manager, told the press I timed my runs remarkably well for a seventeen-year-old, and commented on my 'lovely balance', and I was told a television reporter at the game compared me to George Best in his half-time report and got a right bollocking from his studio for 'talking rubbish'. The gaffer told us we'd been 'magnificent' for half an hour and, ever the perfectionist, wanted to know why we hadn't kept it up. As he left the dressing room, it was Neil Webb, I think, always a bit of a rebel, who muttered after him: 'miserable git'.

Whether the gaffer was happy or not, the result put us four points clear of Liverpool at the top of the table and stretched our unbeaten start to seven matches. It was to go on and on and, for the first time for longer than many at Old Trafford could remember, United were genuine title contenders.

In September we began the defence of the Cup-Winners' Cup against Athinaikos. Because of the old UEFA 3+2 rule limiting the number of non-Englishmen we could play, I missed both legs, a 0–0 draw in Greece and a comfortable 2–0 win at home that put us safely through. In the next round we were drawn against Atletico Madrid, and again I wasn't selected for the first game, which was a bit of a disaster. I went to Madrid and watched as we got stuffed 3–0. They took the lead after half an hour, then we came back into it quite well, but they ended up getting two more in the last three minutes. Paulo Futre, the Portuguese striker, scored two, but it was Germany's Bernd Schuster, in midfield, who really impressed me. Atletico had a good team then, they were top of the Spanish league, and we were left facing a real uphill battle in the second leg. We needed to score goals, and I played this time, getting a real welcome to the big league. I can't remember who their right-back was, but he was quite tasty and in the first couple of minutes he tackled me from behind and went right through me. I thought, 'Right, I'll have you next time.' Not long after that we got in a tangle and I made my point. Next thing I knew, we had a free-kick on the right and I was at the back post, waiting to attack the ball, and as I'm looking for it to come over he smacked me right on the bridge of my nose with his elbow. He wouldn't get away with it now, with all the cameras around, but nobody spotted it then. I thought, 'That's enough. I won't be doing him again.' He was too streetwise for me, too experienced.

After the first leg, the outcome was pretty much a foregone conclusion, and all we could manage in the return was a 1–1 draw. That was my introduction to European competition, and at about the same time, in October '91, I made my senior debut for Wales in a European Championship qualifier against Germany in Nuremberg. Four months earlier, before I got in the squad, Wales had one of the best results in their history when they beat the Germans 1–0 in Cardiff, but now we were away, and nowhere near full strength, so it was a daunting introduction for me, as the youngest player ever to appear for Wales, aged seventeen years and eleven months. It was not much of a start, because I was a substitute and didn't get on until the eighty-fourth minute, when, with Wales chasing the game, I replaced Eric Young, the Crystal Palace centre-half. The occasion still meant a huge amount to me, though. We didn't have anything like our full team that night, with Mark Aizlewood, David Phillips, Clayton Blackmore and Peter Nicholas all missing, and Gavin Maguire playing out of position, at right-back. The Germans, on the other hand, all seemed to be famous names: Brehme, Kohler, Buchwald, Matthäus, Effenberg, Möller, Riedle, Völler and so on.

Terry Yorath was our manager and I liked him a lot, he was a good man. I know he had a difficult relationship with Alex Ferguson over my selection for Wales, and I sensed that he was very careful about how he treated me. I was only seventeen and the gaffer didn't want me to burn out early so sometimes it wasn't possible to play in all the internationals. He has never liked me playing friendly internationals, and I know all my Wales managers have had a big problem with that but he has never stopped me playing. Personally, I never had any problems with Terry, and I also got on really well with his assistant, Peter Shreeves, who had a warm personality and made me feel really at home. I was nervous – I think anybody would be, making their debut against Germany – but Terry and Peter both did their best to settle me down, saying the way I was playing for United would be good enough for them. Terry told me just to go out and enjoy it, and that's what I tried to do. I wasn't on for long, but I managed a few nice touches, and made sure I swapped shirts with Effenberg at the end.

Back at United, my next goal came in a Rumbelows Cup tie at home to Cambridge. It was my first appearance in the competition we all knew as the League Cup, and I opened the scoring in a routine 3–0 win. I remember Dion Dublin playing and making a real impression for Cambridge – so much so that the gaffer signed him at the end of that season.

In the First Division we were flying. We were unbeaten in our first twelve league games, but then we hit a brick wall in the Cup-Winners' Cup. That 3–0 stuffing in Spain shook our confidence, and a combination of the result, the travelling and the physical knocks we'd picked up left us 'leggy' and vulnerable three days later, when we went to Hillsborough and lost 3–2. The backbone of the team was shaky. We were without Ince and Hughes, and Bruce and Robson were both carrying injuries from Madrid. Wednesday, who were fifth in the table and on a run of seven straight wins at home, were up for it, and caught us at the right time.

Sparky Hughes and Mark Robins were both suspended,

so Choccy McClair was moved from midfield to play up front, between Kanchelskis and me, in an unusual 3–4–3 formation. We led 2–1 at half-time, McClair scoring both, but Wednesday were stronger in the second half, and Nigel Jemson scored twice to win it for them.

That defeat cost us top spot, Leeds taking over the leadership after three successive wins, but we hit back hard, beating Sheffield United 2–0 at home to go back to the top when Leeds could only draw 0–0 with Wimbledon.

By this stage I was starting to feel that I belonged, that I really was part of the team. In those days we used to socialize together a lot more than the players do now, by which I mean go out together for a drink. There were some real social animals in that side, people like Robbo, Brucey, Webby and Sharpey, and I was gradually joining in. It happened more after away games than when we played at home. We'd all leave our cars at the Four Seasons Hotel at Hale, near Manchester airport, and when we got back the team bus would park there and we'd all go into the Irish bar they had, called Mulligans. Robbo always made it plain every pre-season that all the lads would be expected to go for at least one beer after a game. It was a bonding thing, done to foster team spirit. We don't do it any more. The gaffer banned it around 1996.

Lee Sharpe was my running mate on nights out and, being two years old than me, he led me into a few scrapes. He was a good lad, but I think he wasted the tremendous natural talent he had. We were mates, but following his lead was going to get me into real trouble towards the end of this, my first season as a first-team regular.

Back on the pitch, after losing to Atletico and Sheffield Wednesday, we responded like potential champions, with six wins and two draws in our next eight league games. We were scoring goals for fun, too, sixteen of them in four matches, including a 6–3 victory at Oldham on Boxing Day, which kept us top of the table. I remember getting our sixth on a freezing cold day at Boundary Park – for some reason it's always 'brass monkeys' there. We were playing really well, and were happy enough with a 1–1 draw at Leeds, our closest rivals, on 29 December. That kept our noses in front of Howard Wilkinson's team, but then we started to lose our way. On New Year's Day we were beaten 4–1 at home by Queens Park Rangers, an ordinary team who were fifteenth in the table at the time. The gaffer blamed what went wrong on the pitch at Old Trafford, which he took to calling the cabbage patch. The muddy, uneven surface obviously didn't suit our passing game. We were short of an aerial threat up front, especially when Sparky was out. There were rumours that the gaffer tried to sign Mick Harford from Luton. Harford was a tremendous header of the ball, as well as one of the toughest guys around, which gave him a real presence and authority in the box. I think he'd have enjoyed playing with our wingers. I know I would have enjoyed playing with him. I wouldn't have had much trouble finding him!

Partly because of the pitch, and the dread we had of playing on it – dreading playing at home! – we started dropping points in games we were expected to win, drawing home games against Sheffield Wednesday, Chelsea, Wimbledon and Manchester City. We were still going strong in the Rumbelows Cup, where I scored in our 3–1 win at Leeds in the fifth round, which came in the middle of a series of three games in seventeen days against them. Ten days before that cup tie, we drew 1–1 at Elland Road in the league, and in our third meeting we beat them 1–0 in the third round of the FA Cup, Sparky getting the only goal.

February was a bad month. Of the five league games we

played, we managed to win only one, 2–0 at home to Crystal Palace, which enabled Leeds to close the gap at the top to two points. We also went out of the FA Cup, drawing a fourth-round replay against Southampton 2–2, only to lose on penalties when Tim Flowers saved mine. That was a big disappointment for an eighteen-year-old, but there was still plenty to play for. Not only were we top of the league, we booked our place in the final of the Rumbelows Cup by beating Middlesbrough in the semis. My mate Sharpey scored our first goal and I got the winner.

In March we were still dropping points in the league, losing at Nottingham Forest and drawing with Wimbledon and QPR, and it was a worry that Sparky, our main striker, had suddenly stopped scoring. To our relief, we hit form again at the end of the month, when a 3–1 win at Norwich took us back to the top of the table, a point clear of Leeds with a game in hand.

My first cup final, not counting the FA Youth Cup, was on 12 April 1992, when we played Forest at Wembley in the Rumbelows. It was a good competition for me and my home entertainment system! If you were man of the match, the sponsors, Rumbelows, gave you £500 to spend on a TV or a hi-fi, whatever. I still laugh about that now with Roy Keane who was another beneficiary of Rumbelows' generosity. He was playing for Forest then and he got three man-of-the-match awards on the way to the final, and I did the same. I kitted my bedroom out with a big telly and a new stereo. I also got a nice bonus from my first boot sponsors, Puma, for getting to the final.

Some people say that United don't take the League Cup as seriously these days, but it's a good opportunity to blood new players. Back then, though, the trophy cabinet had been empty for so long any trophy was very welcome, we couldn't afford to be fussy. The occasion was one to remember for me, but the match wasn't. Both teams were without their inspirational captains – Robbo was injured for us, as was Stuart Pearce for them – and we coped better without ours. Paul Ince and Mike Phelan, who was preferred to Neil Webb, gave us the edge in midfield, where Roy Keane was unable to get Forest's famous passing game going. Peter Schmeichel had almost nothing to do, and the only goal of an ordinary game came in the fourteenth minute, when I ran forward and shaped to shoot, but reversed the ball into Brian McClair's path. Choccy took it in his stride and tucked away what was his twenty-third goal of the season. He had a knack for scoring, he'd get all sorts of scruffy goals. He was a natural scorer, always in the right place at the right time. He had a very dry sense of humour – and most of it still went right over my head. I always got on with him OK, but he'd say something and I'd think, 'What's he on about?' I'm still not sure! Sharpey got on for Andrei Kanchelskis late in the final, but we had one eye on the crucial league games that were coming up, and one goal always seemed likely to be enough. It was a cup final, but it just seemed to peter out.

There wasn't much to treasure in the memory, but it was the first time I had come across Keaney, and he was typically welcoming. I remember getting the ball and nutmegging him (though he still denies it!). He came straight through me from behind. As I lay on the ground, he looked down at me and said, 'Get up, you soft git', or words to that effect. So not much has changed there! I tell him now that I sat on the floor thinking, 'Who is this muppet?' He says he doesn't remember it, and *certainly* won't have it that I 'megged him, but he just doesn't want to face facts! I still give him stick about it to this day.

Me as a baby

And as a toddler with my Aunt Hayley. We were like brother and sister

At Bristol Zoo with my Nan,
my mum's mother

With Hayley and Nan

And me sporting another classic T-shirt design

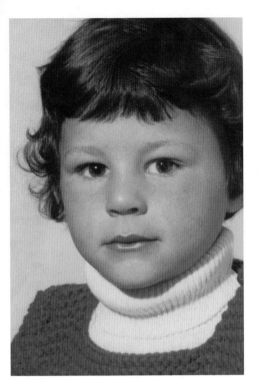
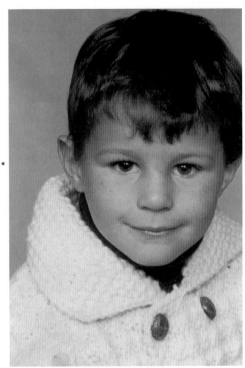

Growing up

Me and my brother Rhodri

My dad, Danny
Wilson, playing
rugby for Cardiff
in 1976

Playing for Deans, my schoolboy club side

And Salford Under-15s

For Salford Under-11s

The England captain

With Nan in Cardiff, wearing an England Schoolboys blazer

Playing for England Under-15s. I knew I'd one day be playing for Wales

My first start for United against Manchester City in 1991

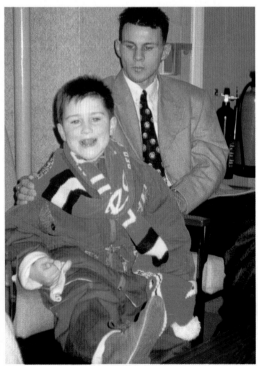

The Rumbelows Cup Final against Nottingham Forest in 1992. The first time I made Roy Keane's acquaintance

In the players' lounge at Old Trafford with my cousin Calum

United win the league for the first time in twenty-six years in 1993

The gaffer with the Premier League trophy

Celebrating with Incey again

With Eric – the best player I've played with

Forest had their revenge when they beat us 2–1 at home on Easter Monday, when I played up front with McClair, who got our goal. Sparky was having a bad run, and was left out after going fourteen games without scoring. As I remember it, we played quite well, but the Forest 'keeper, Mark Crossley, had a blinder. The gaffer didn't give us a bollocking, he said we were unlucky, but the dressing room was like a morgue.

On the way home Sharpey suggested we go to Blackpool to forget about it, and after a miserable afternoon's work, I didn't need much persuasion. We went, a pair of young idiots together. It was not like we had been drinking or even planning a big night out, we were both driving after all. It was still light when we got there, and we didn't stay long. We had a bite to eat and got back to Manchester by nine o'clock at the latest. No harm there – or so we thought.

Two days later we played West Ham away and another defeat, 1–0 this time, put us out of contention for the league. On the Thursday, the gaffer sent me and Lee to a charity evening that Bernard Manning was running in a real rough place in Manchester, and that same night the gaffer was at a dinner in Morecambe, chatting to someone on the top table. The conversation went: 'I saw a couple of your lads on Monday in Blackpool.' That got his attention.

'Did you? Who was that, then?'

'Sharpe and Giggs.'

'No, it couldn't have been. They had a game on Wednesday, they'd have been at home in bed.'

'No, it was definitely them. They had identical Suzuki jeeps. They had a couple of girls and a few of their mates with them.'

The news had definitely spoiled his evening out. The gaffer could barely contain his fury. Meanwhile, we'd gone to the Bernard Manning function, done the raffle and presented a few cheques, and wrapped it up by about ten o'clock, unaware that there was a storm brewing. Afterwards we went back to Lee's house, in Hale Barns, near Altrincham. There were a few girls and a few of the United apprentices there, and we were planning to go to a nightclub in Stockport, which was always busy on a Thursday night.

At least, that was the plan. After the gaffer had been told the Blackpool story and put two and two together to make five, he was so angry that he drove straight from Morecambe to Sharpey's house. It was a new estate and there was no number on the door but that didn't put him off. He just kept on knocking on door after door in search of Lee's place. And every wrong one made him more and more angry. Finally, when he knocked on the right door he was volcanic. One of my mates answered and didn't recognize him at first.

'Is this Lee Sharpe's house?'

'You what, mate?' came the reply.

The gaffer just barged straight past him and into the kitchen, where I was leaning against the fridge, talking to a couple of girls.

My mate, who had been pushed out of the way, realizing his mistake, ran upstairs to Lee's room, where he found him preening himself in front of the mirror.

'What's up?' Lee asked him.

'The bloody gaffer has just turned up.' Lee thought it was a wind-up.

'Oh yeah, of course he has.'

Downstairs it was bedlam. The gaffer threw *everyone* out – some of them our non-footballing mates and girls who were nothing to do with him. But he was a man on a mission. Unstoppable. 'Go on, get out. Out!' he shouted. 'Go home. This is no fucking party house.' Three young apprentices who were upstairs getting ready to go out, hid in the wardrobes and never got caught. They were still there when, with everybody else gone, the gaffer came downstairs and sat me on the settee with Lee opposite and absolutely slaughtered him, just ripped him to shreds. He was so angry I really thought he was going to hit Lee. He was shouting in his face, poking him in the chest. 'You're an absolute disgrace, you've done it this time. You're out of this house and going back into digs. You can't be trusted to live on your own because you've no self-control.' He'd been in trouble before, but this was my first scrape and I was shitting myself.

Then he turned on me. 'As for you, you're going down the same path as him, and it will ruin you. I'm going to ring your mum straight away and get you sorted out. I'll see you in my office tomorrow morning.' He really monstered both of us. I had my car outside and I had to drive home to my mum's in a right state, shaking from head to foot. The little Escort only had an 1100 engine but she was racing along. At one stage I looked down at the speedo in disbelief! The pistons were about to explode through the bonnet and I hadn't even noticed. Going over Trafford bridge I thought I was going to take off.

I pulled up at the house and ran in.

'Mum, the gaffer is going to ring in a minute. He's just caught me with Sharpey, about to go out.' As I was talking, the phone rang. It was him. He told her everything, but I needn't have worried about her reaction. Despite the gaffer's rage, my behaviour left her unruffled. She'd seen much worse from my dad, and she wasn't that bothered. A couple of young lads going out for the night didn't seem like such a big deal to her. That's not the way the gaffer saw it.

We both got fined, I think it was a month's wages. Despite the fact that two weeks was supposed to be the maximum, the gaffer split the offences and docked us two weeks for going to Blackpool before a match and another two for what happened that night. The striking thing was that he didn't hold it against me despite his strength of feeling. He was completely fine with me almost immediately. With Lee it was different, though. He always liked a night out, the gaffer knew what he was doing, and he ran out of patience with him in the end. It was a real pity Lee couldn't just buckle down a bit more and cut out the socializing. He had a good career, and played for England, but I don't think he achieved anything like as much as he should have done. The season I broke into the team he'd just won Young Player of the Year, he was in the England squad at nineteen, and I remember sitting on the bench and watching him in awe. He was so quick, strong and such a good crosser of the ball. I sat there thinking: 'How am I ever going to get into this team with him around? He's a left-winger, like me, and he's flying out there.' I got a lucky break when he had real trouble with a hernia, and was out for the best part of eighteen months. He was still very young but after that injury he never got that electric pace back.

The loss to Forest had been a major setback for United, enabling Leeds to go a point clear at the top. We still had a game in hand, with three left to play to Leeds' two, but now the wheels really came off. Our game in hand was at West Ham, who were bottom of the table at the time, and were to finish there, so everybody expected us to win without too much trouble. So much for theory. It was our fourth game in seven days, and we were knackered. The gaffer dropped Neil Webb. He wasn't happy about it, but it was the right decision. With West Ham fighting for survival, it turned into a real battle, and that wasn't Webby's sort of game. Fair play to them, they really got stuck into us, and we could have no complaints with the result – even if their goal was a fluke. It came when a clearance from Gary Pallister hit Kenny Brown on the knee and flew past Schmeichel from the edge of the penalty area. The nearest we came to scoring was when Sharpey ran through and put the ball in the net, but was ruled offside.

That was it, we knew we'd blown the title. Bobby Charlton went round the dressing room, thanking each player individually for their efforts. It was a nice touch from the great man, but we were all too gutted to take much notice. Mathematically, we still had a chance, but it was out of our hands. Even if we won our last two games, away to Liverpool and at home to Tottenham, we had to rely on either Sheffield United or Norwich beating Leeds in one of their last two. It was possible, but none of us thought it was going to happen, and our morale and form had disintegrated to such an extent that we lost our third game on the trot, 2–0 at Anfield, of all places. After the game, as we walked out to the coach, what I thought was a supporter asked me for an autograph. I signed it and he tore it up in my face. Leeds, who won 3–2 at Sheffield United, were champions with a game to spare. We did manage to win our last match, 3–1 at home to Tottenham, but so did Leeds, so we finished four points behind them, in second place.

Runners-up in the league and Rumbelows Cup winners meant it was a good season by anybody's standards, but somehow it didn't feel that way. The title was the club's priority, and we'd missed out. Personally, I had plenty to put on Mum's mantelpiece. The players' union, the PFA, made me Young Player of the Year, and I was still young enough to play in the FA Youth Cup Final, where United beat Crystal Palace at home and away. I played in the second leg, which we won 3–2. In that team with me were Gary

Neville, David Beckham, Nicky Butt, Keith Gillespie and Robbie Savage, all of whom were a year or so younger than me. It wouldn't be a bad six-a-side team, would it? That class of '92 was a credit to Eric Harrison and the youth system the gaffer had put in place. I'd be seeing a lot more of them all.

Paradise

I was part of the team now, and if what people were saying about me was true, an integral part too. I'd started thirty-two of United's forty-two league games in 1991–2 and got on as sub in six more. In all competitions I'd made fifty-one appearances – more than Steve Bruce, Paul Ince or Andrei Kanchelskis. I'm a very private person, shy really, and suddenly it seemed everybody wanted to know me. I started to ask myself why. Were people so friendly because they genuinely liked me, or just because I was a footballer? I wouldn't tolerate hangers-on, so they were never a problem, but I found everyone's attitude towards me was changing in a way I didn't like. People who used to go to school with me, who I'd known for years, were different with me. 'Oh, you've changed,' they'd say. 'Success has changed you.' It hadn't, it was their attitude to me and perception of me that had changed because I was a well-known footballer. I found that very difficult to come to terms with at first, I couldn't get my head around it. I just wanted to talk to people normally, but I found myself watching what I was saying all the time, desperate not to sound like a name-dropper or Billy Big-Time. It's not a problem now because I keep to a close-knit circle of friends, most of whom have known me for years and treat me like any other mate, not a celebrity. Things had changed so fast, though, and I was being forced to adjust very quickly.

I started earning a lot more money than my friends, and I had to be careful about that as well. Your natural instinct, especially with mates, is to be generous – because you can be – but it's easy to get carried away without really thinking. I had to stop myself saying, 'I'll get these drinks in' all the time, or if we went shopping and someone said, 'I like that,' I'd want to say, 'Have it, I'll get it.' There were a couple of close mates I'd go shopping with and buy a pair of jeans or a jumper for. That has never really bothered me, and I don't think it bothered them either. They accepted without embarrassment. As with everything else that was changing, it just took a little getting used to. The 1992–3 season was the year the old First Division became the FA Premier League, but United fans have other reasons to remember it with affection. The first of these was the arrival of their greatest hero of the modern era, Eric Cantona. The gaffer had been after another striker for some time, and pointed out that our goals had tailed off badly the previous season, when we scored forty-two in the first half of the season and only half as many after that. He tried for Alan Shearer, who went to Blackburn instead, and also for David Hirst, of Sheffield Wednesday, who was on fire at the time. Eventually he settled for Dion Dublin, who had played well for Cambridge against us during our Rumbelows Cup run. Dion was a good lad, well liked by everyone at the club, and we were delighted for him when he got off to a good start, scoring the winner at Southampton in August. Tall and strong, with a good touch, he was a real handful for the best of defenders, and I know the gaffer thought a lot of him. It hit everybody hard when he broke a leg in only his sixth game, at home to Crystal Palace. The break was a bad one, and it was obvious he was going to be out for a long time. We all felt a deep, genuine sympathy for him, but football can be a hard business. We needed goals and he had to be replaced.

Eric had scored a hat-trick for Leeds against Liverpool in

the Charity Shield the previous month, so everybody knew all about him. On television the previous season, I'd seen him score a lovely goal that any player would have been proud of, that was the first time I noticed him. Then he got the hat-trick at Wembley and suddenly everybody seemed to be talking about him.

While Eric was all the rage though, our season got off to an awful start. We lost our first two league matches, to Sheffield United and Everton, then drawing 1–1 at home to Ipswich, so after three games we were twentieth in the table, with one point and two goals. The gaffer wasn't a happy man, and wasn't good at hiding it. We all knew something was going to happen. We recovered well, winning the next five on the trot, but then fell away again, and when we played Leeds at home at the start of September, Steve Bruce and Gary Pallister raved about Eric and went to the gaffer and said how tough he was to mark, and what a good player he was. The gaffer took note of that and made his move in November, after a bad run in which we drew five league games in succession, then lost the next two. Also during that time we'd gone out of the Coca-Cola Cup, as the League Cup had now become, losing over two legs to Brighton.

I know the gaffer tried again for Hirst before getting Eric, and he had been talking to the chairman about getting Peter Beardsley, from Everton. And then Howard Wilkinson, the Leeds manager, phoned asking about Denis Irwin. The gaffer took advantage of the opening to ask whether or not Eric was available. I think it was a pretty tongue-in-cheek inquiry so he was pretty surprised when Leeds said yes. Of course, getting Eric proved to be a masterstroke. It seems amazing now that the fee, £1m, was exactly the same as we had paid for Dion. Value for money or what? We had had only one win in over two months from mid-September when he signed. He was registered too late to play in our next game, away to Arsenal, but he came with us to London and trained with the team on the morning of the match. He was brilliant in everything he did, and the other players took to him immediately. He had given us the lift we needed, and we won 1–0, Sparky getting the goal.

Straight after the Arsenal game we went to Portugal for a golfing break, and while we were over there we played a friendly against Benfica. Eric came with us, and it was a valuable getting-to-know-you exercise for him and the rest of us. Four or five days away with the lads helped him no end. As soon as we got there we all went out to a casino for a laugh and a few beers and he seemed to be at home straight away – nothing like the aloof figure of legend. When we got back, his first appearance was as a substitute in the Manchester derby at home on 6 December 1992. Who made way for him? None other than yours truly. I'd broken a bone in my foot and had to go off at half-time. I cut inside, had a shot and my foot hit Steve McMahon's studs. It's probably the worst injury I've ever had, but it gave Eric his chance. We won the game with goals from Ince and Hughes, but as the gaffer put it later, it was Eric who had 'illuminated' Old Trafford, and after that 'Ooh-aah Cantona' became the fans' favourite chant. Eric was in the team for good, never a substitute again. He was in from the start at home to Norwich, who were the league leaders, when a 1–0 victory lifted us to third in the table, and he scored his first goal for the club in a 1–1 draw at Chelsea on 19 December. Up and running, he scored again in each of the next three league games as we rattled in twelve goals against Sheffield Wednesday, Coventry and Tottenham to go top of the table for the first time in early January.

We were a team on fire, and it was Eric who had been

the inspiration. Nobody could have predicted the fantastic effect he would have. Everyone remembers how he used to strut around the pitch, arrogant and super-confident in his own ability, with his collar turned up, but he was never cocky with us, just one of the lads. He would join in with the banter and come out for a few drinks. After the game he'd always be there.

Normally, the new lads joining the club stay at the Mottram Hall Hotel, south of Manchester, but Eric used the Novotel in Worsley. Just round the corner from where I bought my own house. It was one of six, a new development built on the site of an old farm, half a mile from where I went to school. I bought it off plan. I paid £60,000 for the plot of land and £100,000 to have it built, so £160,000 in all. The architect lived in the main farmhouse, so I knew he wasn't going to build rubbish next door, and it turned out to be a great investment. Anyway, I'd pick Eric up for training, or for games, and we'd talk. To the media, he used to pretend that he couldn't speak English, but that was just to get out of doing interviews. He knew it would stop him being pestered. With us, his English was good right from the start. His family were still in Leeds, and Worsley is convenient for the M62, so he could get home in twenty-five minutes. Eventually he had a house in Boothstown, which is just next to Worsley. I guess he liked the area.

I wouldn't say I was best mates with Eric, but I certainly spent more time with him than the others at first because of where he lived. Peter Schmeichel was the one who went on to become his real pal. They roomed together on trips, so they got to know each other well, and they were similar personalities. Off the pitch they were quiet and reserved, on it they were just the opposite.

I realized immediately what a good player Eric was – how

strong and how quick he was. I couldn't believe a big man could have such pace. Once he got going, nobody could outrun him. He was one of those guys whose speed is deceptive. You suddenly notice how far they've travelled before you'd really thought they were moving quickly. For a winger, like me, his partnership with Sparky was a dream because you could ping the ball up to either of them and they'd bring it under instant control, whatever the angle. If I saw Denis Irwin on the ball, about to knock it up to Eric or Sparky, I'd always make a run because I knew they'd hold it up and play me in. Eric would receive the ball, turn in one movement and lay it off. For me, he was fantastic to play with. Because of his vision, you just knew he'd read your run and play you in.

He was a match-winner, a great player. All the great players do it when it matters, and Eric did. So did Peter Schmeichel, Bryan Robson and Sparky from that team. They all did it when the team needed them. When we were looking to him, Eric would score.

Inspired by the boost he had given us, we stayed top of the league until the end of January '93, but then lost the leadership by going down 2–1 at Ipswich, who were a decent side, in fourth place, but fell away badly to finish sixteenth. Norwich went top again, and our minds inevitably went back to the previous season, when we had blown our title chances. Manchester United were bigger than Norwich City. Surely we had to be better than them?

The nerves were jangling, and we had a terrible struggle to beat Sheffield United 2–1 at home in our next game, when Eric got a late winner. Two days later we had to go to Leeds, which is always a horrible fixture for us, and the atmosphere was made even worse this time by Eric's return to Elland Road. The crowd's hostility towards him was evil, and we were all just happy to get away from the place safe and sound, and with a goalless draw too. Fortunately for us Norwich slipped up, too, losing 3–0 at Southampton, and our other title rivals, Aston Villa, were beaten 1–0 at Crystal Palace. We realized we weren't the only ones feeling the pressure.

We thought we had cracked it with three successive wins, against Southampton, when I scored both goals, Middlesbrough (I scored again) and away to Liverpool, who were having a terrible season under Graeme Souness. Astonishingly, they were only three points off the relegation places. Beating them put us back on top, a point ahead of Villa at the same time as Norwich's challenge faltered, with a 3–1 defeat at QPR.

The title was there for the taking, but no one seemed to want to grab it. We stumbled badly, losing 1–0 at Oldham, making it just three points from four games. In the middle of that run, Villa came to Old Trafford, and with the two teams level on points, with all to play for, it was billed as the match of the season. Villa always worried me more than Norwich. Ron Atkinson had put together a strong, experienced team, and they gave us a lot of trouble. We'd already lost to them twice that season – they put us out of the Coca-Cola Cup in the third round. Before this third game we worked hard on our tactics all week. The gaffer had me on the right wing, from where he wanted me to cut in on my left foot, with Lee Sharpe on the other wing. Andrei was out of the side at that stage. The plan was to play men in behind Paul McGrath and Shaun Teale, two excellent central defenders who were great when facing the danger, but not so good when they were turned. Mark Bosnich, who had played in the reserves with me, was now in goal at Villa, and he kept us out until the second half, when Steve Staunton, who always had a powerful shot, gave them the lead with a real screamer. We were lucky when Mark Hughes equalized with a header, to keep us joint top. Like I said, he was a player who delivered when the team needed it. Norwich stayed two points behind.

So the league was still wide open, and the following week the race took another turn when Norwich beat Villa 1–0 and we could only draw 0–0 at home to Arsenal. It meant Norwich went top again, and that, going into April we faced another 'match of the season'. But, this time, at Carrow Road we would be without Sparky, who was suspended. The gaffer still chose to have a go at them and put out one of the most attacking sides he had picked all season, featuring me, Kanchelskis, Sharpe, Cantona and McClair. The bold approach worked. I played up front with Eric, with Andrei and Lee on the wings, and Choccy just behind, and we produced our best performance for weeks to beat Norwich 3–1. We played them off the park and were 3–0 up, with the outcome beyond doubt, after only twenty-one minutes. They tried to play an offside trap, but our pace did them again and again. I got the first goal, Kanchelskis and Cantona the others. It was exactly what we needed and did wonders for our confidence.

The following game, at home to Sheffield Wednesday, was a real nail-biter. We missed a stack of chances in the first half, and in the second they took the lead with a penalty, after Incey had fouled Chris Waddle. The gaffer sent on Robbo with twenty minutes left and we bombarded them, but the goals wouldn't come. When Steve Bruce equalized, with a typically brave header, there was seven minutes of normal time left, but we played on and on, long after all the other Premier League matches had finished. The referee had pulled a muscle I think, and had to be replaced, which took time, and there was a lot of stoppages for injuries, so the gaffer spent the latter stages making an exaggerated show of looking at his watch, and pointing to it with that wide-eyed look of his. They had heard on the bench that Villa had been held to a draw at home to Coventry, and the gaffer was signalling that a draw would do us, too, but then with seven minutes of added time played I took a free-kick out on the left. On reaching the goalmouth, the ball was deflected by a defender out to the right, from where big Pally, of all people, crossed it back into the middle for his mate Brucey to head in the winner. There was bedlam all round the stadium, with Brian Kidd doing a war dance on the pitch. After that result, we felt luck was with us.

We put in a storming finish to the season. It was all but decided with two games still to play when we went to Crystal Palace and beat them 2–0. Villa were away to Blackburn that day, with an earlier kick-off than ours, and they were 2–0 down before we started. At half-time in our game the gaffer was able to tell us that Blackburn were 3–0 up, and we knew there and then that we'd be champions. Our fans knew it too, they were going nuts all through the second half. That night we had a four-point lead at the top of the table with only two matches to play. Norwich had blown up and were out of it after losing 3–1 at Ipswich. Again Villa had to play first. I don't think it would be allowed today, the games would have to be simultaneous for reasons of fairness, but back then television dictated that Villa would play Oldham on the Sunday and Blackburn would come to us the following day. Oldham was always going to be a difficult game for Big Ron and his team. They had beaten us in March, and Joe Royle had them scrapping for their lives (they eventually avoided relegation by one place). Still, we all assumed Villa would get at least one point. We were wrong, Oldham won 1–0, with a goal from Nicky Henry, and we were champions without playing.

We'd won it the day before our game against Blackburn, when Villa lost. We weren't playing, but I couldn't watch the Villa match on television, and went to a pub, the Bridgewater in Worsley, with a couple of my mates. I was there when I got a phone call, telling me the result. I rang Incey to ask what all the lads were doing, and he said: 'Get over to Brucey's house.' I didn't know where he lived, I didn't know south Manchester at all, but I got directions and set off with the mates from the pub. When we arrived, all the players were there with their wives and girlfriends, drinking the captain's champagne. That went on all night, until about six o'clock in the morning on the day we were playing Blackburn. I was driving, so I went home at about one a.m., which was earlier than most, but still hardly ideal preparation for the game.

I remember driving in to Old Trafford, where by this time the parking arrangements had changed. We didn't use the old car park, opposite the ground, we had to drive to reception where our cars were parked for us. Getting through the crowds took ages. There were red and white banners and flags everywhere – most of them seemed to have Eric's head in the middle. The fans were so excited they were rocking and shaking the players' cars as they came in. They were trying to get into my car, it was a bit scary and the stewards had to intervene to get me into the ground. It was then that we realized it was going to be a crazy occasion. We beat Blackburn 3–1. The result was just the icing on the cake, and Old Trafford went mad. The relief and the intensity of the celebration was on a scale we'll never see again.

What it meant to United to win the league after all those years had become apparent to me the previous season, when we lost it to Leeds. After that, I went away on holiday and United fans kept coming up to me saying, 'Ryan, are we ever going to win the league?' That went on every day of my holiday. I couldn't believe the number of people who approached me and said, 'We've got to do it next season. Got to.' That really brought it home to me what a massive thing it would be for Man United to win the title, and how much it meant to the supporters. For a club of our size, twenty-six years was ridiculous.

After the game we had another party. We went to a hotel called the Amblehurst, which Robbo used a lot. He knew the owner of the place, so we all went there. By that time I was really friendly with Incey, and the two of us had agreed that if we won the league we'd wear something outrageous, so we bought these shocking jackets. Mine was a loud, blue and white striped thing, his was even worse, so we both got loads of stick all night. I left my car at the Amblehurst, and spent the night at Clayton Blackmore's house. I slept in the clothes I'd been wearing, forgetting that Clayton had a cat. I had black trousers on, and woke up with white cat hairs all over me. I looked like something the cat had dragged in! Clayton asked: 'What are you doing today?' and I told him I was going home. He said, 'A lot of the lads are going to Chester races, do you fancy coming?' So I went, still wearing the clothes I'd slept in.

But first we went back to the Amblehurst for a champagne breakfast! Then off to Chester races with the rest of the players. The gaffer didn't go. I don't think he was into horseracing that much then. The celebrations were fantastic, the best I've ever known, and carried on for days.

It had been an historic season for the club and a great one for me, personally. I'd started forty of our forty-two league games, got on as substitute in another one, and played forty-six matches in all competitions, getting eleven goals, which put me ahead of Eric and second only to Sparky, who was leading scorer with sixteen. I was a regular with the top club in the country and an automatic selection for Wales. The PFA again voted me Young Player of the Year, as did football's major sponsors at the time, Barclays, who presented me with their Silver Eagle Trophy and a cheque for £5,000 at the Savoy Hotel, in London. I felt I had arrived.

The Family

My brother, Rhodri, also started a career as a professional footballer, with Torquay United, before ending up at Mossley, a good non-league club. Growing up, he was always interested in the game, but not obsessed, like I was. He's right-footed and plays up front or on the right wing, similar in style to me. We went to the same school, where he soon got a bit of a reputation. He has always been a bit of a lad. I had my football to keep me on the straight and narrow, he strayed and got into a lot of trouble at school.

It's only recently that I've come to terms with the upbringing we had, and realized the effects it must have had on my brother. Our dad went when Rhodri was very young, times were hard financially, and Mum had to do two jobs, as a barmaid at a pub called the Henry Boddington's and as an auxiliary nurse at Pendlebury Children's Hospital, to make ends meet, so there wasn't the constant parental attention and influence that most kids have.

On top of that, both of us had to cope with another emotional upheaval when, a couple of years after Dad left, a new man came into Mum's life, Richard Johnson. I have to admit neither of us liked that, and I think it was a difficult time for everybody involved. It was hard for him, hard for me and Rhodri, and particularly hard for Mum. She had two sons at an awkward age, she had found someone she wanted to be with, and before long she moved into his house. She did, I didn't. I was fifteen, and I chose to spend a lot of time at our old place on my own. But Rhodri would go with my mum to Richard's house. He had a really nice place in Swinton, near my school, with a leather suite, state-of-the-art TV and video and a lovely kitchen. We were quite poor really, we had a pay-meter for the electricity and no central heating, so at Richard's house it was nice to experience another style of living. He was a freelance chef who specialized in making cakes, he was very creative at that, but he wasn't at all interested in football, so it was hard – really hard – we had so little in common and we definitely didn't get on at first. So much so that I went to live with Paul Ince for a while. Rhodri, though, didn't have the same opportunities to escape the unsettling domestic situation.

I'd been happy with things for a long time, just the three of us living together, and now Mum was interested in someone else. Richard tried his best with me, but I just didn't want to know him. He didn't have a chance. Trying to build bridges, he took us on a foreign holiday, to the Greek island of Zante, but even that nearly ended in disaster. A group of us went: Richard and Mum, me and Rhodri and two of my mates. I'd been there two days, I think, when I came off a motor bike. It was the summer I'd just left school to join United. My two mates had bikes at home, so as soon as we got over there they said, 'Let's go and hire one each.' They got two scooters, I was on the back of one and when we were out in the middle of nowhere, half-way up a mountain, I said, 'Come on, let me have a go.' They let me, I skidded and came off, cutting my arm to bits, hurting my knee and ruining my holiday. It didn't seem that way at the time, but I was lucky. If the injury to my knee had been worse, it could have been a real nightmare, costing me my place at United. As it was, I managed to hide the bandages from Mum for a day or so, but eventually she came into the bedroom I was sharing with my mates, saw blood on the sheets and said, 'Where's that from?' I had to tell her, and got a verbal hammering. Mum was always strict with me. Because she was only seventeen when she had me, she seemed more like my big sister than my mother, and we've always had arguments, always bickered, but she has always had the last word. Worse than the bollocking on this occasion was the way my holiday was ruined. I couldn't sunbathe, my arm was in a right state, so I learned a lesson the hard way. I haven't been on a bike since.

I don't think Richard was too impressed. He'd made the effort, taking us all on holiday, and I'd messed up, but, fair play to him, he didn't make a fuss. Eventually there came a stage when I realized he was good for my mum, and it was nice to see her happy again. He worked hard, looked after her and my attitude to him thawed. We were never best mates, but we got on. Eventually they got married and moved from Richard's house, which was a bachelor pad really, to a bigger property just 200 yards down the road. It was an old, derelict cottage which he refurbished completely. He kitted it out beautifully, and it was something me and our kid weren't used to. We suddenly had a really nice house, and for the first time in my life I was proud to invite my friends home and comfortable about inviting girlfriends back.

But Rhodri never got on with Richard. And it was worse for him than me in that respect. He was younger than me and he never came to terms with the stepdad thing really.

At the time I didn't appreciate the pressures Rhodri was under, and if I'm honest I feel a bit sorry for what he had to cope with. Apart from what was going on at home, he was always being compared with me, right through school, and when he played football it was always: 'He will never be as good as his brother.' He still has to live with that now, and possibly because of it he's got a short temper – our dad's temper – and he's been in a few scrapes. People locally know who he is, and sometimes when he's out he'll hear people have a pop at me, maybe just to wind him up. Unfortunately, he's not the kind of person who can just walk away from it, he's got to fight them. He's got into a lot of trouble like that.

He was expelled from school and has never really had a stable job. He was an apprentice at Torquay and he really enjoyed it down there. Our grandparents would go down to visit him quite often, because it's a nice part of the country. I saw him play once, against Birmingham at St Andrews. I couldn't see him often because I was usually playing at the same time. He played really well, but I know he wasn't happy with the money he was getting there, and he left under a bit of a cloud.

After that things went downhill for him. He carried on playing for the non-league scene, but he was no better at controlling his temper or walking away from a potential confrontation. And this ended in a pub brawl that led to a nine-month prison sentence. He was in trouble again and again after that and we fell out badly. I told him he was letting down his family, and especially our mum. But blood's thicker than water, and we've patched things up. We're mates again now, and over the past three or four years we've been closer than ever. As long as he was hanging around with the wrong crowd trouble was always on the horizon. I suggested to him a few years ago that he'd be better off leaving it behind and associating with my mates because they're all sensible lads. To his great credit he's done that and I see him a fair bit now. We all play golf together. Rhodri is better than me – a bit of a bandit playing off a fourteen handicap. I'm a genuine sixteen. He lives with his girlfriend in his own house, near Worsley, picking up £100 a game for Mossley and making ends meet in partnership with a mate, selling cars via the internet, which suits him because his office is his phone. So I'm happy to say he's doing OK. I have to say that I admire the way he's pulled things together. I can only guess how distressing he found Dad's leaving and the unsettling effect it had on him at a vulnerable age. He was always scarred by that, but never had the lifeline football gave me. Maybe some of the problems he has had were the product of our father's influence. He didn't exactly set the right sort of example. I'm also aware that I concentrated entirely on my football when I was growing up and wasn't the most helpful of elder brothers. To be fair to myself, I was too young to realize how hard he was finding things. His personality is different from mine. I can snap and lose my rag sometimes, but it doesn't happen that often. With Rhodri, his first instinct is to snap. Fortunately, he has learned to control his temper over the years, and he's a better man for it. He has matured and settled down, and fair play to him for that. He always was a caring and loving person, but in his tearaway days that side of him didn't come across as much as it does now.

It's a great relief, and source of pride, to me that he has conquered his demons and is building a good life for himself. He is enjoying his football, and was Player of the Year for Mossley last season. They love him up there. Wherever he has played he's been popular because he's the sort of player people love to watch. If I get the chance, by which I mean if United haven't got a game, I go and watch him. That's something I plan to do a lot more in future. We used to fight all the time, and fell out for a spell, but we're closer than ever now.

Like Rhodri, I had to learn who to hang out with. Just

before I got into the first team, and then for a while when I was in it, Sharpey was always the one, but after I'd got into a few scrapes with him the penny dropped. Nobody told me to steer clear of him, and we stayed friendly, but not like we had been. We drifted apart and I became closer to Incey, who took me under his wing. Me and Paul hit it off instantly and became roommates on trips, then best mates, and spent a lot of time together. I lived at his house, in Bramhall, for a couple of months, which was great. He had this massive place in Cheshire. It was 1992 and he and his wife, Claire, had just had their son, Thomas. It was a good time, I really enjoyed it. They didn't even charge me for my keep. Mind you, I had to endure Claire's cooking with a grateful smile, so that was probably payment enough!

I was still with Sue then, and the four of us got on really well. I remember we all went to Malta together for a few days on some sort of supporters' function. Back home, we'd go to a place called Coco Savannah in Stockport, which was a popular place with the younger players, but we didn't go out that much because Incey and Claire had just had Thomas, so we spent a lot of time in the house. He had a snooker room and we played a fair bit of that. I'm not much good but he is. At every club you'll have your friendships. At our place there was me and Incey, Robbo and Brucey, Clayton and Sparky. There were no cliques, though. We'd all go for a few beers at Mulligans.

When I left Incey's I went back to the cottage with Mum and Richard for a while, and things were all right. For me, in the long run, the thing that shone through was the love that existed between my mum and Richard. They had a daughter, my stepsister, Bethany, who was born in 1992. She inherited Richard's dyslexia, but has conquered it and done well at school, with the help of a tutor. When I was twenty I bought the house in Worsley. It needed quite a lot of work, so while I was waiting for the builders to finish it, I went on holiday to Marbella with a few mates – none of them players – and that was when I met up with TV presenter Dani Behr. Earlier that year she'd interviewed me on TV in Manchester and we seemed to get on OK, but I didn't chat her up or anything like that. But then when I was in Marbella she just happened to be out there filming for another TV programme. We bumped into each other in a bar in Puerto Banus. I was with all my mates and she was with her film crew. Anyway, we got chatting again and arranged to meet when we got home. We ended up going on holiday together, to Antigua, about two weeks after that. I didn't think there was any point hanging about and I couldn't blame the builders this time! We stayed at a lovely hotel called the Blue Waters. She was earning more than me then, so I'm not even sure I paid for it. Dani never actually moved in with me, but she'd come up and stay in Worsley when the season started, or in the summer I'd go down to her place in London. We were quite an item – or so the media seemed to think. But not for long.

Double Bubble

In July '93 the gaffer made an outstanding signing when Roy Keane arrived from Nottingham Forest for £4m. Roy is a couple of years older than me, and he'd already had three full seasons at the top level, establishing himself as the sort of box-to-box midfielder we needed to replace Bryan Robson.

That summer I signed a three-year boot deal with Reebok, worth about £300,000. I'd just completed two years with Puma, and Martin Buchan, the old United player, looked after me there. That was all before I had an agent. The gaffer said Martin was someone we could trust and so Puma was an easy choice. Now, though, after a couple of good seasons, all the various sportswear companies were in for me. Reebok came up with the best offer, and I was able to use some of the money to buy that house in Worsley.

United now went on a pre-season trip to South Africa and did a couple of soccer schools in Soweto. That was an eye-opener for me. The players split up into groups of four and five and went to different places in the townships. The young footballers we saw had no trainers, some were wearing odd shoes, others didn't have any shoes at all. The pitches were little more than gravel, there was no grass. The conditions could hardly have been worse, but the kids were all smiles. Their happiness to see us and to take part was a humbling, but also rewarding and hugely enjoyable experience. I'd never done anything like it. A lot of them were really skilful, despite their disadvantages. They were all black lads. I was struck by how the whites play rugby while football is the blacks' game out there – a reminder of the country's past. Despite the obvious poverty, I never felt uncomfortable, because everybody made us feel so welcome. If that hadn't been the case, the conditions might have worried us a bit more, but they were happy, so we were. They just wanted to play football, which suited me just fine. And they loved it when we joined in with their games and showed them a few of our drills. We were out there for ten days and I loved it. It was a good experience for me and helped put my changing fortunes into perspective.

The showpiece at the centre of the trip was a match against Arsenal, played in Johannesburg in front of a packed crowd of 65,000 people. Although I wasn't playing, I was in the changing room before the game against Kaiser Chiefs when word came down that Nelson Mandela wanted to meet me and the gaffer. We went up to meet him in his VIP box. It was a huge privilege to shake the great man's hand and talk to him in person, and a memory that will always stay with me. During the game the fans were over-enthusiastic and so was Bryan Robson. He got sent off, which just goes to show that Robbo didn't do friendlies! As if we needed a reminder. It was also further evidence that Manchester United v. Arsenal was always a bit spicy, even in those days. We lost this one 2–0 and Roy, who had joined us a couple of days late, struggled a bit for fitness in the game. I remember him doing a lot of extra running in the days afterwards. It must have been really hard work in the heat out there and it was an early indication for me of his commitment.

On our return from South Africa we had to play Arsenal again, in the Charity Shield at Wembley. This time it went to penalties. David Seaman took one for them and missed and we won 5–4 but that's all I can remember about it really. The trouble is that I hate all pre-season games, the Charity Shield included. The weather is always too hot. On top of that, I never liked playing at Wembley anyway, it wasn't a dribbler's pitch. The grass always looked beautiful, but it was too long and the ball held up in it. It was bad news for me.

With all of that over, we got started the defence of the title with a 2–0 win at Norwich, where I got our first goal of the season proper, then three days later Roy marked his home debut by scoring twice against Sheffield United. He had been known as a goalscorer at Forest, and now he was off to a great start. I think the trip to South Africa had been a big help for him. Away with us for ten days, he got to know the lads and settled in nicely. They were different days then, and there was more room for socializing. And that suited Roy. He used to like a few beers – he wasn't the only one – and the attitude to that was pretty relaxed in the early nineties. We had a fair bit of spare time while we were out there, so there were a couple of decent nights out and a trip to the races too. By the time the season began, Roy Keane was well and truly bonded. United through and through.

I scored again in our third game, against Newcastle, and at the end of August we seemed to be carrying on where we had left off in May, top of the table with four wins and a draw from our first five games. On 1 September Lee Sharpe scored his fourth goal in three matches as we beat West Ham 3–0 at home. We were flying.

The following week I was on international duty with Wales, when we resumed our World Cup qualifying campaign against the Czechs in Cardiff. Wales had got off to a horrible start in Group 4, losing our first match 5–1 to Romania in Bucharest, but went some way towards repairing our morale by stuffing the Faroe Islands 6–0. I got on as sub, for Mark Bowen, and I didn't play in Cyprus, where we won 1–0, which left me back on the bench for the 2–0 defeat by Belgium in Brussels. When the Belgians came to Cardiff for the return, I got a start at last and scored our first goal in a 2–0 win, so I stayed in the team for the 1–1 draw against Czechoslovakia in Ostrava, where Sparky got our goal. A routine 3–0 win in the Faroes had put us in a decent position in the group, joint second with Romania on nine points, behind Belgium, who had fourteen, by the time the Czechs came to Cardiff on 8 September 1993.

The Czechs were a good side at the time, but so were we, and we knew we had a great chance of qualifying. But as is so often the case, luck wasn't with us. We conceded an early goal. I equalized midway through the first half, then Ian Rush gave us the lead before half-time, and it looked good. We seemed to be well set for a solid win and qualification without needing anything from our last game, against Romania. But then a player called Dubovsky pinged an unbelievable free-kick into the top corner. I'll never forget it, I was stood right behind it and knew it was going in from the moment he struck it. It turned out to be a costly draw. But there had been other mistakes. When we played the Czechs away, we'd been 1–0 up through Sparky, but then let in a stupid equalizer, so we had plenty of chances to qualify – we seemed intent on making it difficult for ourselves.

Back at United, we lost 1–0 at Chelsea – our first defeat in seventeen league games – but were still joint top with Arsenal, and in the middle of September we celebrated our return to the European Cup after twenty-five years by beating Honved 3–2 in Hungary. Roy Keane, already a big hit with the fans, scored twice. I played, but all I can remember

77

is Mike Phelan coming on to replace me. We beat them again in the return, when Steve Bruce scored with two headers, and went through easily.

In October, just before my twentieth birthday, I agreed a new five-year contract, and Lee Sharpe got a new deal the same day. I was now on £350,000 a year, or nearly £7,000 a week.

A 2–1 win at home to Spurs put us seven points clear in the league, but then we had a real jolt when Galatasaray came to Old Trafford in the second round of the European Cup. After a quarter of an hour we were 2–0 up and coasting, but then we became over-confident and lost our focus, and they hit back hard to lead 3–2. In the end, we needed a late goal from Eric to salvage a draw. We've played Galatasaray a few times, and for some reason it's always a nightmare. Especially away, and that was still to come. In the league we were still going great guns, and a 2–1 home win against QPR gave us an eleven-point advantage over Norwich, who were second, but the beginning of November took us to Istanbul. I'd never seen anything like it. It was a bad trip from the time we arrived to the minute we left. It was a four-and-a-half-hour flight from Manchester, and when we got to Istanbul airport it was early evening. I couldn't believe the scenes, with hundreds of Turkish fans with vicious looks on their faces waiting to give us a hostile reception. The 'Welcome to Hell' banners were bad enough, but they were spitting at us and throwing coins and other things. When we got on the coach they were rocking it and throwing stuff at the windows. The security was a joke and the atmosphere hellish and intimidating.

The night before the game the Turkish fans were ringing our hotel to disturb the players' sleep, and the hotel staff were putting them through to our rooms every time. We'd gone to reception and asked them to block all calls, but they ignored that. I was rooming with Incey, and he was getting more and more wound up. In the end he snapped and hit back: 'Come on then,' he told the callers. 'You know where I am and which room I'm in, come and have a go if you think you're hard enough. I'll be waiting for you.' He was too. I wouldn't have fancied their chances. Meanwhile, I was under the bedsheets going: 'No, no. Don't,' and making sure the door of the room was double locked. If they weren't on the telephone they were outside our hotel, chanting and letting rip with their car horns all night. None of us got any sleep.

For the game, the atmosphere in and around the stadium was designed to intimidate us. The kick-off wasn't until eight p.m., but the ground was full all afternoon, the fans working themselves up into a frenzy. The game was rubbish, a 0–0 draw putting us out on away goals. At the final whistle Eric had a go at the refreee, who I felt had been scared to give us a decision, and was a right 'homer'. Then it all kicked off in the tunnel. Bare concrete surrounded us as we walked down stairs that led towards the changing rooms under the pitch. As we were coming off the field, fans bombarded us with all sorts of missiles and filth. All the police were interested in was lining the walls of the tunnel. Eric had gone, mentally, after the confrontation with the ref. Already at boiling point. So when a policeman pushed him he just snapped. He was cracked over the head with a police baton, and then things really started to get nasty. Robbo was in there immediately, trying to calm things down, but the police were pushing and shoving our players, looking for a reaction to give them the excuse to wade in and really sort us out. It was total chaos. All of us piled in together and then our security men arrived and ushered us down to the dressing room and it was over. While it lasted it was a horrible, scary situation because we were trapped in the tunnel with nowhere to go. When we complained, some people said it was sour grapes because we'd gone out, but that was wrong. We complained because we were mistreated and threatened. The trip was miserable from start to finish. And without a silver lining.

Going out of the European Cup was a colossal downer, but we showed our character four days later when we were 2–0 down at Maine Road and came back to win the Manchester derby 3–2. It was a relief to be in Manchester again. Even Maine Road! Niall Quinn thought he had won it for them, but two goals from Eric brought it back to 2–2 and then Roy settled it for us in the eighty-seventh minute. I didn't start that day. I hadn't played well against Galatasaray and the gaffer left me out and brought back Andrei to play with Lee. I came on as a sub when we were 2–1 down and with my first touch I set up Eric for his second goal. It was one of the great derbies – for us, anyway! We were eleven points clear in the league; nothing was going to stop us now.

Life is full of ups and downs. There was Istanbul, then ten days after the exhilaration of the derby came what is likely to remain the biggest disappointment of my career. On 17 November 1993 Romania came to Cardiff for the match which should have taken Wales to the 1994 World Cup. We've not been in the finals of the greatest tournament of them all since 1958, but despite making it tougher with our result against the Czechs, we were at home and we fancied ourselves. My mates and my family were all there – well, I don't know about my dad, because we'd lost contact by then. We needed to win against the Romanians to qualify and we were confident. Yes, they'd beaten us 5–1 in Bucharest, but we'd come on in leaps and bounds since, and had players who belonged on the biggest stage of them all. Neville Southall, Ian Rush, Dean Saunders and Gary Speed were all at the peak of their powers, as was Sparky, who was out, injured. Even without him, we thought we were good enough, and we should have been.

In the first half, to be honest, we got a bit of a doing, and they went 1–0 up through Gheorghe Hagi, whose shot slipped under big Neville's body. In the second half we played a lot better, and Deano equalized at close range on the hour from my free-kick. Their morale collapsed, and I could see from their body language that they didn't want to know. Within a couple of minutes we got a penalty, when Dan Petrescu tripped Gary Speed. Poor Paul Bodin will always be remembered for missing it. He didn't miss the target totally, he hit the bar, but the poor lad might as well have missed by a mile for all the good it did us. Had the penalty gone in, I think we'd have won by three or four, but if-onlys don't count. Instead, they won it with a late goal from Florin Raducioiu and we were out.

I was completely gutted by the defeat, but I was young and was sure there would be other World Cups. This had just been my first shot at it. But some of the others were crying and inconsolable, really distraught. Neville, who was thirty-five, and had been the best goalkeeper in the world, knew it was his last chance. Ian Rush was thirty-two and knew he wouldn't be around four years later. Sparky was thirty-one and Deano rising thirty too. They both thought the same thing. It was a desperately sad night for them but it wasn't the worst of it.

I remember somebody calling the result a tragedy, but they were wrong about that. The real tragedy that night occurred off the pitch. A spectator sitting in the stadium was hit and killed by a rocket-type flare some idiot fired off.

Driving home afterwards, I got stopped by the police and done for speeding near Birmingham on the M5. I'll never forget it, this copper stopped me and said, 'Where have you been?' I told him I'd just got knocked out of the World Cup, and he said, 'I'm doing you anyway, you were clocked at ninety-three in a seventy limit. By the way, can I have your autograph?' Ninety-three on a motorway at midnight with nobody about. And the copper was full of it. He said, 'I wasn't chasing you, I was chasing someone else but you got in the way.' I looked at him and went, 'Yeah, right. Just give me the ticket, you've no chance.'

It was a bad time to be a Welsh footballer, and the Welsh FA made it even worse when they sacked Terry Yorath as manager and replaced him with John Toshack. I didn't know Toshack, or even much about him really, all I knew was that we had improved greatly under Terry and he didn't deserve to go. I enjoyed playing for him and his assistant, Peter Shreeves. Not only were they knowledgeable about football, they were very good with the younger players, making them feel instantly at home and part of everything, even if they weren't playing. The training and the atmosphere were always good.

It was after their sacking that I started to feel disillusioned about playing for Wales and I didn't really enjoy international football. Terry's replacement was always going to get a rough ride and that was exactly what happened to Toshack. I wasn't injured but I didn't play in the one game he was in charge, a 3–1 defeat against Norway at Ninian Park, when the fans booed him and chanted Terry Yorath's name. I didn't go, I watched it on the telly. John resigned after one game in charge, which came as a surprise to me and the rest of the players.

An Englishman, Mike Smith, was appointed to replace

him. Mike had managed Wales before, in the seventies, and I knew him from my youth-team days. He'd had a lot to do with Welsh football at grass-roots level and was a really nice bloke, but not the sort to inspire big-name players like Mark Hughes, Ian Rush and Neville Southall. I think he only agreed to take the job again while the Welsh FA looked for someone else.

By the time my twentieth birthday came around, on 29 November, our lead in the league had stretched to fourteen points, which was how it stood at the end of '93. We were going from strength to strength. We'd won the league the season before with the best team in the country, and now we had Roy Keane, who had made us even better. When we were all fit, we knew there was nobody to touch us. Confidence had replaced the nerves and apprehension that used to hold us back before we won that first title. It was a fantastic team we had that year, and we went out expecting to win every game we played. We didn't win them all, of course and at the beginning of January we had a sensational tussle away to Liverpool, where we ended up relieved to get a point. I remember the game very well but not for the best of reasons. Sparky was injured and I played alongside Eric in attack. We went 3–0 up pretty early, with me getting the second, but then Nigel Clough pulled two back before half-time, and after that the Anfield atmosphere took over and a towering, unstoppable header from Neil Ruddock made it 3–3. Even then we could still have won it. With about two minutes to go the ball came to me on the edge of the box and I hit a great shot which was heading for the top corner until Bruce Grobbelaar took off and made a fantastic save, knocking it away for a corner. What I hadn't spotted was that Eric was free, in a better position. Unfortunately the gaffer had and so I got a right bollocking after the game for not passing to him. But as he tore strips off me, Paul Ince waded in on my behalf and had a go at the gaffer: 'How can you give him stick?' he argued. 'He was man of the match, he ran his legs off all night.' However well intentioned, the intervention probably wasn't wise, and the gaffer turned on him. The two of them started arguing, which wasn't unusual in those days. Neither of them was prepared to give any ground. 'Say nothing,' I thought to myself as I watched them lock horns. 'You're better off out of this.'

The death of Sir Matt Busby a fortnight later, on 20 January 1994, touched everyone associated with the club. I was too young to have known him well, but I was very much aware of the huge part he had played in United's history, and everyone was deeply affected by his passing. He would always go to that youth tournament in Switzerland, where I first met him. Also, as president of the club he always kept an office at Old Trafford, between the general office and the wages department. In order to get your wages you had to pass Sir Matt. Coming up the stairs, if you could smell the thick tobacco smoke from his pipe you knew he'd be there. He always made a point of catching your eye and smiling. He still seemed proud of the young lads on the team, even though his responsibility for bringing them on had long passed. We all had a great respect for him. He may have been a legend but to us he was almost a grandfatherly figure. Two days after his death we played Everton at Old Trafford. There were floral tributes to Sir Matt outside the ground and a minute's silence before the kick-off, when the Everton supporters were brilliant. You could have heard a pin drop in the stadium. After that the atmosphere was very subdued, but the gaffer told us beforehand to go out and play the way the great man would have wanted, and we did. There was a pride and passion in our game that day, creating loads of chances. I'm not sure why, but we only took one of them, when I scored with a header, but that 1–0 win took us sixteen points clear of Blackburn at the top.

Sir Matt's funeral was a very emotional affair, attended by everyone associated with the club and friends and high-profile representatives from everywhere else. Despite the sadness at Old Trafford, the season marched on. I don't think Sir Matt would have had it any other way. The previous day we had reached the semi-finals of the Coca-Cola Cup by beating Portsmouth 1–0 at Fratton Park, and at the end of January a 2–0 win at Norwich put us into the fifth round of the FA Cup, so a treble, which had never been done before, was very much on. It would be something to dedicate to the great man's memory.

The Norwich game was remarkable not so much for the result as for a terrible foul by Eric on one of their midfield players, Jeremy Goss. Jeremy played with me for Wales, and he was the sort who wouldn't hurt a fly. He was the last person who you'd expect to be on the receiving end of a foul from Eric. I wasn't sure exactly what had happened at the time, but slow-motion replays on BBC television looked terrible, and Jimmy Hill accused Eric of 'vicious play'. The gaffer's always been unshakeable in his defence of his players, but the flipside of that is that he gets his say behind closed doors. For public consumption, the gaffer called Jimmy a 'prat', but privately he wasn't at all impressed by what Eric had done, and let him know it in no uncertain terms. Unfortunately, the behaviour was to get much worse. And it wouldn't just be Eric next time the gaffer had cause to speak his mind.

In the first leg of our Coca-Cola semi, against Sheffield Wednesday, at home, I got the only goal early on. Wednesday had a good team then, with Stuart Pearce, Des Walker,

Carlton Palmer, Andy Sinton, Chris Waddle and David Hirst, all England internationals, but we were better on the day, and I remember going round their 'keeper, Kevin Pressman, and leaving myself with a really tight angle, but managing to slide it in at the back post. After that, we went to Hillsborough for the return and hammered them 4–1 for a 5–1 aggregate. Andrei Kanchelskis was on fire that day. That was a good performance, but we gave an even better one to win 3–0 at Wimbledon in the fifth round of the FA Cup. Eric scored with a tremendous volley, but it's our third goal that gets shown almost every year on TV. According to the gaffer, there were twenty-seven passes in the move before Denis Irwin finished in a way I'd have been proud of. He cut inside, played a one-two, dummied the 'keeper and stuck it in. Not only were we top of the league by a comfortable margin, we were in the Coca-Cola final and were now made 6–5 favourites for the FA Cup. The media talked a lot about the treble, but the players were thinking more in terms of winning two trophies – the championship and one other. The gaffer kept reminding us that United had never done a double of any sort. The confidence was definitely there. On our day, no one could live with us.

We were brought back down to earth with a bump in March, when Chelsea ruined our unbeaten home record. Gavin Peacock, who had got the winner when we lost at their place, did it again, and by now our lead in the league, which had been sixteen points in January, was down to just four. Blackburn were our problem, they were on the charge, with eight wins and a draw from their last ten games. In the FA Cup we beat Charlton, who weren't in the top division then, 3–1 despite having Peter Schmeichel sent off just before half-time, with the score still 0–0. Peter charged 40 yards out of his area, took the man before the ball and had to go, but it made no difference to the outcome. The gaffer took off Paul Parker and sent on Les Sealey in goal and with ten men we won easily enough in the end, thanks largely to Andrei, who scored twice.

In mid-March, after thrashing Sheffield Wednesday 5–0, we had a seven-point lead over Blackburn, but now our discipline really went haywire, threatening to ruin all our good work, and that was when the gaffer had to read the riot act. Eric was sent off for stamping on Swindon's John Moncur, then red-carded again three days later for clashing with Tony Adams in a bad-tempered 2–2 draw at Arsenal, where Roy Keane's booking took him over the top under the totting-up process. That meant he would miss our FA Cup semi-final against Oldham. We took only a point apiece from the games with Swindon and Arsenal, and so our lead over Blackburn was down to six points, but they had a game in hand.

The gaffer really lost his rag with Eric over the Swindon thing, and told him in typically forthright fashion to sort himself out, or else. But it wasn't only Eric who had the hair-dryer treatment. Sir Alex had a phrase for Schmeichel, Ince, Robson, Keane, Hughes and Cantona: he said they could start a fight in an empty house. That fighting spirit could serve us well, but it could also be our undoing and the gaffer knew it. Unless we kept a lid on our discipline we'd throw it all away. He called all of them into his office to lay down the law: 'That's enough,' he told them. 'No more.' No room for argument.

The team we had that season was full of fiery characters. Me and Sharpey were still young, but the rest were battle-hardened old pros – experienced, clever and determined men who couldn't stand losing and would do anything in their power to prevent it. They were prepared to take on their own teammates, as well as the opposition, if they felt someone was in the wrong. Schmeichel would have a go at Bruce and Pallister, Ince would be bollocking everyone and Sparky was always ready for a fight. In training and in the dressing room they were fine, it was during the games that the Jekyll and Hyde thing seemed to come over them.

The positive aspect of our 2–2 draw at Highbury was that Lee Sharpe, who had been out for seventeen games after a hernia operation, returned to score twice. He was still a fine player, still a great crosser of the ball, but that injury cost him the extra surge of pace that made him outstanding, and in my opinion he was never the same after it. Before, I'd watch him in training and he could give Denis Irwin five yards and just steam past him, and Denis was quick. I don't think Lee recovered properly from the hernia. It wasn't just the seventeen games he missed, he was out on and off for eighteen months and never quite got back that blistering speed he had when he was nineteen. Of course, his lifestyle didn't help. He never looked after himself as well as he should have done and in the end that's always going to catch up with you.

The day before we played the Coca-Cola final, Blackburn beat Swindon 3–1 to keep the pressure on, then at Wembley it all went pear-shaped. We just didn't turn up and Villa fully deserved their 3–1 win. I was disappointed with my own performance too and couldn't complain when Lee came on to replace me. They were a decent team certainly. We'd had to fight them off in the championship the previous season, and Dalian Atkinson and Dean Saunders got the better of us on the day but we should have been able to compete. Andrei was sent off in the last minute, for handball on our goalline, but it was over as a contest well before then. We'd never looked like winning.

The result was obviously a downer as much in the way we lost as the result itself. We needed a lift in order to maintain our momentum, and we got one forty-eight hours later when Blackburn lost 4–1 at Wimbledon. The following day we took full advantage, beating Liverpool at home 1–0 with a goal from Incey, and with a six-point lead we were cruising again – or at least we *thought* so. At the beginning of April we were the fools. We had to go to Ewood Park for a real crunch game and, with Eric starting a three-match suspension, we were well beaten, 2–0, Alan Shearer scoring both. That meant the gap was down to three points with seven games left.

In the FA Cup semi-finals the following week, Chelsea beat Luton 2–0 with two goals from Gavin Peacock, who proved that it wasn't only us he scored against! We had a real struggle against Oldham at Wembley. Joe Royle had Oldham well up for it, and at the end of normal time the match was goalless. We hadn't looked like scoring until, in extra time, after Oldham had taken the lead through Neil Pointon, Sparky came up with the sort of goal only he could get. He was leaning back, his body shape was all wrong and his technique defied logic when he got both power and dip into a volley which was a goal from the second it left his boot. Conceding so late absolutely destroyed Oldham, and we battered them in the replay, winning 4–1 at Maine Road.

Before that, though, there was real drama when Blackburn beat Aston Villa 1–0 to draw level with us on seventy-nine points. Remember we'd been sixteen clear at one stage. Now we had a real fight on our hands. We still had a slight advantage, with a game in hand and a superior goal difference and everybody – even the gaffer – was a bit more relaxed about the situation than they would have been the year before, because now we knew what it took to win the league. We all felt that if we stayed calm and played as well as we could, we'd be OK. It was just a matter of keeping our nerve.

It was easier said than done though. On the same day in mid-April both contenders lost. We went down 1–0 at Wimbledon and Blackburn 3–1 at Southampton. The crucial difference was that we recovered well and they didn't. Eric, back after his ban, scored both goals in a 2–0 derby win at home to Man City and the following day Blackburn were held 1–1 at home by QPR. We were two points ahead of them, with a home game in hand. More importantly, we were playing well, while Blackburn faltered. They won just one of their last five, and the title was ours with two games to spare, when they lost at Coventry the day after I'd got our winner at Ipswich.

We still had home fixtures to complete against South-ampton and Coventry, but the championship was in the bag, and a lot of the lads went out to celebrate the night before the Southampton match. That sort of thing was usually unheard of, but Steve Bruce rang the gaffer and asked if it was OK to go out. 'All right,' he said, 'but don't go mad because we still want to win tomorrow!' I didn't go with them this time, and instead went to my local pub, The Bridgewater, with my mates.

The real celebrations could wait. In the Cup final we were up against Chelsea, who had beaten us twice in the league that season, and fancied their chances at Wembley. They still fancied themselves with the game an hour old and goalless. They had been the better side up to then, and our friend Peacock hit the crossbar. As he struck the shot I thought, 'Oh no, not him again!' but it rebounded out and suddenly we buried them. Eric scored two penalties in the space of seven minutes and they never looked like coming back from that. The first penalty came when I nutmegged

Eddie Newton to release Denis Irwin, who was clearly brought down inside the area. The second was for a non-existent push on Andrei. Chelsea were broken by the unfairness of that one and Sparky made it 3–0, then Choccy McClair, on for Andrei, completed the scoring.

The gaffer's choice of subs must have been difficult. Robbo was leaving at the end of the season, after so much sterling service, and everybody expected him to be one of the two permitted at the time. I certainly thought it would be him and Lee Sharpe. Even at thirty-seven, he was still a massive presence at the club, and we always missed him if he wasn't there, on the bench or wherever. He still had the priceless ability to come on and inspire all those around him. He had what Roy Keane acquired after him – we all felt we had a much better chance when they were in the team, and it wasn't as if he was finished either. Don't forget, Robbo played on at Middlesbrough after that season.

But Lee and Choccy were picked instead at Wembley. I know Robbo was hurt by it too. It was a shame. It would have been the perfect send-off for him, as club captain, to go up and collect the cup with Steve Brucey, our team captain. It's something Liverpool did with Jamie Redknapp later on, but it didn't happen this time.

It had been a fantastic season by a marvellous team. We had been top in every table that was published bar one. After our third match, against Newcastle, who held us 1–1 at home, we were third, but after that nobody could catch us. Whenever we were at full strength, as we were in the Cup final, we were never beaten. Just for the record, that team was: Schmeichel, Parker, Bruce, Pallister, Irwin, Kanchelskis, Ince, Keane, Giggs, Cantona, Hughes. I've heard the gaffer say it is the best team he's had here, and I wouldn't argue with that. It had everything: pace all the way through the side, a fierce competitive streak and the unique, match-winning skills of Cantona. I had my best season too, scoring 17 goals in 57 appearances in all competitions. In the league it was 13 in 38. Eric was leading scorer, with 25 in 48 in league and cup, followed by Sparky with 21 in 55, Sharpey with 11 in 41 and Andrei's 10 in 46. We had goals from everywhere. There was every reason to look forward with confidence to what lay ahead and, at the end of the season, Peter Schmeichel signed a new contract for another four years and Andrei Kanchelskis for another five. Unfortunately, one of them turned out to be taking the piss.

The George Best Treatment

I was still living with my mum when the fans began giving me the pop star treatment. I was nineteen when fan mail, birthday and Valentine's cards began to arrive by the sackful. On Valentine's Day that year I got nearly 3,000 cards, all sent to the club. The girls on reception at Old Trafford would ring me at the training ground to tell me, 'You've got to come and pick up these bloody cards.' Each player has his own cubby-hole for mail but mine couldn't cope. The other lads gave me loads of stick because while Denis Irwin or Steve Bruce were getting five or six letters, I'd be getting bin-liners full. Even Sharpey only got half as many as were pouring in for me. It wasn't just women either. Men would write too, although on the whole their letters were about football! I tried to read as many as I could, but there wasn't enough time to get through them all. Instead I'd bring home the sacks and give them to Mum. I'm not even sure what she did with them. For all I know she might still be hoarding them in the garage. Generally speaking though, her dad – my grandfather – has always been in charge of that side of things. He answers the majority of the fans' letters. And when I'm playing for Wales in Cardiff I use the opportunity to go to his house and sign autographs, photos and the rest. Grandad is on the firm – I'm happier keeping it in the family.

I've been lucky that the vast majority of the attention I've had has been good-natured. But I did get stalked by a fan once. Thank God it never got out of hand. It was a woman from London who would turn up at every away game. Every time I got off the team coach, she'd be there waiting for me. It was never scary, but she was always there, and she'd shout my name and give me a letter or a little gift. Eventually she got into trouble with the police, and it emerged in the newspaper coverage that she was stalking me, Ayrton Senna and Michael Jackson at the same time. I suppose that explains where she was when we played at home: she was rotating the three of us!

Despite people's best intentions, things could become unnerving. I did a promotional appearance in Slough which was very hairy. So many people turned up they had to shut the M4 exit. The police came and tried to shut it down. 'You're going to have to stop this now,' they told us. 'They're queueing for more than a mile at the motorway junction, and it's causing traffic problems on the motorway.' Fortunately the pop star thing was only at its peak for a couple of years, in '93 and '94. Later, of course, Becks took over, and it *really* snowballed for him, especially after he met Victoria. At one time I was probably doing too much of that stuff. It wasn't just Reebok; I had promotional contracts with a soft drinks manufacturer, the makers of the meat substitute Quorn – five or six other big companies – so I was doing a personal appearance somewhere every other week.

United were OK about it, but I was beginning to have my doubts. By this time I had an agent, Harry Swales. The gaffer knew and trusted him, and he was instrumental in getting the two of us together. Harry became my agent just after I signed my deal with Reebok. He had been agent to the England football team in the seventies, and now he looked after Robbo. I was getting letters from lots of different agents and I'd give them all to the gaffer and say, 'What do you think?' Quite a few of them were from people he didn't get on with, so they went straight in the bin. Sir Alex helped me with a lot of my deals early on, but it got to the point where he didn't have time for it all, and he thought Harry was the best person to take it on. I met Harry in the manager's office at The Cliff, just to see how we got on. He wasn't like the rest of them at all. He had big white sideburns and a moustache, was over seventy and in semi-retirement. I liked him immediately. Harry Swales is a real gentleman, the last of a dying breed. He has never been out to make a quick killing, either for himself or for any of his clients. The players he has looked after – myself, Kevin Keegan, Bryan Robson – have been in it for the long haul, and Harry has handled our careers with long-term security in mind. He goes the safe route when it comes to contracts, preferring long deals to the quick big hit. His clients have all become friends, more than business associates, and it never ceases to amaze me when he does a sponsorship deal for me how many of the people we deal with he has worked with before. They all get to know and trust him, and use him because they know they can work with him. He's dead straight, there's no risks with him. We've never needed a contract, we shake hands on everything. That's enough. We've always said that if there's a problem between us we'll talk it through, but we've never needed to. He's like family really. He takes a percentage from any commercial deals he does for me, but nothing from my income from United. He says I earn, and deserve, all that. I'll never understand footballers giving their agents a cut from their contracts. At first Harry said, 'No, I don't want to do it. I don't need all that at my age.' I had to talk him into making money, which must be a first for an agent!

Eventually, though, the extra workload became too much

for me. That point came when I was shooting a video for my own soccer school, in association with Bobby Charlton, who had them everywhere. We were filming in pre-season and the video was really hard work. I was turning up at six o'clock in the morning, filming for three hours, then going for pre-season training, which is always exhausting, and after training I was going back to film some more. That went on for the first week of pre-season training, at the end of which I was totally knackered. I had to ring Harry and say: 'Enough is enough, I can't do any more of this.'

Right from the outset, when I first joined United, the gaffer had been very protective. I think the club had learned their lesson when George Best was left to his own devices and went off the rails, and they weren't going to let it happen with me. George, for example, was doing interviews when he was seventeen; I wasn't allowed to do my first until I was twenty. It became a bit of a big thing in itself. The fact that I wasn't doing them became the story. When I did start the gaffer chose carefully who it was with. Hugh McIlvanney of the *Sunday Times* was someone he'd known for years. He trusted him. I spoke with him over lunch in December 1993 and I remember telling him that I thought Wales would qualify for the '94 World Cup and that I would end up playing in Italy one day. So much for the wisdom of youth!

For as long as it lasted, I loved not needing to bother with the interviews all the other players were doing; it was nice to be able to go straight home after training or matches without all that. It couldn't last for ever though, and not having my say started bothering me. I was getting a bit of stick from the media for 'snubbing' them, and I'm sure the fans were beginning to wonder if I was dumb. But getting it wrong in an interview can explode in your face, and I was lucky in that I had been able to watch how Robbo and

Brucey handled them. It was easy for them, they were so clever in the way they deflected awkward lines of questioning and avoided controversy. I looked at how they did it and decided that was the way to go about it.

Trying to conduct interviews on my own terms was particularly important because of my relationship with Dani Behr. It was in the papers a lot, even though it lasted less than six months. Dani would come up to stay at my house in Worsley for four or five days at a time, but I found it difficult because, while I would go training, she'd stay in bed all morning, then when I got home at lunchtime she was raring to go. 'Right,' she'd ask, 'where are we going? Let's go out for a bit of lunch.' After running around all morning, I just wanted to stay at home and relax in the afternoon, so it never really worked. It couldn't. I'd have to devote maybe four or five days entirely to her, and I just wasn't able to do that and play football to the best of my ability as well. We just seemed to be at cross purposes, and I have to say that put me off proper relationships for a long time. I had a few, of course, but none of the girls ever moved in with me. Home remained off limits. I probably wasn't ready for a long-term relationship, but things were made especially hard because we lived so far apart and were both trying to build our own careers.

The only person who lived with me was Bernie Taylor, a mate from school who had a couple of restaurants in Worsley – a tapas bar and an Italian. He lived at my place for eighteen months or so and we still managed to be great friends at the end of it. So perhaps there's hope for me yet.

I wouldn't say I was wary of *women* after Dani. I had a good few one-night stands which gave the lie to that idea. I know some of the lads worry about gold-diggers who make a beeline for footballers because of the money we earn, but that has never bothered me. There were a few of them I didn't spot, but usually I could.

It was about a year after Dani before I got into my next serious relationship. Davinia Taylor later became well known as an actress in *Hollyoaks*, but at the time she was still at college. Her mum and dad were from Liverpool, but she grew up in Wigan, and we met at a bar-restaurant in Manchester called Johnsons. I was twenty-two, she was seventeen, and I was with her, on an off, for nearly eighteen months. We were quite serious, but she was very young, and it never got to the stage where I was tempted to ask her to move in with me. She may not have even wanted to! That said, she did stay over at my place a lot.

In those days my grandparents, my mum and my mates would come to home games, and we'd meet up in the players' lounge afterwards. I used to go in there after every match, something I don't do any more. Incredibly, I've never gone in there for a drink, not even once. Quite a few of the players did, though. In the early days of my United career it was definitely the done thing. They'd have a few – whisky, brandy or whatever – but the culture has changed, and it's a half pint of lager at most now. Or so I'm told. When I used to go in there it was more just a place to meet up and unwind after the game. It never became more than that for me. If I wanted to go out and socialize, I'd move on to somewhere in town with mates outside football.

I did have friends at the club too. When I was twenty or twenty-one the closest were Incey, and after him Nicky Butt. I've always got on well with Nicky, even when I was in the first team and he was in the reserves. Don't be fooled by his public image: he's not such a quiet lad, not at all. He and Paul Scholes don't really bother with interviews, and when they do they say very little, so people get the wrong impression of them. Out of the spotlight they join in with the banter and give as good as they get. They like a laugh as much as the rest.

In 1996 Becks bought the house just behind me in Worsley. I saw a lot more of him after that. One night I had a few of my mates with me at my place, watching TV when the phone rang. It was Becks and he didn't sound too happy. 'I think there's someone trying to get into the house,' he told me. My mates and I sprang into action. We all ran round there straight away and checked the place out, but we couldn't see anything. If there had been burglars, they'd gone. And just as well too. They'd have had a nasty shock if we'd caught them, because my mates are a bit handy. Me? I'd taken a baseball bat with me. Just in case.

It didn't have anything to do with that incident, but I moved house soon afterwards. I gave the house in Worsley to my mum and moved out into the country, to a place called Blackrod, not far from Bolton's Reebok Stadium. If Becks had trouble again, he'd have to fend for himself!

Welsh Wails

I lost a lot of my enthusiasm for playing for Wales when the Welsh FA sacked Terry Yorath. He had done a good job and was so close to taking us to the 1994 World Cup. Terry was a proud, passionate Welshman who had captained the team himself for a long time. He was well liked and all the players had great respect for him. The Welsh manager's job is a tough one, but we could see knew what he was doing. He was clever enough tactically to make the best of limited resources, and that was vital.

Unfortunately, little of the above applied to those who followed him. As I mentioned, John Toshack lasted only one game. His replacement, Mike Smith, was a nice man, but not equipped for the job. It was when he took over from Toshack that the rot really set in. We got off to a decent start in our qualifying group for the 1996 European Championship, beating Albania 2–0 in Cardiff, where I scored the second goal, but then we lost 3–2 away to Moldova and were thrashed 5–0 by Georgia in Tbilisi. I missed those two defeats, with an ankle injury, and was absent again when Bulgaria came to Cardiff and won 3–0. The big news at that game was Vinnie Jones being picked for the first time. He had discovered Welsh ancestry somewhere or other. Unlike some, though, I didn't have particularly strong views about it. He qualified, he didn't make up the rules, so why not? We didn't have a lot of Premier League players available, some good ones had retired, and he came in and did all right for us. Our poor results weren't down to him in any significant way, we just didn't have the quality in numbers needed to succeed in international football.

I was back when the Bulgarians beat us 3–1 in Sofia in the return. They were a good team then, but we were very poor, and after four successive defeats morale was at rock bottom. We'd gone from being organized and hard to beat under Terry Yorath to a demoralized rabble. Goals were flying in against us left, right and centre. We were going out on to the pitch and not expecting to win. After playing for United I found that particularly hard. We finished next to bottom of that qualifying group, so it was hardly a surprise when the Welsh FA sacked Mike Smith in June '95.

Two months later, after a lot of talk about Ron Atkinson and Howard Kendall, they appointed Bobby Gould, who had been out of work for ages and now became Wales' fourth manager in two years. What we needed was an experienced man who could handle big players like Rush and Hughes. Atkinson or Kendall would certainly have fitted the bill. Bobby, though, I wasn't sure about. I wasn't against him from the start – I think you have to give any manager a chance before you make your mind up about him; Mike Smith and John Toshack came and went so quickly we couldn't really make a proper judgement. We needed a bit of stability, so, like all the players, I wanted to give Bobby the benefit of the doubt. No one was keener than me to see it work out. But he never recaptured the spirit, or the effectiveness, we had under Terry. We never had the depth or intensity of Terry's preparation, whereby each player knew exactly what was expected of him, and what he should be doing. Worst of all, of course, Bobby's results were poor. To say the least.

In November '96, before a World Cup qualifier in Holland, it got to the ridiculous stage where Bobby decided we should choose who was to captain Wales in a players' ballot. Barry Horne, the regular captain, was injured, and in their vote the players picked Vinnie Jones to replace him. I wasn't on the trip, so I don't know how it happened, but I have to say I wouldn't have voted for Vinnie. There were other players in that team who were much better equipped for the job and who deserved the honour more. In the circumstances, it didn't surprise me that Wales went down to their worst-ever World Cup defeat, losing 7–1 in Eindhoven. We were that bad in those days.

The first time there was a real fuss about me pulling out of the squad was in February '97, when we had a friendly against the Republic of Ireland in Cardiff. After that it was a big deal every time, as if people were just waiting to make a song and dance about it. It was a difficult situation for me. At that time, whenever I played two games in one week I always seemed to pick up an injury, so the gaffer and I sat down and looked at it game by game. If the international was a friendly, the feeling was that I didn't have to play. Obviously I wanted to play for my country as often as I could, but to be honest I felt the medical care we got with Wales was never as good as it was with United. Not just that, but the preparation – the training and the pitches used, everything really – was never top-class, which it should have been. It echoed the situation that Roy Keane complained about with the Irish. The two of us used to talk about it a lot, sharing our frustrations about our countries' respective set-ups. Nothing, we agreed, was as good as it should have been.

It made it easier to decide that, if I wasn't 100 per cent fit, I wouldn't risk joining up with Wales. I'd gone through a couple of years playing with niggly little injuries, or coming back too soon, and I suffered for it. I had to look after myself, so I took a conscious decision that I would take care of my own interests better. If I turned up for Wales with a dodgy hamstring or whatever, I'd always be under pressure to play and certainly felt obliged to. I've done it a few times, gone away with Wales and been injured, and I'm always the one who loses out.

People aren't aware of my medical situation, and I don't blame them for that. My hamstrings have been a problem for years, and I've always suffered from delayed fatigue with them. If I played an international or a Champions League match on a Wednesday, the hamstring – it's usually the right one, but occasionally the left – would start playing me up the following night, by Friday it would be even worse and on the Saturday I'd just be getting over it when I was due to play again. After playing in midweek, especially in a tough European game, I'd know that my hamstring was going to be really tight on the Friday, and for the last three or four years, the gaffer has taken one look at me and said, 'Right, we'll rest you tomorrow.' But the United squad wasn't always as big as it has been recently. Until recently he had no choice sometimes other than to put me on the bench or say: 'Just give us an hour and you can come off.' There have been many games when I've just about got away with it, but a lot more where I haven't. There were three occasions, for some reason all against Derby at home, when a hamstring went late on in the game, and people would ask me, 'If it was down to fatigue, how come it didn't go after ten minutes?' but it doesn't work like that. I know when the problem is going to flare up, it's always when it's cold or when the leg feels tired.

It took about six or seven years, but eventually the penny dropped, and I said to myself, 'You're doing yourself no favours here, you've got to start looking after number one,' and because I've done that, the last three years have been my best, injury-wise.

In March '97 we blew our chances of getting to the World Cup by losing 2–1 to Belgium in the last international staged at Cardiff Arms Park. I played, and more memorable than the result was a row between Bobby Gould and Nathan Blake, the black striker then with Bolton, who accused Gould of making racist remarks. I'm no fan of Gould, but I don't think he's a racist. He did use the phrase 'black so-and-so', but the way he said it wasn't really racist. I think it all got blown out of proportion because Nathan didn't like him anyway – not many of us did. The Welsh FA took it seriously enough to hold an investigation, but after Gould apologized, considered the matter closed.

Big Neville Southall was also talking about retiring from international football around then, and probably wishes he had. He was pulled off at half-time when we lost our World Cup qualifier 6–4 to Turkey in Istanbul. Despite the score-line, he'd managed to keep us in the game. If he hadn't been there in the first half, it could have been ten. It was the craziest game I've ever been involved in. Bobby Gould, the tactical genius, played me at left wing-back, which lasted all of twenty minutes. They had a right-winger and a right-back who kept bombing on at me, and I was constantly out-numbered. Once I started to push on, we did all right. Having been 2–0 down after eight minutes, we fought back to lead 4–3. At that stage Dean Saunders tried to play me through and his pass got cut out, they broke away and scored for 4–4.

When Gould took Neville off at half-time he sent on Paul Jones, who hadn't started a match for us then. Nev definitely wasn't happy about the decision, and said so. It was his last match for Wales, and a sad way to bow out after ninety-two caps. I didn't really get to know him that well. To be honest, I found him a bit strange, but then he was famous for that! As a goalkeeper, though, he was the main man for a long time, and I'd put him right up there with Peter Schmeichel as the best I've ever seen. The two of them had days when you just couldn't beat them in training. When they were in the zone, they were that good they'd be saving shots and laughing at you. Nev was unbelievable for Wales, sparing us some real hidings with the saves he made. For a few years I've no doubt he was the best 'keeper in the world. Huge. I guess that gave him the right to be peculiar.

He was definitely eccentric. In the mid-nineties, before the clubs put their foot down about when they would release players, we'd meet up on a Thursday for international matches the following Wednesday, so we'd go out at the weekend. I remember sitting with some of the lads in a club in Cardiff called Jacksons. I looked up and at the end of the bar there was Nev, with a Thermos flask of tea. He didn't drink alcohol, so he sat there with a cup of tea. It took some bottle, mind you. Imagine the stick he got off the lads!

Bobby Gould seemed to do a lot of things just for effect. It was typical of him when he picked a lad called Ryan Green to beat my record as the youngest player called on by Wales. Ryan, like me, came from Cardiff, but we didn't have much else in common. He'd been a pro with Wolves for seven months when Gould chose him and hadn't even played for the first team. Gould told the media, 'I've unearthed a real gem,' but I don't think the boy has been mentioned since. Last I heard, he was playing non-league football. It was a typical Gould stunt. Soon after that his mate Vinnie retired, after winning nine caps for Wales. Vinnie's brief career typified Bobby's time in charge. I liked Bobby personally, but things never gelled under him. They never felt settled. His own lack of international experience as a player meant that he had to work hard to earn respect from the dressing room, while his English roots meant he would always have a battle to win over the fans. Neither had been a disadvantage suffered by Terry.

Fergie's Fledglings

When I first got into United's first team I still took great interest in the apprentices I'd played with in the FA Youth Cup-winning side, and the other young lads who were coming through. It was much easier to follow their progress in those days, when we were all at The Cliff. If we had a game on a Sunday, we'd train on the Saturday, then stay behind and watch the youth team or the A team play afterwards. Most of the senior players would do that.

Within the space of two years or so, a lot of those youngsters had joined me in the first team. In chronological order, they made their debuts as follows: Gary Neville, Paul Scholes, David Beckham, Nicky Butt, Keith Gillespie, Ben Thornley, Phil Neville, and it was the 1994–5 season when they started to make their mark. Everybody knew the gaffer was really excited about their potential, and now he decided to put his faith in youth. There were no really big signings in the summer of '94. David May, at £1.4m from Blackburn, was our only buy. We had proved the previous season that our squad was good enough, and there were good young players pushing for a place. Signing Roy Keane a year earlier had given us the edge, all we needed was to keep going the same way.

We played in a pre-season tournament at Ibrox, which I remember for two reasons. One was Eric getting sent off in the game against the hosts, Rangers, for a two-footed tackle. Like Robbo he was another one of those players who don't do friendlies. The other reason was that before the match

I'd come in early from the warm-up, which I tend to do, and I was just getting my kit when I felt a tap on my shoulder. I turned round and it was Sean Connery towering over me. He was at the game as a guest of the gaffer, who introduced him to all the players. It's not that I'm star-struck, but Connery definitely did it for me. He's a legend. Sadly, I didn't really manage to make the most of the opportunity. I just managed to blurt out, 'Pleased to meet you,' and that was it. I doubt it was quite as memorable for him!

We beat Blackburn 2–0 in the Charity Shield in another friendly that was anything but. There were seven yellow cards and Incey was fined for overdoing his celebrations after scoring. Blackburn were not just local rivals, they were spending big, intent on taking our title, and by this stage there was a bit of feeling between the two sides.

In the league, we had a decent start, beating QPR and then Spurs, but Newcastle got away to a flier, winning their first six games. Meanwhile we lost 2–1 at Leeds and beat Gothenburg 4–2 in our first group match in the Champions League, when I scored twice. It didn't seem so at the time, but a more significant match than either of these two was the Coca-Cola Cup tie away to Port Vale towards the end of September. That was when the gaffer decided it was time to give the young players a go. Paul Scholes made his first appearance that night, but also in the starting line-up were David Beckham, Gary Neville, Nicky Butt, Keith Gillespie and Simon Davies. There were only five senior players in the starting line-up – Gary Walsh, Roy Keane, Denis Irwin, David May and Choccy McClair – but the lads did the club proud and won 2–1. Scholesy made it a debut to remember by scoring twice.

In our next league game though we lost 3–2 at Ipswich, which put us fourth, behind Newcastle, Blackburn and

Nottingham Forest. There was no panic, though. Winning two championships had made us much more relaxed, and we never really worried if other teams got away to better starts. We knew that if we played well, we'd soon go on a run of our own which would take some beating. Previously, we'd worry about teams getting ahead of us, but experience had taught us to bide our time. We had the confidence to do it too.

In the Champions League, a goalless draw away to Galatasaray was as uneventful as our last visit had been dramatic. The Barcelona game that followed, though, was something of a minor classic. I didn't play, and the gaffer surprised us all by dropping Steve Bruce and using Paul Parker to mark Romario, their star striker. The theory was that Paul's extra pace was more likely to deal with the Brazilian, but it didn't go to plan. Sparky headed us into the lead, but Romario broke clear to equalize. The gaffer was furious afterwards because Paul was supposed to mark Romario man to man, but had passed him on to Gary Pallister, who was beaten for pace. Bakero, the midfielder Incey was picking up, put them ahead, and it took a clever, backheeled equalizer from Sharpey to get us the point which kept us top of Group A.

It was a disappointing result, but we came back well in the league, ending Blackburn's 100 per cent home record by winning 4–2 at Ewood Park, then ruining Newcastle's unbeaten start to the season by beating them 2–0 at our place. Everything seemed to be fine, but at the beginning of November we came unstuck in a big way, when we travelled to Barcelona. In fairness, we were not at full strength because of the limitation on 'foreigners' that applied at the time. Because of that, Gary Walsh played in goal instead of Peter Schmeichel. The gaffer thought their full-backs, Albert Ferrer and Sergi, were vulnerable to opponents running in behind them, and told me and Andrei to pass the ball infield and run past our markers for the return. The other key part of his game plan was for Incey to pick up their dangerous runners from midfield.

None of it worked, they took us to pieces to win 4–0. It's a lonely place, the Nou Camp, when you're getting a stuffing from them. They had two quality strikers, Romario and the Bulgarian Stoichkov, who gave Bruce and Pallister a right run-around. As soon as we went a goal down, that was it. We never got a look in. After the game the gaffer picked our performance to pieces. A number of players came into the firing line, including Incey. But he took exception to it. I think it was at that point that he and the gaffer began to fall out big time, when the relationship began to deteriorate irreparably. It certainly kicked off in the dressing room between them afterwards, when strong words were spoken on both sides. Incey wasn't one to stand there and take a bollocking; he'd always have his say back, and that only made the gaffer worse.

Someone was always going to suffer after our humiliation in Spain, and we came back and thrashed Man City 5–0 for the club's biggest-ever derby win, Andrei getting a hat-trick. That put us second in the table, two points behind Newcastle, and in mid-November we went top when we beat Crystal Palace 3–0 at home. At the same time Newcastle, who had been setting the pace all season, lost 3–2 to Wimbledon.

However, just as things were looking up in the league the Champions League brought us down to earth with a bump. We needed a draw in Gothenburg to have a chance of going through to the quarter-finals, and all was well at 1–1, but then we lost our discipline, both positional and mental, and were hit twice on the counter to lose 3–1, with Incey sent off for dissent. I didn't play in that game, but I remember Jesper Blomqvist causing us problems and scoring. I was out injured for nearly four weeks at that time, and sat out the 0–0 draw at Arsenal which enabled Blackburn to go top.

It was my twenty-first birthday three days later, on 29 November, and I had a big party in a function room at The Oaks, in Walkden, just up the road from where I lived. All the players came and all my mates, and it was a good party. A very good party, actually!

In December we beat Galatasaray 4–0 at home, but still went out of the European Cup, which was hard to come to terms with. I missed that game, too, in what turned out to be my worst season for injuries. I picked up a calf strain when we played at Ipswich near the end of September. It was all new to me. I'd never really been injured before, and I didn't know how to handle it, what the recovery process required, so I kept coming back too quickly. I wanted to get back, thought I was all right, but would break down again. It was that season when I first started having trouble with my hamstrings as well, so it was a bad time from that point of view.

At the end of the year we were second in the league, three points behind Blackburn, then the gaffer stunned everyone by signing Andy Cole. That came as a total surprise. It seemed very strange – not strange that we should want him, but very odd that Newcastle, who were fourth in the table and challenging for the title, should let him go. We've always had a TV in our dressing room, and at that time we'd come in after our games, look at the screen for the other results, and Cole seemed to score for Newcastle every single time. We could all understand the gaffer wanting him because he was something we didn't have – a six-yard-box predator. Keith Gillespie went the other way as a makeweight in the deal, which wasn't such a surprise because he was hardly getting a game for us.

By agreement between the two clubs, neither Andy nor Keith was involved when we played at Newcastle less than a week later and drew 1–1, in a match notable chiefly for Mark Hughes' knee ligament injury, which kept him out of the team for four league matches at a vital time. That was a shock to us all because Sparky never got injured, never missed a game. It was a good job we took on Andy when we did. He made his debut in a 1–0 win against the league leaders, Blackburn, at Old Trafford. I made the goal for Eric. I was dribbling at Henning Berg, lost possession to him, and when he tried to run away with the ball I caught up and slide-tackled him and won it back. I got up off the ground and crossed it for Eric, who was at the back post, to head it in.

We were now just two points off the lead, and confident that we could catch Blackburn, but on a never-to-be-forgotten day in January our challenge blew up in our faces at Selhurst Park. The match against Crystal Palace had been niggly right from the kick-off. Their centre-halves, Richard Shaw and Chris Coleman, the Welsh mate I knew as 'Cooky', were dishing it out from the start. There was a lot of sly, aggravating stuff, shirt-pulling and that sort of thing, and I know the gaffer complained to the referee about it at half-time.

Four minutes into the second half, when Eric was through and had his shirt pulled again by Shaw, it was once too often. He kicked out in retaliation and was sent off. I didn't see what happened next, and I know most of the other players didn't because we were either remonstrating with the referee or concentrating on reorganizing the team to play with ten men. We know now, of course, that a Palace

My first big
sponsorship deal
with Reebok

Meeting Nelson Mandela in South Africa – a huge honour

Completing the double in 1994

Robbo bids us farewell in 1994. He'd been a big influence on me

Celebrating the 1996 title with Roy Keane

With Neville Southall. A Welsh teammate and, for a while, the best keeper in the world

With Dani Behr

Playing the role of roadside
flower-seller for a Reebok
ad campaign

And Davinia Taylor

A Champions League classic. Celebrating a goal in United's 1998 3–3 thriller against Barca

My favourite goal – in the 1999 FA Cup final against Arsenal

The treble is on. Celebrating the championship in 1999

And afterwards in the dressing room with Teddy,
Becks, my half-sister Bethany and Becks's son
Brooklyn

Celebrating the double with the 1999 FA Cup win against Newcastle

With Mum and the silverware so far

Harry Swayles, my agent,
and I hold the cup

The treble!

fan had a go at Eric, and he jumped into the crowd and attacked the guy: feet first.

I didn't see Eric leap into the stands. All I saw was Peter Schmeichel escorting him off. When we got back to the dressing room after the game Eric wasn't agitated, and seemed unaffected by what had happened. It was the same on the plane travelling back to Manchester. Nothing was said because none of us, the gaffer included, realized the seriousness of what had gone on. Word just hadn't got through and Eric was giving nothing away. It wasn't until I got the chance to see it on telly, when I got home that night, that I could see how bad it was. I couldn't believe what I'd seen. The club had to react the next morning, and banned Eric for the rest of the season, but because none of the players had ever seen anything like it, we had no idea if that was the end of the matter or not. It wasn't, of course. It would be a long time before we had Eric back in the side again.

Looking back now, I'm sure the fact that he wasn't allowed to play again that season cost us the title. In one mad moment we lost our inspiration, our talisman. In passing judgement on what Eric did, I think it's important to remember that the spectator he had a go at wasn't exactly whiter than white. He had provoked the attack with a stream of abuse, and it later emerged that he had a conviction for assault with intent to rob. Hardly a paragon of virtue.

Three days after the Palace match, with the drama over the kung-fu kick still unfolding, we beat Wrexham 5–2 in the fourth round of the FA Cup, a match notable as Phil Neville's debut. The following week Andy Cole's first goal for United was the winner at home to Aston Villa. Eric was the subject of huge amounts of attention and in February, he dominated the front pages of the newspapers again after a scuffle with an ITN reporter. But on the same day United climbed almost unnoticed to the top of the table by winning the Manchester derby 3–0 at Maine Road. The bookmakers now made us title favourites, and few would have been inclined to dispute that after we set a Premiership record by hammering Ipswich 9–0 in March. Andy Cole scored five. We should probably have got even more. It has to be said we play loads of games at Old Trafford when we create fifteen chances. The difference on this occasion was just that we put most of them away. I'm still embarrassed that I didn't get on the scoresheet!

Despite our avalanche of goals, Blackburn were still top of the league, needing only one to beat Aston Villa and stay three points clear. Wins against Arsenal and Chelsea while we were beating QPR in the FA Cup stretched that to six points, then we did ourselves no favours by losing 2–0 at Liverpool in mid-March. It's no real excuse, and I'm not using it as one, but the Selhurst Park saga inevitably became a distraction. At the end of February the FA extended Eric's ban until 30 September and fined him £10,000. Then in March the police charged Incey with assault for his supporting role in the fracas. Eric was bailed, pending an appeal against his two-week prison sentence, as was Incey, pending trial on 25 May. Eric won his appeal on 31 March, and had his sentence amended to 120 hours' community service, a 'result' he marked in his own inimitable way by lecturing the media about trawlers and sardines! The players loved that. The older lads, like Brucey and Pally, gave him some stick about it, which he found very funny. He was taking the piss, which he liked to do with the press, and not just the press, to be honest. If someone came up to him and he didn't know them, or didn't want to speak to them, he'd put on this act that he couldn't speak English: 'I don't understand you,' he'd say in his thick French accent, when in fact he knew exactly what they were saying. He spoke English very well.

While the post-Palace soap opera was going on, the rest of us played football. Eric was allowed to train with us throughout, and seemed to take it all in his stride. Footballers as a breed just get on with it, really. You take whatever life throws at you and use your football to get away from it all. The game is our refuge, I suppose.

At first, we didn't seem to miss Eric. We had Andy to play with Sparky, who was back after injury, so it wasn't that bad. It was later on that his loss was critical, when the league became so tight. He trained with us every day, then minibuses full of kids would arrive at The Cliff and Eric would stay on to do his community service, coaching them for two or three hours. The United coaches helped him, but it was definitely hard work for him. He had to serve every minute of his sentence and wasn't allowed to miss a session.

At the beginning of April Becks made his league debut in a 0–0 draw at home to Leeds, which was two points dropped, and a couple of days later Blackburn won to go eight points clear at the top with six games left to play. We were definitely worried now. We played Crystal Palace, of all people, in the semi-finals of the FA Cup, and there was a lot of bad feeling over what had happened at Selhurst Park, only a couple of months earlier. I remember both managers appealing for calm before the match, which was at Villa Park. It didn't prevent fighting on the day and the tragic death of a Palace fan. We came from behind twice to get a 2–2 draw, then won the replay 2–0, despite Keaney getting sent off for stamping on Gareth Southgate. Roy apologized to the rest of us in the dressing room afterwards for letting the team down, and it was accepted without question. Nobody would ever have a go at him about his behaviour. They couldn't, really, most of them were getting sent off themselves! Not me, of course. I've only been sent off once in my career, and that was playing for Wales, against Norway, for two yellow cards. I have my own painful reasons for remembering that semi-final. It was the first time I pulled the hamstring that still gives me trouble today.

In the title race, Blackburn seemed to lose their nerve at Easter, when they lost 3–2 at home to Manchester City, then 2–0 at West Ham, but we failed to take maximum advantage, dropping two points at home to Chelsea, so by the end of April Blackburn were six points clear. The position was a false one, though, because we had two games in hand, and now we applied the pressure. With six regulars out, we won 3–2 at Coventry, Andy scoring two, then David May, a former Blackburn player, got the goal that beat Sheffield Wednesday to take us to within two points of the top with two to play.

A couple of things happened to rock the boat at a time when we could have done without it. First Inter Milan came in for Eric, and there was a lot of talk about him leaving before he finally put it to bed by signing a new three-year contract. Obviously he wasn't happy at the time: he wasn't playing, which left a big hole in his life, and he hated the constant press intrusions. They were swarming over him. By this stage he'd moved out of the hotel and lived five houses away from my best mate on a normal estate, not far from Worsley, in Boothstown – nothing grand or flash. The people who lived around there were brilliant with him, but it was the sort of house where you step out of the front door straight on to the road. There was no driveway or anything to provide him with a degree of privacy. Most days reporters or photographers were there waiting for him. He really hated that. And there was a time when we thought he'd pack his bags because of it, but looking back now, I don't think he ever really intended to leave.

Much worse than the speculation about Eric's future was the behaviour of Andrei Kanchelskis. He had been injured and out of the team since playing for the Ukraine in late March, and now he slagged off the gaffer in the papers about not getting enough games, and said he couldn't play for him any more. He was fined for that and became even more stroppy, eventually demanding a transfer. There was speculation about Andrei's reasons for wanting to go because his contract meant he was entitled to a proportion of the profits from any transfer. That prospect wasn't what was motivating him, though, because in his eagerness to leave he'd said he was prepared to waive the payment. His attitude meant he wasn't considered for the run-in, which was unfortunate timing because I'd been injured in the Cup semi-final and missed the last six league games.

Blackburn beat Newcastle 1–0 in their last home match, with Alan Shearer's thirty-sixth goal of the season. At that time Shearer was just frightening, the complete centre-forward and the best finisher around. He's the best striker there's been in the Premier League, no question. There has been nobody near him. He had it all, scoring every type of goal. The gaffer tried to sign him twice, and the mind boggles at what we might have achieved if he had come here.

A late penalty from Denis Irwin gave us a 2–1 win in our last home game, against Southampton, which meant that the championship was to be decided on the final day. High drama. If we won and Blackburn didn't, the title was ours again. We were at West Ham, where we'd lost the league three years earlier, and where we always seem to have trouble, and Blackburn had Liverpool at Anfield, which was still a real fortress at the time. The gaffer surprised everyone by leaving out Sparky, so we were playing the decisive match without me, Kanchelskis, Hughes and Cantona, which placed a heavy burden on Andy Cole's shoulders.

I was at home, watching the two games at the same time on split-screen TV. The hamstring injury was pretty bad, and the gaffer said he'd rather keep me back in the hope that I'd be fit for the Cup final. But not being there with the lads was a terrible experience on a nail-biting afternoon that put my emotions through the wringer. Andy Cole hit a post and then West Ham took the lead, against the run of play, through Michael Hughes. Meanwhile, at Anfield, Shearer had put Blackburn in front, and at half-time it seemed to be all over. But then we fought back and equalized through Choccy McClair, and Liverpool did likewise, with a goal from John Barnes. Now all we needed was to score once to be champions again, and the lads laid siege to Ludek Miklosko's goal, only to find the Czech giant in inspired form. Liverpool did us a big favour by winning 2–1, Jamie Redknapp scoring late on, but not even the introduction of Sparky from the bench could break the deadlock at Upton Park, and Blackburn were champions by a single point. They deserved it because they finished top, which means that over the season they were the better team, but we still feel that if Eric had been available we'd have won it. It's not unreasonable to suppose that during the run-in he would have scored the extra goals that would have tipped the balance. He'd done it in the past after all. He wasn't around when we needed him.

Losing the title definitely affected us in the Cup final. In that situation, if you win the league, you're confident going to the final; if you don't you travel with the feeling that it's not your year. My hamstring still wasn't right, I wasn't even

60 per cent fit, but the squad was down to the bare bones – Nicky Butt had to play on the right – so I was on the bench at Wembley, where the final, against Everton, was one of the worst I can remember. I got on at half-time, for Steve Bruce, and I know now that I shouldn't have taken any part. After my first run the hamstring went completely and I played for nearly 45 minutes with one leg totally lame. It was the FA Cup final, so adrenaline got me through it, and I knew I had six weeks off afterwards so I stayed on, but I shouldn't have done. I was still feeling it the next pre-season, and I've had trouble with it on and off ever since.

Everton were ordinary, they had just finished fifteenth in the league, and we should have beaten them, but Neville Southall played out of his skin, making some great saves, and we lost 1–0 to a goal from Paul Rideout. Among others, the gaffer blamed Incey, who, contrary to instructions, he said, was getting too far forward, losing possession and enabling Everton to break away and score. Funnily enough, the party after that final was the best we've ever had. We'd gone so close in the league and the FA Cup, and the gaffer gave us his blessing. 'It's been a long, hard season,' he told us. 'Make sure you enjoy yourselves tonight and we'll bounce back with a vengeance in August.' That was all the permission we needed. So we had an all-nighter at the Royal Lancaster Hotel in London. The lads had a great time.

The final was the last straw as far as the gaffer and Incey were concerned, and my old mate was sold to Inter Milan the following month. He had been immense for us. For one, maybe two seasons he was our best player. At that time there was nobody better, or stronger, than him and Roy Keane. Of the two, Roy was the replacement for Bryan Robson. He'd scored his share of goals for Forest, and we were looking for him to get forward and do the same for us. So Incey ended up being the sitting midfielder, which he didn't like. He thought he was better than that and wanted to get forward and score goals himself. Unfortunately for him, he became so effective in the holding role that it had to be his position. He was so quick and mobile, and such a good tackler. He'd tackle, maybe go to ground, get up in an instant and give the ball to one of the flair players like me. At least, that's what I told him his job was!

He has called himself 'the Guv'nor' for as long as I can remember. It never bothered me, I thought it was just a cocky cockney thing, but I know it got up certain people's noses. Not a lot of people said anything about it, which they should have done if they didn't like it. I can't remember him coming in one day and saying, 'Call me the Guv'nor from now on.' But he started answering his phone, 'Guv here,' his car registration was 'GUV 8' and he had it on his boots. Incey never did things by halves, and he went the whole hog with that. The gaffer hated it, and of course Incey knew that and seemed to put it on all the more. But there was only one 'guv'nor' at Manchester United, and when they fell out it was inevitable that there would be only one winner. That didn't stop it being a great shame, however. Whenever Incey has come back to play at Old Trafford he has always been booed. That's unfair after what he did for the club at such an important time in the team's development. It's down to his Liverpool connection, of course, but he doesn't deserve that sort of treatment here. I've always thought United supporters were fair about ex-players coming back, but they never have been with him.

We'd been so close to winning the double again, but had ended up with nothing, and the sense of disappointment throughout the club was overwhelming. Personally, it was my worst season to date. I'd scored just four goals in thirty-nine appearances, down from seventeen in fifty-seven the previous year. It was because I was coming back from injuries too soon. Often I wasn't fully fit and hadn't trained, and I need to train properly to be at my best. It was a stop-start season for me and I knew I could do better. I had to.

'You Don't Win Anything with Kids'

The summer of '95 was a difficult time for Alex Ferguson. Not only had we won nothing the previous season but now three of the fans' favourites – Paul Ince, Mark Hughes and Andrei Kanchelskis – all left at once. Incey's departure to Italy was no surprise, given the collapse in his relationship with the gaffer, but the supporters didn't like Andrei going to Everton, and were even more upset when Sparky upped and left for Chelsea. Then, to make matters worse, Eric asked for a transfer. What triggered that was the FA's ruling that for the full duration of his ban he couldn't play in practice matches, not even behind closed doors at The Cliff. The club had organized games against Rochdale, Bury and Oldham to keep him in shape, and the decision that he wasn't allowed to take part under the terms of his suspension really pissed him off. He was training all week with no games at the end of it, and he wasn't having that. It was only when the FA eventually decided he could play in those practice matches after all that Eric agreed to stay.

Meanwhile, there was so much upheaval that the local paper, the *Manchester Evening News*, ran a poll asking readers whether the boss had lost the plot and should be sacked, which was ludicrous of course. Most of the people who responded were probably City fans, having a laugh. I imagine it made their day.

Looking for replacements, the gaffer inquired about Stan Collymore at Nottingham Forest, who instead joined Liverpool for a British record fee of £8.5m, and also Darren

Anderton at Tottenham, who would have been the replacement for Andrei on the right. The gaffer tends to sign players who have done well against us – Eric and Andy and Dion Dublin are all good examples. Collymore and Anderton both came into that category, too. Neither came in the end, but it's interesting to think that, had Anderton signed, Becks would almost certainly have had to wait a bit longer for his chance.

On opening day I was still out with my hamstring trouble when, without reinforcements, we lost 3–1 at Aston Villa. Becks scored our goal in a team that also included the Neville brothers, Nicky Butt and Paul Scholes, and it was after this game that Alan Hansen made his famous remark on *Match of the Day* that 'You don't win anything with kids.' How he must have regretted that rush to judgement as, kids and all, we won eight and drew two of our next ten league games! To be fair, even the gaffer has said since that he understood what Alan meant. At United we all knew how good our young players were, but there were doubts in all our minds after losing Ince, Hughes and Kanchelskis. That was a lot of experience, as well as quality, gone. Those three were very strong mentally, they were never fazed by anything that was thrown at them, and it was asking a lot for novices to take over.

It was difficult to separate this new draft in terms of ability, but I suppose everybody had their favourites. Nicky Butt was a good replacement for Incey – he was as tough as they come, loved a tackle and could pass the ball. Scholes was in the Cantona mould, Becks could cross it better than anyone and Gary Neville was a natural leader. My favourite was Paul Scholes. For me, he was great to play with, I'd swap passes with him more than anyone else. If you made a run, he would always spot it and play you in. At schoolboy level people were always worried about his size. He was small, so where did you play him? He was shuttled between midfield and attack, whereas he was perfect for what we came to know as the Cantona role, just off the front.

All the young players slotted into the team really easily. Four or five of them coming in together helped – they were able to support each other rather than being alone and overawed. I'd played in the same youth team as them, but I was a year older. I was mates with Nicky Butt, but when they were apprentices I had never been as close to Gaz, Becks or Scholesy. We didn't really become friends until they got in the team.

Becks was the only one who didn't come from around Manchester, and I remember a lot of us taking the piss out of him because he lost his cockney accent so quickly and started speaking like a 'Manc'. We know that didn't last, but he didn't start talking like a southerner again until Teddy Sheringham joined us. Becks never got treated differently because he was from London, but he did get a lot of stick. He coped with that well though, he was always a confident lad. They all were, really – I think it's their mental strength that set them apart. It soon became apparent that we weren't missing the big players who had gone, the young replacements had done that well. It was then that I realized they could go all the way, not just with United but with England.

Becks had played centre midfield in the youth team, and always wanted to play there in the first team, but the gaffer kept him on the right, and I think that's his best position. His ability to cross the ball is second to none, and that would be lost in the middle. He also gets forward more playing on the right, which means he hurts the opposition more. A lot of the Wales players – Chris Coleman was one – used to say to me that Becks' crosses were a nightmare for defenders because they were so quick and powerful. It has always been his great strength.

Early on in 1995–6 we had two games with a bit of feeling back to back, at Blackburn and Everton. Blackburn had just pipped us for the league, so we loved winning 2–1 at their place, despite having Roy Keane sent off. The seven bookings tell you what sort of match that was. Blackburn is always a great away game for United, we take a lot of fans and it's always a spicey occasion. Next came Everton, who had beaten us in the Cup final, and who now had a certain Andrei Kanchelskis playing for them. I scored in a 3–2 win, but it was Lee Sharpe who enjoyed himself most that day. Not only did he get the other two goals, he also hit Andrei with a challenge that dislocated our old mate's shoulder. There had been a lot of pre-match hype about Andrei playing against us, and what he was going to do. I have to admit that there was a fair bit of ill-feeling towards him, but nothing came of it. Andrei was only on the field for fourteen minutes.

Beating Bolton 3–0 at home now made it five league wins on the trot. Paul Scholes scored two that day, and I got the other one. The team was younger than ever – I remember Terry Cooke played. We were going strong in the league, but went out of the Coca-Cola and UEFA Cups very early. By now the gaffer had got into the habit of playing the reserves in the Coca-Cola, and York City beat us over two legs with a team that cost less than £100,000. More serious was the elimination by Rotor Volgograd in the first round of the UEFA tournament, which left us out of Europe in September. Nearly everybody involved was glad to forget those games – everyone bar Peter Schmeichel that is. In the second leg against Rotor, the big goalkeeper charged upfield for a corner and equalized with a header for 2–2. It was not enough – we went out on the away goals rule – but the viking, as the gaffer called him, had the satisfaction of preserving our record in European competition, where we had never lost at home. He never let us forget it!

A week later it was the Eric Cantona show. Out for eight months, he could hardly have scripted his comeback better. We were at home to Liverpool, always a tasty game, and just the stage to bring the best out of a player with a flair for the theatrical. The atmosphere was unbelievable – especially after Nicky Butt scored in the first minute. Liverpool hit back with two belters from Robbie Fowler, but cometh the hour, cometh the man, and midway through the second half I was pulled down in the area by Jamie Redknapp and Eric stepped up and buried the penalty, cool as you like, for a 2–2 draw. 'The King' was back.

In November against Southampton it was my turn to make a splash. Straight from the kick-off I knocked the ball back to Gary Neville and I sprinted down the middle while Eric pulled out to the left. From the half-way line, Gaz knocked a high, crossfield pass to Eric, who headed it inside to me and I hit it on the half-volley. I didn't see the ball go in because a defender came in to block me and knocked me over, so I was on the floor, but when I heard the crowd roar I couldn't believe I'd scored so soon. Sixteen seconds. It was a once-in-a-lifetime thing – I knew I'd never do anything like it again. I was really buzzing and got another goal while I was still on a high. We beat them 4–1. A good result but not such a big deal when we heard Blackburn had thrashed Nottingham Forest 7–0. At the end of November we could only draw 1–1 at Forest, which was the start of a horrible run of five league games without a win. In fairness, there were good reasons for that – we had half a team. Roy Keane and Nicky Butt were suspended, Peter Schmeichel had an elbow operation, and Bruce and Pallister were also injured at the same time. The gaffer was desperate for a centre-half and brought in a Frenchman we'd never heard of, William Prunier, on trial.

Prunier made his debut at home to QPR and did all right in a 2–1 win, but in his second game, on New Year's Day, we lost 4–1 at Tottenham, which was our biggest league defeat for four years, and we never saw him again. After what was one of the shortest United careers on record, the gaffer packed him off, back to France. When Newcastle beat Arsenal 2–0 the following day, they were seven points ahead of us with a game in hand, and the gap got wider and wider. By 20 January they were twelve points clear and seemed to be on an unstoppable charge, but it didn't last. We started clawing the lead back with a charge of our own. We strung together ten successive wins in league and cup, with Eric our inspiration. From 22 January until the day the championship was decided we won seven matches 1–0 and he scored the goal in five of them.

In the FA Cup we came from behind to beat Man City 2–1, Sharpey getting a late winner, then in late February it started to get really interesting in the championship. I scored one of the goals as we beat Everton 2–0 and on the same day Newcastle lost at West Ham, trimming their lead to six points. Kevin Keegan now bought David Batty from Blackburn, presumably to stem the flow of goals against, but Newcastle could only draw 3–3 at Maine Road, and our biggest away win for thirty-six years, 6–0 at Bolton, piled on the pressure. Batty was obviously a good player. He had won the league with Leeds and Blackburn, so he had been there and done it. And he was a tough guy to play against, always in the right place defensively. A good reader of the game. I suppose you could say he was broadly similar to

Nicky Butt, but I think Nicky had a bit more about his game.

At the beginning of March we were on a roll, with five wins on the trot, as we went into the crunch match, away to Newcastle. They had a 100 per cent record at St James' Park, and everybody was saying it was make or break for both teams. As if any extra spice was needed – which it wasn't – Eric and David Ginola didn't get on. They had fallen out when France failed to qualify for the '94 World Cup. Eric blamed Ginola for the mistake which cost them the decisive qualifier, against Bulgaria, and of course the papers had reminded everyone beforehand that there was no love lost between them. Eric usually came out on top when they met, and it was no different this time. Newcastle gave us a battering in the first half, but Peter Schmeichel was magnificent, coming to our rescue again and again, and during the interval the gaffer did his stuff, asking us if Newcastle really had the greater desire to win, because that was how it looked. He said a few more things besides, and the upshot was a vastly improved performance in the second half, when Eric volleyed the only goal from a Phil Neville cross. The gap was now just one point, and while Newcastle still had a game in hand, we had the feeling that they would crack. We had been over the course and finished first before, they hadn't, and experience counts for a lot during the run-in.

A 2–0 win at home to Southampton saw us into the FA Cup semi-finals, then on 16 March we went top of the league for the first time, on goal difference, after Eric's stoppage-time equalizer at QPR. Newcastle overtook us again two days later, but the initiative had changed hands. The momentum was now with us, and when Eric gave us another 1–0 win, at home to Arsenal, Newcastle were unable to respond and lost 2–0 at Highbury three days later.

We now played Chelsea in the semi-finals of the Cup, on a nightmare pitch at Villa Park, like playing in a sandpit. Ruud Gullit gave them the lead, then Cole and Beckham scored to pull it around for us, but it needed a goalline clearance from Eric – the hero again – to see us through.

Newcastle had cracked now and lost for the fourth time in six games when Stan Collymore's last-minute winner gave Liverpool a 4–3 win in a sensational match at Anfield. We were now three points in front, but Newcastle still had a game in hand. Liverpool were third, five points behind us, but dropped out of contention a few days later when they were beaten 1–0 at Coventry.

On Easter Monday Eric scored for the sixth league match in succession for another 1–0 win, against Coventry, and on the same day Newcastle lost 2–1 at Blackburn. I watched it on the telly, and a lad called Graham Fenton, who I've never heard of since, scored twice in the last five minutes.

We were in the box seat now, but we slipped up at Southampton, where we were 3–0 down at half-time. When we came in at half-time, the gaffer's angry reaction was the last thing we expected. 'Right, get that kit off,' he told us. We were playing in the infamous grey away strip. He never liked it and neither did we. It was such a dull colour that it wasn't easy to pick out your teammates against the background of the crowd, but whatever the psychological effect of changing the colour of our shirts, that wasn't the reason we were three goals down. The reality was we didn't play well and gave away bad goals. I was to blame for the first, trying to dribble out of defence. They took the ball off me, and Ken Monkou scored. I made partial amends, pulling one back for us, but we lost 3–1 and Newcastle took full advantage, beating Aston Villa 1–0, which left them three points behind but with a game in hand.

That's when the gaffer really went to work. Campaigns are won on and off the pitch and he knew it. It was all about pressure. After Leeds had given us a real scrap at home, he said he hoped they would be as competitive when they played Newcastle two weeks later. Kevin Keegan took the bait. He got riled by it and, after his team had beaten Leeds 1–0, he went on Sky TV, with eyes bulging like a madman, shouting about the gaffer's mind games, and how he'd 'love it, really love it' if they finished in front of us. The previous day we'd hammered Forest 5–0, and it was obvious that the close race had got to Keegan. You could see he'd 'gone' mentally, and that we were home and dry.

Newcastle could only draw 1–1 at Forest, which meant a point from our final game, at Middlesbrough, would be enough to clinch the title, and I contributed our last goal of the league season as we won easily, 3–0. Newcastle had blown up, and their 1–1 draw at home to Spurs meant they finished four points behind us. It was nice to win it off our own bat on the final day. On the two previous occasions we were champions, we'd been crowned without playing because our rivals had lost, and this was much better – a bigger buzz. The gaffer told us we couldn't have a party to celebrate because we had the Cup final against Liverpool the following week. We ignored him, of course! We were straight off to Mulligans, at the Four Seasons, near the airport, where we had a good few beers. After all, we had the best part of a week to recover!

Wembley that year became known as the White Suit Cup final, because of the gear the Liverpool players wore. Speaking to Ian Rush before the game, I couldn't resist rubbing his nose in it a bit. 'Who chose those suits?' I asked him, smiling. He shot me an embarrassed look and said, 'It certainly wasn't me.' I'd never thought it was. It was the younger players, those who'd been christened the 'Spice Boys', who made the choice, and it was definitely a blunder on their part. Our attitude was: 'Who the hell do they think they are, poncing around like John Travolta?' Liverpool had a good record against us around that time, and they were definitely confident. Over-confident. One of our lads came into our dressing room and said, 'Have you seen their flash suits? They think they've won it already and they're out celebrating.' For us, it was a real wind-up. The match was crap, but we were the better team. Roy Keane sorted them out in midfield and Eric won it with a spectacular shot. Steve Bruce was injured and missed the final, so Eric led us up the famous steps to collect the cup. As he did so, he was spat on by a Liverpool fan, and those of us in the vicinity thought, 'Oh no – here we go again. This is going to be Selhurst Park all over again.' Thankfully, it wasn't. Eric just brushed off the spittle with that contemptuous, disdainful look of his. He had learned his lesson.

The season had been a personal triumph for 'the King'. He scored nineteen goals in thirty-eight appearances, a high percentage of them match-winners. By comparison, Coley had got thirteen in forty-three, and was even dropped, in favour of Paul Scholes, during the run-in. To be fair, Scholes' scoring record that year was fantastic – fourteen in thirty-one games. I'd weighed in with twelve in forty-one, and as a winger I was happy enough with that. It was a dramatic improvement on the four I scored the season before and back to where I wanted to be. This time around I'd had fewer injury problems, I was fitter, and Eric was back, creating a lot more chances for everybody. He was the catalyst.

New Faces

The summer of '96 was one of new beginnings. Steve Bruce left us for Birmingham on a free transfer after nine years of stalwart service and the gaffer freshened up the squad with a sprinkling of new faces. Meanwhile, Arsenal were about to bring in the man who would break our grip on the championship. All sorts of signings were made that year, but without doubt the recruitment of Arsène Wenger was the most significant.

As Brucey left, soon to be followed by Lee Sharpe, who went to Leeds for £4.5m, four newcomers arrived at Old Trafford. The gaffer tried again for Alan Shearer, offering Blackburn £12m, but the best striker in the league went to Newcastle for £15m, forcing United to look elsewhere for reinforcements. Karel Poborsky had stood out for the Czech Republic at Euro '96, and the gaffer bought him for £3.5m from Slavia Prague, presumably on the strength of that. His other signings were Ronnie Johnsen, from Besiktas, for £1.2m, Jordi Cruyff from Barcelona for £800,000 and an unknown Norwegian, Ole Gunnar Solskjaer, from Molde, for £1.5m.

Two of them proved to be superb buys, the other two were not so good. The most expensive of the four, Poborsky, was the biggest disappointment. He would say he never really got a decent run in the side because of the emergence of Becks, but he had his chances, and if he had played up to his international form he wouldn't have been left out so often. To be fair, I suppose he did help to provide the strength in depth we needed, and after leaving us he did well. Jordi was bought as a versatile forward, but with the intention of using him mainly on the left, as an alternative to me. Lee Sharpe was leaving, and the gaffer wanted two wingers for each flank. I think Jordi's best position was just off the front man, but unfortunately for him we didn't play with that formation at the time. In training, he was one of the best I've ever seen – I'm talking about skill rather than running, which was definitely not his strong suit. When we played short-sided games his balance, ability to take people on and finishing were right up there with the very best. You'd come off the training ground thinking, 'What a talent,' but in match situations he never seemed to produce. If he got on as sub for me, or if I was out and he played on the left, he was expected to work up and down the touchline, which he wasn't used to, and didn't like. The United dressing room's the kind of place where everyone just gets on with whatever's expected of them, and Jordi's discomfort wouldn't have gone unnoticed by the gaffer. He made it clear too often that he preferred the way things were done at Barca and that didn't go down well with the lads.

Solskjaer couldn't have been more different. When I saw him for the first time, I honestly thought he'd just signed as an apprentice. He looked so young and fresh-faced. I couldn't believe he was older than me and a first-team player. Nobody had ever heard of him, but what an impact he made. In pre-season training at The Cliff, when we were practising crossing and shooting, he was just unbelievable. In the first finishing session he did with us he scored every time, and every sort of goal – headers, volleys, left foot, right foot, everything. I remember going home that day and telling one of my mates what I'd just seen.

'We've just signed a player and I'm not joking, he's every bit as good, if not better, than Shearer.'

'Right, yeah,' came the unimpressed reply. ''Course you have.'

'Honestly,' I told him. 'Remember his name: Ole Gunnar Solskjaer. He's the best finisher I've ever seen.'

He's also one of the nicest lads you could ever meet. He was very quiet at first, but we soon brought him out of his shell. Unfortunately, he's had terrible luck with injuries.

The fourth signing that summer was Ronnie Johnsen, a top-class defender who did really well for us. He was another player we'd not really heard of before, but for strength and power he was just like Jaap Stam. Those two were awesome. Ronnie could play in midfield as well, which he did a lot in his third year with us.

Just as the 1996–7 season started, Arsenal made what was to be a major signing of their own, although nobody realized it at the time, buying Patrick Vieira from Milan. He has been a top player over the years, but I think Roy Keane has always been better. Roy was the all-round package. We bought him as an attacking midfielder, but he became much more than that. He could defend, organize, win headers *and* score goals. He could do the lot. For me, Roy's natural finishing ability was always an advantage he had over the Frenchman.

Vieira's arrival was overshadowed when Becks scored the most remarkable goal of his career. On the opening day of the season, he lobbed the Wimbledon goalkeeper, Neil Sullivan, from the half-way line. I was out injured and I wasn't at the game, but I read a report on Ceefax of what had happened. I was talking to a mate that night and told him that Becks was supposed to have scored an unbelievable goal. 'Make sure you watch *Match of the Day*,' I told him. I made sure I did the same. When I saw it, I couldn't believe it. I tried it myself once, at Charlton, and hit the crossbar from the half-way line, but that was more of a volley. I'd just scored, and the adrenaline was pumping, otherwise I wouldn't have even attempted it, but the ball came over my shoulder, I hit it sweetly and it came back off the bar for Ole to knock in. It was probably a good job for me that it did result in a goal, because after his success Becks had tried to do it again on a couple of occasions and it hadn't come off. By the third attempt the gaffer was sick of it and gave him a bollocking.

Rating how good that strike was at Wimbledon is difficult. I scored one people still talk about in an FA Cup semi-final against Arsenal when I ran through from half-way, and how can you compare the two? I suppose that the truth is that each goal reflected the particular qualities of the player who scored it. One of Becks' great strengths is his shooting from long range, mine is beating people at speed to score. That's what I'm renowned for. Which is better boils down to a question of personal preference in the end.

Our second game was at home to Everton, when Duncan Ferguson gave us terrible trouble, scoring twice to give them a 2–0 lead before half-time. At his peak, as he was then, he could be unplayable. At 6ft 5ins with a good jump on him, he was unbeatable in the air. But he was good on the deck, too, especially for such a big man. Whether he was running the channels, closing you down or winning his headers, he never gave you a minute's peace. I remember him scoring with a header against us at Goodison once when he jumped higher than the crossbar. What can any defender marking him do about that?

We started the league season with a nine-match unbeaten

run, but there were too many draws, and after five games we were only fifth in the table. Sheffield Wednesday were top – doesn't that seem strange now?

The Champions League began with a 1–0 defeat away to Juventus. I had a shocker and got brought off at half-time. We played 4–3–3, with Jordi on the left, Eric in the middle and Poborsky on the right forming a front three and me, Becks and Nicky Butt in midfield. I kept dribbling with the ball, Deschamps would take it off me, pass it to Zidane, who'd give it to Del Piero, and they'd be in on our goal every time. The gaffer had a right go at me at half-time, and I had a dig back. I didn't feel it was all my fault. The way I saw it I had nobody to pass to because the front three weren't making runs or showing for the ball. We argued about it, and he took me off and put Brian McClair on. So I guess that was an argument I lost. Looking back, though, I have to admit I didn't play well. And when I tried to make excuses I was on a hiding to nothing.

At about this time there was shock in dressing rooms all over the country when Tony Adams came out and admitted he was an alcoholic. I have to say I didn't really believe it. My thinking was: 'He can't be and play the way he does.' He was a great player, one of those you look at and think, 'I fancy my chances against him,' but then find you get nowhere because he's always in the right place at the right time. His positional play and the way he closed you down offered nothing. He would have been brilliant for us. The highest accolade I can give any opponent is wishing they were on our side and he *always* came into that category. The gaffer definitely admired him too. Even when rivalry between United and Arsenal was at its most intense I only ever heard him say good things about Tony Adams. There's no doubt he was Alex Ferguson's kind of player.

Towards the end of September we were fourth in the table going into our Champions League tie at home to Rapid Vienna, where Ole and Becks scored for a straightforward 2–0 win. We had started the season without Andy Cole, who had pneumonia, and now, on his comeback in the reserves, he fractured both legs in a nasty incident involving Liverpool's Neil Ruddock. Fortunately, Ole had started scoring straight away and got both goals in a 2–0 win at home to Spurs which lifted us to third in the table. Liverpool were now top, but we beat them 1–0 at home, with a goal from Becks, to set ourselves up nicely for the Champions League tie away to Fenerbahce. I travelled to Istanbul with the team, but I was injured and sat next to Bobby Charlton in the directors' box. The tannoy blared out music while the game was going on. Bobby couldn't stand it and, when he could take it no more, he told them to turn it off. They did as well! I sat there thinking, 'He's got some pull, him. They listen to him everywhere.' We won easily enough, 2–0, but came home and got the biggest stuffing we'd had for twelve years, 5–0 at Newcastle. Ginola, Ferdinand and Shearer all scored – even their centre-halves, Darren Peacock and Phillipe Albert, got in on the act. I was still injured and didn't play, but I watched it in horror on telly. It was a real body blow – our first defeat of the season and a drubbing. Ginola got a great goal, and Albert chipped Peter Schmeichel, which didn't happen often. At the time, though, Newcastle were capable of doing that to any team, and the three points kept them at the top of the table.

Ginola was an interesting guy, a great crosser with either foot. Newcastle had two very dangerous strikers in the middle, Shearer and Ferdinand, so you wanted to stop him getting the ball to them, but it was very hard because he was genuinely two-footed. He was certainly a big talent, but he didn't like having to defend, and whenever we came up against him we tried to exploit that. Not, it has to be said, with any success this time round.

That 5–0 beating was the start of a terrible run. In our next game, at Southampton, Roy Keane was sent off and we lost 6–3. We didn't even have grey shirts to point to as an excuse this time. We'd conceded eleven goals in two matches, which was unheard of. We always found The Dell a hard place to play. It was a horrible little ground. Whenever we went there it always seemed to be sunny, the sun was in your eyes and the pitch was dry and bobbly. I hated it. The run got worse. United had been unbeaten at home in European competition for forty years, but now that record went, and not to Juventus or anybody like that, but to Fenerbahce, who we'd seen off comfortably over there. To the gaffer's disgust, they beat us 1–0, with a flukey deflection off David May, and three days later we tumbled to our third successive league defeat, 2–1 at home to Chelsea, and dropped to sixth in the table. Chelsea were above us in the league, and now they signed one of my all-time favourites, Gianfranco Zola. It says everything about his ability that whenever we played against him, the gaffer would single him out for special attention. Normally, United would never man-mark anyone, whatever the personnel or the system we were up against, but there were one or two exceptions to the rule. Zidane was one, Zola another. It was usually Ronnie Johnsen or Phil Neville who did it, they were both good at it. We knew we had to nullify Zola because he was pure quality – the sort of player I'd love to have played with. His vision and range of passing were second to none, he was quick and he was strong in a stocky sort of way, and I could easily imagine me making a run and him playing me through. I didn't really know him, we just exchanged hellos after a game, but I still got the impression that he was one of the good guys, too.

Injuries were partly to blame for our bad run. I hadn't played in any of the defeats, and Andy Cole, Roy Keane and Gary Pallister were also out for long periods. Another factor was Eric's dip in form. 'I didn't know I could play so badly,' he confessed with evident self-disgust. The ineffectiveness of Poborsky and Jordi, both of whom were taken off in the Fenerbahce game, wasn't helping either.

I was back when we halted the slide by beating Arsenal at Old Trafford in mid-November, but we hadn't quite nipped it in the bud. Two days later we lost again in the Champions League, 1–0 at home to Juventus, which put us third in our group, behind the Italians and Fenerbahce. At that time, Juve were the team in Europe that everybody was trying to emulate. They were the best because they had the best players. Boksic and Del Piero were brilliant up front and in midfield they had the pair who won everything with France, Deschamps and Zidane. They were the team to beat, and it took us a couple of years before we could make legitimate claims to be of a similar standard.

By the end of November we were down to seventh in the Premier League, and not too many were betting on us retaining our title, but a 3–1 win at home to Leicester signalled the beginning of a charge. We needed to beat Rapid Vienna in Austria to go through to the last eight in the Champions League, and we did it, but at a price. On a freezing cold night in Vienna I scored midway through the first half, sidefooting in when I was one-on-one with the 'keeper. Eric made it 2–0, but Roy Keane's knee was cut to the bone by a horrific tackle, and he was out for the next few games. The game wasn't only won in their half. Peter Schmeichel made a save that everyone likened to Gordon

Banks' from Pelé at the 1970 World Cup. Without it, the result might have been different.

Back home, we had a great Christmas, thrashing Sunderland 5–0, with Ole and Eric getting two apiece, winning 4–0 at Nottingham Forest, where Andy scored on his return, then beating Leeds 1–0 at home to go second in the table, two points behind Liverpool.

On New Year's Day, Arsenal overtook us when Ian Wright scored his 200th league goal. He was some item. Incey knew him well, and I had a few nights out with the two of them. Wrighty was hilarious, loud and larger than life, and great company. As a player, he was a top goalscorer, but I don't think he ever scored against us. It was the same with Ian Rush, another great striker who just couldn't do it against United.

In January we had two wins in succession against Spurs, at home in the FA Cup then at their place in the league, and at the end of the month I scored against Coventry and then Wimbledon as we went to the top of the table, a point ahead of Arsenal. At about this time Andrei Kanchelskis left Everton for Fiorentina. He hadn't stayed in Liverpool long, and we all wondered about why he was moving again so soon. We were on a roll, unbeaten in thirteen matches in the league, so it was a nasty shock to the system when we went out of the FA Cup in a replay at Wimbledon. They had a decent side then – they were sixth in the Premiership – but we were at full strength, and certainly didn't expect to lose in the competition, other than in the final, for the first time for four years.

It didn't seem to affect our progress in the league, though, and we bounced back by winning 2–1 at Arsenal, inflicting their first home defeat of the season. It was a good result, but the match is remembered for all the wrong reasons.

That Peter Schmeichel and Ian Wright didn't get on was no secret, but a bad, two-footed challenge by the striker hurt Peter and provoked a real storm. The feud simmered away for the rest of the game before boiling over at the end when they had a right go at each other as the players left the field. In the papers the following day it was reported that Peter had been a racist, a claim Wright did nothing to pour water on. The first thing that has to be said is that the challenge on the 'keeper was a nasty one. Wrighty was never going to get the ball and went over the top. He was a fiery character, and I think it bothered him that he'd never scored against us. Some players are like that, they just lose it, and he was one of those. But I just can't imagine Peter making racist remarks, he wouldn't do that. It sounded to me as if Wright was happy to let the 'racist' row deflect attention from his own mistake.

We played Chelsea three days later, so we stayed down south, at Bisham Abbey, where England used to stay before home games. It's the only time I've known us do that, and it brought home how important the two games were to us. We drew 1–1 with Chelsea, then beat Coventry 3–1 at home, which stretched our unbeaten run in the league to sixteen matches and took us four points clear of Liverpool at the top. That meant we were on a high going into our Champions League quarter-final at home to Porto at the beginning of March. The Portuguese champions were the form team in the competition, having come through the group stage unbeaten, with five wins and a draw in their six games. They had knocked out AC Milan, which is always an achievement, and when we got them in the draw we thought it was going to be hard to get through. They had a good Brazilian striker, Jardel, who was scoring a lot of goals, but we met them at a good time. There was three months between the group and knockout stages, and in that gap they had gone off the boil. Their form had dipped and we were on fire. I played in centre midfield with Ole on the left and Eric and Andy up front. The gaffer told me to break forward from deep and use the spaces left when Ole and Andy stretched them out wide. And it worked. So well in fact that it's probably the best game I've ever had for United. My passing was spot on, I was winning tackles and I got our third goal in a sensational 4–0 win. The ball was played down the line to Eric, and I'd made a 60-yard run, overlapping him. He waited for me to go past and played me in for a shot which went in at the near post. The satisfaction and exhilaration that comes from playing like that is huge. The gaffer said afterwards that he'd never seen me play better. It wasn't as an orthodox central midfielder, it was one of those occasions when we attacked from every angle, interchanging positions, and our play flowed from every direction. Everything we tried came off and we were all over them. I don't know why it all came together in the way it did that night, but they never stood a chance.

From the sublime to the ridiculous: we came back and lost 2–1 at Sunderland. I didn't play – it's a prime example of my hamstring problem. In big, high-tempo European games when I played well, I knew I'd suffer for it afterwards, and although I travelled to the north-east with the rest of the lads, hoping it would settle down, it was the worst it has ever felt.

With a four-goal cushion, the return leg against Porto was never going to trouble us. I went, but I was one of those rested for a routine goalless draw. Towards the end of March Liverpool closed to within three points of us with a 2–1 win at Arsenal. People remember it as the match when Robbie Fowler fell over, got up and signalled to the referee that he hadn't been fouled by David Seaman, but was awarded a penalty anyway! I know Fowler got on well with Seaman, but refusing a penalty is not a thing I'd do. Referees get enough wrong the other way, and in the end the luck evens itself out. There was no foul, and to be fair to Fowler I don't think he dived, he just lost his balance, which can happen.

Early in April, Liverpool blew their title chances by losing at home to Coventry, who were bottom of the table at the time. Our old mate Dion Dublin did us a favour, getting the winner, but at the time we were more interested in the Champions League semi-finals, where we were up against Borussia Dortmund. The first leg was over there. I had a double hernia operation at the end of that season and I shouldn't have played. It was in Germany that the problem really flared up. I could feel something wrong in my stomach but couldn't work out what it was. In training the day before the game I tried to sprint, but the explosiveness just wasn't there. The gaffer felt it was worth taking a chance and played me anyway. By this stage in the season I wasn't the only one with problems. During the same session Peter Schmeichel and David May both picked up injuries which put them out of the side. Raimond Van der Gouw and Ronny Johnsen deputized. In the match I had no power at all. It was such a weird feeling. I can remember Nicky Butt shooting against a post, and if that had gone in, we might have been OK, but it didn't and they won 1–0 with a deflected goal. I came off, and I didn't play again in the league that season.

Without me, the lads overpowered Liverpool 3–1 at Anfield, Pally scoring with two headers. Their defence and particularly their goalkeeper, David James, were known to be vulnerable at set pieces, and we worked a lot on our corners before that game, with Becks targeting Pally's runs to the near post. It was one of those nice occasions when all the work pays off. On the same day Arsenal were held 1–1 at home by Blackburn, which left us five points ahead with a game in hand.

If the trip to Germany had been disappointing, the return against Dortmund, at Old Trafford, was a disaster. One down from the first leg, we knew we couldn't afford to concede again, but they scored after seven minutes. We lost 1–0, after missing enough chances to have won five matches. According to the gaffer, who keeps count of such things, we were one-on-one with their 'keeper *fifteen* times, and still we couldn't score. I wasn't really fit, but as a last throw of the dice I was sent on, in place of Ole. I was no better than anyone else. I had a couple of chances but made a mess of them both. The worst miss was probably by Eric, though. His form had been disappointing for quite some time, and he made a simple decision. The day after the second leg he went to see the gaffer, and told him he was going to retire at the end of the season.

In the league, Middlesbrough came to Old Trafford and were 3–1 up in forty minutes, but Gary Neville scored his first goal for the club and Ole's equalizer, midway through the second half, left us needing to win one of our last two games to be sure of the title. As it turned out, we did it without playing when Liverpool lost 2–1 at Wimbledon and the other team still in contention, Newcastle, were held 0–0 at West Ham.

A fourth title in five years had consolidated our position as the dominant force in English football, but some saw it as the end of an era, with Eric confirming his retirement, a week before his thirty-first birthday. Were we surprised? Life with Eric was one long surprise. You never knew what he would do next. There were no farewells or anything like that, and I didn't really believe he meant it until he failed to turn up the following season. He was a fit lad, and he could definitely have gone on longer.

My own form that season had been disappointing. Strangely enough, in the middle of it I had my best game for United, against Porto, but otherwise it seemed to be stop-start all the time, and I never really got into my stride. That feeling was borne out by my stats – just three goals in twenty-six league appearances. I knew I was better than that.

Gunned Down

The near-impossible task of filling Eric Cantona's boots fell to Teddy Sheringham, the England striker, who cost £3.5m from Tottenham. Teddy made quite an entrance when he turned up for training for the first time driving a Ferrari. In doing so he broke a taboo and set a precedent because up until then the gaffer had always had this thing about footballers driving flash cars – he didn't like it. He preferred his players to be like Bruce and Pallister, both of whom were Mercedes men. I went to and from training every day in a Jeep – I didn't let on that I had an Aston Martin at home! But as soon as Teddy arrived in his new toy, it was a case of open season – 'If he can have one, so can I' – and I went straight out and bought a Ferrari too. Becks meanwhile went with a new Porsche.

When Ted turned up like that, a lot of people thought, 'Typical flash cockney,' but he wasn't like that. I liked him straight from the off, and he was definitely the sort of player I really enjoyed playing with – his vision and passing ability were top drawer. But no matter how good he was, that first season was always going to be hard for him. How could anybody follow Eric, the fans' favourite? They weren't like for like either. Although they were both clever players, and played the same role, Eric was quick, and Teddy has never been that. Teddy's timing in the air was better than Eric's and he was a great talker on the pitch, too. One of his first games for us was a pre-season friendly against Inter Milan and during the game he was always talking, always thinking.

'When you go forward,' he'd say, 'don't worry about getting back, I'll fill in for you,' things like that. I liked him instantly as a footballer.

Our other major signing that summer was Henning Berg, the Blackburn defender, who cost £5m. The gaffer had always liked him, and had tried to sign him before. He was a good, experienced centre-half who went on to play a hundred times for Norway. At around this time Incey came back from Italy and signed for Liverpool. We'd lost touch when he was out there, but now we picked up our old friendship, and met up for nights out.

Our first league game took Teddy back to Tottenham, where they booed him throughout and he missed a penalty. Some players would have been gutted by that, but it was water off a duck's back to a strong character like Teddy, and it certainly didn't affect us, as we won 2–0. We made a decent start to the season, and were top of the table in mid-September, when we went to Slovakia and beat Kosice 3–0 in the Champions League. After that, we had the first indication of what was to come when Arsenal hammered West Ham 4–0 and we lost 1–0 at Leeds in a match which ended Roy Keane's season almost before it had begun. Roy snapped the cruciate ligament in his right knee in an incident involving Alf Inge Haaland, which would have serious repercussions years later. Losing our inspirational captain was a huge blow: he was not just a leader but an important player in his own right. Then, as if it weren't enough, we were knocked off the top of the table by Arsenal at the same time.

It was hardly the best way to approach a Champions League visit from Juventus. And we got off to a terrible start in the game. Alessandro Del Piero stunned Old Trafford into silence by scoring in the first minute. But we turned it around brilliantly. I wanted to have a good game more than anybody, having had a stinker against them the previous year, and I did. The whole team played really well. The feeling among the players was that, if we were ever going to win the European Cup, we'd need to beat this particular team. Juventus were the benchmark, and that night at Old Trafford gave us the belief that we could not only live with, but beat, the best. Teddy equalized, then Paul Scholes put us 2–1 up. I scored our third in the eighty-ninth minute. There was still time for Zidane to make it 3–2 with a fabulous free-kick, but we won the game after going behind.

We kept our 100 per cent record in the group by beating Feyenoord 2–1 at home, and three days later jumped from third to top of the league by thrashing Barnsley 7–0. Andy Cole got a hat-trick and I scored two. We were capable of stuffing anybody at that time, and to prove Barnsley was no fluke we put six past Sheffield Wednesday in our next game to go four points clear.

That sort of form stood us in good stead in Europe, and we won 3–1 away to Feyenoord, with Andy getting another hat-trick. The match, though, is not really remembered for his goals. Certainly my abiding memory is of a dreadful tackle by Paul Bosvelt which wrecked Denis Irwin's knee ligaments, putting him out of the team for two months. All the lads were angry about that. It was a nasty tackle on a player who was one of the nicest in the game, and it really took the shine off a good night. We played well again, and I think the confidence we drew from beating Juventus had us thinking we could beat anyone in Europe. It seems remarkable now to think that we were doing it without Roy Keane, who was out for the season. You never wanted to be without Keaney, but in his place Nicky Butt and Paul Scholes really came into their own in centre midfield.

Coming back from Rotterdam on a high, we were immediately brought down to earth by a 3–2 defeat at Arsenal, who were one place behind us, running second. It was 2–2 at half-time, Teddy Sheringham scoring twice for us, then David Platt got the winner, with a header, just before the end. It was especially galling to lose three points to our main rivals, particularly when it didn't reflect our run of form. When we beat Blackburn 4–0, we'd scored twenty-four goals in the last five league matches, and our form was just as impressive in the Champions League, where a 3–0 victory at home to Kosice enabled us to qualify with a game to spare. The fixture in question was away to Juventus where, with nothing to play for, we lost 1–0. Unlike us, Juve were definitely up for it – if they hadn't won, they wouldn't have gone through with us.

At Christmas we had a six-point lead over Blackburn at the top of the table, with Arsenal down in sixth. Karel Poborsky wasn't getting a game with Becks doing so well on the right, so it was no real surprise when he was sold to Benfica for £3m. Then things seemed to come unstuck.

I'm not sure why, but we suddenly started leaking goals. We let in two in the last five minutes to lose 3–2 at Coventry, then allowed Chelsea to score three in the last twelve minutes in an FA Cup tie at Stamford Bridge. Fortunately we'd taken a 5–0 lead before that, but the gaffer didn't like this sudden defensive sloppiness, which was seen again when we lost successive league games to Southampton and Leicester. A draw against Bolton made it one point from a possible nine, and now the pack were closing in, with Chelsea our closest challengers. As it happened, we needn't have worried about them, because they immediately lost four on the bounce and sunk like a stone. It was their London rivals we needed to watch. It was now that Arsène Wenger's Arsenal made their charge. Sixth at Christmas, they put together an amazing run of results that we were unable to match.

Towards the end of February we had successive wins against Derby and Chelsea, and all seemed to be well. We were still nine points clear of Arsenal, although they had two games in hand. But now injuries hit us hard. In the Derby game, after I'd scored, my hamstring went, and Jordi fractured a bone in his foot. Then the following week, against Chelsea, Gary Pallister had to come off with a back problem which would keep him out for a month. There were a few others struggling for fitness too, and the gaffer was forced to field an under-strength team, featuring lads like Clegg, Twiss, Nevland and Thornley, for an FA Cup replay against Barnsley, which we lost 3–2.

For all our problems, we had stretched our lead in the league to eleven points by beating Chelsea 1–0, with Phil Neville's first goal for the club, and at the beginning of March one Manchester bookie, Fred Done, started paying out on the bets he had taken on us to win the league. Poor Fred was Done in more ways than one!

The match that really undid us that season was the Champions League quarter-final away to Monaco. Gary Pallister and I missed the game, injured, and although the 0–0 draw out there was a decent result, a rock-hard pitch took its toll on a few of our lads, notably Denis Irwin, who had to miss the next game when, with *eight* players carrying minor knocks and strains, we lost 2–0 at Sheffield Wednesday.

The trouble was that Arsenal were really flying now. They came to Old Trafford in mid-March, second in the table and unbeaten since December. If they beat us, the winning of the title would be in their own hands for the first time. I had to sit it out again and injuries elsewhere meant we had a young lad, John Curtis, picking up Marc Overmars. It wouldn't have been an easy job for an experienced defender with a hundred caps. And when Overmars got away from John in the second half, his goal gave them the result they needed. Peter Schmeichel went charging upfield in search of a last-gasp equalizer then pulled a hamstring running back. Arsenal were still six points behind us, but with three games in hand we needed them to lose. And they were winning every time they stepped on to a football pitch. In second leg of our Champions League quarter-final, Monaco could hardly believe their luck. They were playing a United team with no Schmeichel, Pallister, Keane and Giggs. Paul Scholes, too, was well below maximum fitness and was only able to manage one half of the game. They took the lead very early, through David Trezeguet, and although Ole equalized in the second half, we never looked like scoring again, and went out on the away goals rule. At full strength, we were a better team than Monaco. We'd shown that in beating Juventus, but we were clearly missing important players on the night. We had Phil Neville on the left wing. Enough said!

Out of Europe we now had only the league left to play for, and the outlook there wasn't too rosy, either. In beating Bolton 1–0, Arsenal kept their eighth clean sheet in succession – a Premier League record. It left them just three points behind with two games in hand, which meant we had to keep winning and hope they'd slip up somewhere. It's no fun, feeling the hot breath on the back of your neck, we were looking over our shoulders all the time, and Arsenal's clean sheets did worry us. We were thinking, 'Who the hell is going to score against them, let alone beat them?'

I was fit again for the match at Blackburn in April, when we came back from a goal down to win 3–1, but four days later we could only draw 1–1 at home to Liverpool, despite the fact that they were down to ten men for most of the game after Michael Owen had been sent off for a bad tackle.

Arsenal took full advantage, beating Newcastle 3–1, and cranking up the pressure with a big win at Blackburn, where they were three up after fourteen minutes. They were now just one point behind us with two games in hand, and they'd turned the tables on us. They were in the position we like to be in, hunting down the leaders and playing the best football. And this time it was us who cracked. We dropped two more points at home to Newcastle, and Arsenal swept past us when they stuffed Wimbledon 5–0. We'd been knocked off the top for the first time in six months, and although we managed to win our last three games, there was no stopping Arsenal, who clinched the title with a tenth successive victory, 4–0 at home to Everton. Everybody remembers the fourth goal, right at the end, when Tony Adams ran through and scored like a striker. That was just rubbing salt into the wound.

Arsenal fully deserved to win the league, which they did with two matches to spare. They were an exciting counter-attacking team, with a strong back four, Vieira and Petit to pull the strings in midfield and the pace of Overmars and Anelka, who could murder anybody on the break. They also had the Footballer of the Year, Dennis Bergkamp, who made and scored great goals. He was their Cantona, Sheringham or Zola. I think that team was even harder to play against than the Arsenal side that went through the season unbeaten in 2003–4. They were so good defensively that you never got any chances against them, while at the same time they created plenty. It was a crushing combination.

That season was a hard one for Teddy, who suffered more than most because of our injuries. Eric had the same problem when our regular wingers weren't playing – that sort of player relies on wingers more than any other sort – and in the season we're taking about, Becks played quite a lot in centre midfield and I was out for important games and I know Teddy missed us, and I sympathized with his situation. The crowd got on his back, saying he was no Cantona – but they'd got him wrong. He won them round in the end, of course.

Individually, it had been Bergkamp's season. I have to say that, like Ian Wright, he has never done particularly well against us, but that doesn't stop him being a fine player and a rare talent. He scores some great goals. If there were more players of his quality around, I'm sure more teams would play with that withdrawn forward knitting the attack and the midfield together, bringing others into the game.

I'm sure his fear of flying is one of the reasons Arsenal haven't done as well as they would have liked in Europe – they play half their games without their best player. I honestly can't imagine our gaffer putting up with it. I hate flying, but I've never refused to do it. Instead, me and Incey used to hold hands and shut our eyes as the plane raced down the runway and into the air. Pally was just as bad. The three of us would all sit there, shaking, while everyone laughed.

Just before the end of the 1997–8 season, the gaffer signed Jaap Stam, from PSV Eindhoven, for a club record £10.75m. The players didn't know much about him, so we asked Jordi, who knew him from Holland, and he said he was the best centre-half he'd ever seen. 'Surely he can't be that good,' we thought, 'otherwise we'd have heard of him,' but he was. From the moment he arrived he was brilliant. He was a beast of a man. Put him and Ronnie Johnsen together and the ball might get past, but no player would.

As Jaap came, Choccy McClair left, after eleven years

with the club. He'd not been first choice for two or three seasons, but the gaffer loved him because he could always be relied upon to do a job for the team. He looked on him as a lucky charm – Choccy would be having a horrible game, then somehow he'd pop up with the winning goal. Always sad to see a player like him move on. Especially as I still hadn't got his sense of humour. From day one it just flew straight over my head!

Wales Captain

Despite all my non-appearances, Wales thought enough of me to make me captain for the final World Cup qualifier, against Belgium in Brussels in October '97. Sadly, we had long since dropped out of contention, and were certain to finish fourth in the group, which Holland won, so perhaps the honour – which was definitely how I saw it – was really a cosmetic exercise, designed to encourage me to play more often in future. There was never any doubt in my own mind about my desire to do so.

We lost 3–2, but it wasn't a bad game, and we should have had a point from it. They were 2–0 up at half-time, but we stepped things up in the second half. When I was brought down in the box, Mark Pembridge tucked away the penalty, then I equalized on the hour. I should have scored again but was off target. It was costly. A goal from Marc Wilmots finished us off.

It was an unsatisfactory was to begin as Wales captain, and I'd love to say that things got better, but the second time I did the job, against Norway in September 2001, it was even worse. It was a World Cup qualifier in Oslo, an important match. We'd gone 2–1 up through Robbie Savage and Craig Bellamy, then threw it away, losing 3–2. I picked up two bookings – and a red card – through sheer frustration. It's the only time in my career that I've been sent off. Things didn't improve much when I was made captain for a third time to mark my fiftieth cap. We lost 2–0 at home to Austria, but at least I managed to stay on the pitch this time.

Bobby Gould had resigned as manager in June '99, after we were beaten 4–0 by Italy in Bologna. I was up front with Dean Saunders that day, and at half-time Gould tore into both of us, saying we weren't showing – weren't taking up the right positions for the rest of the team to be able to pass to us. We tried to tell him that the ball was taking too long to get up to us, that we were making our runs and not getting picked out – a normal football argument in other words – but he came in after the game and said we were a disgrace and that he was calling it a day. Mentally, the lads all punched the air in delight. Certainly nobody tried to talk him out of it, he wasn't a popular man. I get on with most people, and I didn't think he was a horrible person, but I never rated him as a manager. Strange, inexplicable decisions meant there was no stability to the side. Too much changed from game to game, and we'd turn up not knowing what formation or which players he'd be trying this time. It just felt so disorganized. If only I'd known that it was up to me and Dean Saunders, we could have nipped it in the bud earlier!

Anyway, while they looked for a new manager, the Welsh FA put Neville Southall and Mark Hughes jointly in charge for our match at home to Denmark, which was played at Anfield the following week. I had a lot more respect for the two of them, but they didn't have much time to turn things around. We lost again.

I never felt that the arrangements made for the Welsh team were as professional as they should have been. The arrangements for a European Championship qualifier away to Belarus in 1999 were a perfect example. For some reason we always seemed to fly from Stansted. I don't know why, because it wasn't exactly convenient for any of us. I can only assume it was cheaper. This time, after the journey to Essex that we could have all done without, we tried to check in, only to discover that we had exceeded our baggage allowance by a ton and a half. Cue red faces all around. We couldn't take all that extra weight, so we had to ask thirteen fans if they would mind catching another plane. A few of them had been on the pop too, and were the worse for wear, so when Sparky had to break the news to them I thought there was going to be trouble. At least one of them thought it was worth fighting for. And who could blame him? Flights to Minsk weren't exactly stacking up. Fortunately, Sparky diffused the agro, but what a position to put your manager in. But it was typical of the general approach. Overweight by a few pounds you could understand, but a ton and a half! That's the weight of a car! It's never the best idea to put players and fans on the same plane anyway. It's just asking for trouble. Sparky was furious and demanded changes, and it was certainly the last time we flew from Stansted. After all that, though, we won the game 2–1, and I got the winner just before the end. That same season Wales called up Ipswich's David Johnson, even though he'd already played for England B and Jamaica. Needless to say, he never played for us once that came to light. Another cock-up.

Things improved a lot under Sparky. He made the whole set-up much more professional. After he was given a four-year contract in November '99, the first thing he did was to bring in Eric Harrison, my old tutor at United, as his number two. That was a really good move. Eric had learned his trade at the best club in the country, under the best manager, and knew how to organize things. He wouldn't settle for second best.

Early on in the Wales job, Sparky tried to take advantage of his good relationship with the gaffer by picking me for a friendly international away to Qatar. Much to my embarrassment, in nine years as a Welsh international, I hadn't played a single friendly. The Welsh public and media would never let me forget it, which was fair enough, but it came about because successive Wales managers hadn't kept their word. The gaffer would agree with them that I could play one half – something Sven-Göran Eriksson does a lot with England – but then they'd keep me on for longer, and he wasn't having that. So in February 2000, when Sparky announced that he was picking me to go to Qatar, rather than risk exacerbating my back trouble and hamstring problem with a long flight, I decided I couldn't go.

But I did finally get to play in my first friendly the following month, when I scored, in the first football international played at the new Millennium Stadium in Cardiff. The goal didn't count for much – we lost 2–1 to Finland. We weren't helped by the pitch. It was dreadful. It slotted together in blocks, like a jigsaw, but the pieces didn't sit evenly, and I actually injured myself in training before a match against Brazil when my studs caught in the turf and the jolt hurt my thigh. I had *really* wanted to play in that one too. I mean, everyone wants the chance to play the Brazilians. And of course the injury made the gaffer even more reluctant to release me subsequently.

Our bid to qualify for the 2002 World Cup got off to a depressing start when we lost 2–1 in Belarus, where we'd drawn the previous year. Craig Bellamy was unlucky to be sent off by the Italian referee, which did nothing for our cause, and it was the eighty-ninth minute before Gary Speed got our only goal. It was *exactly* the sort of game we needed to be winning if we were going to get anywhere.

By June 2001 Wales hadn't won a World Cup tie for five years, and that record didn't improve when we lost to Poland in Cardiff. Nathan Blake gave us an early lead, then I missed an open goal. Things definitely got worse for Sparky before they got better, but they started to look up when we got a good 1–1 draw with the Ukraine in Kiev. The result was an improvement, but it was a game we should have won. We played well enough, we just didn't finish them off. It was symptomatic of another failed campaign.

Our hopes that our luck might change when it came to qualification for Euro 2004 were dashed by a horrible draw. We were in with Italy, Yugoslavia, Finland and Azerbaijan. We've learned to always expect the worst from the seeding system. And that's not going to change until we do manage to qualify for something. As things stand we will always get a top team, a difficult one that nobody wants to play and a third seed better than us. But there's only one way to change that. It's down to us.

Occasionally, we get tantalizing tastes of what we are missing by failing to get to a major championship. In February 2002, for example, we played Argentina in Cardiff and drew 1–1 in front of a crowd of 65,000. All right, it was a friendly, but it was a pretty competitive one. They took it seriously, and we had our strongest side out for once and deserved the result. Julio Cruz equalized for them after Craig Bellamy had given us the lead, but we played well, and it made all of us wonder what we might be capable of if we ever got to a big tournament.

Another occasion like that came in May 2002, when we beat Germany 1–0 at the Millennium. The Germans were on their way to the World Cup, and used the game as a full-scale dress rehearsal. They were strong, but we won with a goal scored by Cardiff's Robbie Earnshaw on his debut. Earnie later went to West Brom and carried on scoring in the Premier League. For some reason, though, he hadn't been a regular starter for West Brom. I'm not sure why not, because he strikes me as a natural goalscorer, blessed with good technique and two good feet. He's also quick, which is a great asset. As a bloke, you couldn't dislike him, he's a lovely lad. He's obsessed with football, lives for the game. He could tell you about every player at every club – he's a bit of an anorak like that. Craig Bellamy is exactly the same, maybe even worse. Ask him any question about football and he'll know the answer. 'You won't catch me out on football,' he'll tell you. He's right too!

Sparky retired as a player in July 2002, to concentrate full-time on managing Wales, and I really thought that could be the start of something good. It certainly looked that way when in our first qualifier for Euro 2004 we won 2–0 in Finland. John Hartson and Simon Davies were our scorers, and I was particularly impressed with Davies, a player I've got a lot of time for. His progress at Tottenham was held up by injury and illness, but when he plays for Wales he gives us good balance by providing width on the right. We played with me on the left, Bellamy on the right and Hartson at centre-forward with Speed, Pembridge and Davies across the midfield. Simon is also capable of scoring some very good goals, which he did in Helsinki, and in October 2002 he was named Welsh Footballer of the Year, an honour he fully deserved.

One of the highlights of my international career came later that month. There was a huge sense of anticipation surrounding the arrival of the Italian team in Cardiff. It was the kind of big event that the Millennium Stadium was built for. We went into the game really confident after the result in Finland. The system Sparky was using suited all the players and worked a treat. We got off to a great start, cheered on by a full-voiced home crowd, when Simon Davies scored early on. Alessandro Del Piero equalized before half-time, but then Craig Bellamy got the winner after about seventy minutes. It was a great result, and a top performance.

After beating Italy, we all felt we had it in us to qualify, and that belief grew stronger when we went to Azerbaijan and won 2–0, which left us unbeaten in eight games. Big John Hartson scored again in Baku. He's a good lad. That people have the wrong impression of him after that awful incident in training at West Ham, when he booted Eyal Berkovic in the face, is perhaps unsurprising. But while I don't know what Berkovic said or did to John that day, if anything – we've never discussed it – his reaction was totally out of character. He's a quiet one off the field, and doesn't have much to say for himself, although he does enjoy a bit of karaoke. I like him as a player, and his record speaks for itself. Wherever he's been, he's always scored goals, and it's been the same at international level.

Sparky signed a new four-year contract with Wales in January 2003, which all the players saw as good news. The manager was committed and determined to achieve something positive, and so were we. When we got back on track with the qualifiers at the end of March, we stuffed Azerbaijan 4–0 in Cardiff. We had now enjoyed a ten-match unbeaten run, stretching back twenty months, and that fuelled our confidence.

It meant it was all the more annoying when the run came to an end in meaningless fashion at the end of May 2003, when a half-strength team lost 2–0 to the United States in San Diego. The fixture was a waste of time, and it was one friendly I definitely didn't mind missing. Who knew whether it shook us, but when we resumed the European qualifying campaign in August, it was with a defeat to Serbia-Montenegro in Belgrade. It was a scrappy, tight game, and we nearly snatched something out of it. At 1–0 down in the last minute Earnshaw took the ball round the 'keeper and his shot seemed certain to go in until Dejan Stefanovic, of Portsmouth, dived across the goalline and diverted it over the bar with his big toe. If we'd got a draw there, I think we'd have been on the plane to the finals, but that first competitive defeat took the wind out of our sails at exactly the wrong time. Next up we had Italy away. And they had a score to settle.

There was a row before that game over Craig Bellamy's fitness. He had a knee problem that prevented him from playing twice in one week, and Newcastle didn't want to release him, but with the two countries neck and neck at the top of Group 9 we had to dig our heels in, and Sparky got his way in the end. Not that it mattered much, we were outclassed in Milan and lost 4–0. We held our own in the first half, when Buffon made a lucky save from me and it was goalless at half-time, but then the floodgates opened. Filippo Inzaghi ran riot to score a hat-trick in the space of eleven minutes. In the heat of the San Siro it was asking a lot of our defenders, like Mark Delaney and Robert Page, to shackle a player like Inzaghi in the mood he was in. And of course once we fell behind and started chasing the game, we stopped protecting the defence as well as we usually did. After the highpoint at Cardiff and missed opportunities in Bosnia and Serbia-Montenegro, the sense of deflation after such a heavy defeat was immense.

After that result, we knew we wouldn't win the group, and were looking to qualify through the play-offs. Four days later we played Finland in Cardiff. We'd beaten them in Helsinki and confidently expected to do so at home but, after Simon Davies had given us a third-minute lead, Jason Koumas was sent off, and they battered us in the second half. We didn't play well, and the truth was that they deserved their late equalizer. They created a lot of chances, and it took some good saves from Paul Jones just to earn us our point. Liverpool's Sami Hyypia was a giant for them at the back, well equipped to take care of John Hartson, but at times they seemed to have *ten* Sami Hyypias. They were that big as a team.

A month later we suffered a real hammer blow when Serbia-Montenegro came to Cardiff and beat us 3–2. We were without some important players, like Mark Pembridge, Simon Davies, Robbie Savage and Andy Melville, but we should have done better. It's the story of my international career. It was so disappointing to know that we had thrown away the possibility of automatic qualification after getting off to such a good start in the group. At least, though, we had made it to the play-offs, where we were drawn against Russia. The first leg was in Moscow.

We travelled east looking for a draw and got it, 0–0. We weren't really an attacking force at all, we just ran our socks off to deny them space and keep them out. The only memorable thing about it from our point of view was a clash I had with a player called Vadim Evseev, who fouled me then collapsed dramatically when I stuck out an elbow. He wasn't really hurt, but the Russians made a big thing out of it and tried to get me banned for the return. Their jumping up and down worked to an extent, because UEFA charged me with misconduct, but it did them no good because I was allowed to play in the second game. Later, I was banned for two matches, which meant I missed the World Cup qualifiers away to Azerbaijan and at home to Northern Ireland. I've got to say that missing the trip to Baku was no hardship – in fact some of the lads gave me stick, saying I'd done a 'Becks' and got banned deliberately! I hadn't, I'm not that clever!

At the time, though, we thought 0–0 over there was a great result against a good side. We all worked incredibly hard that night – probably too hard, because we were knackered for the home leg, which was only four days later. The return leg against the Russians was a disaster. We didn't play at all well in Cardiff. They outclassed us, and we lost 1–0. They made a few changes to the team and were much fresher than us. We seemed jaded by comparison and never really got out of first gear. They scored midway through the first half through Evseev – that's how hurt he had been by my elbow – which meant we now had to get two, and our team just wasn't set up to do it. With hindsight, we were probably a bit too cautious in playing with only John Hartson up front, and when Robbie Earnshaw and then Nathan Blake came on in the second half, it was too little, too late.

The result was a crushing disappointment. We'd started the campaign so well, beating Italy at home and Finland away, but we just ran out of energy, and fresh players to bring in, when it mattered. For me, it was even worse than the Romania game, which cost us a place at the '94 World Cup. I was gutted then, but I was only nineteen and I knew I'd get another chance. Now I was about to turn thirty, and there weren't many chances left. I knew how they'd all felt in '94. We knew that if we'd played how we were capable of playing – as we had earlier in the campaign – we'd have beaten the Russians. The story wasn't over just yet though.

Towards the end of January it was revealed that one of the Russian players, Igor Titov, had failed a drugs test during the play-offs, and the Welsh FA immediately applied to UEFA to have us reinstated in their place. At the time, I thought we had a case – if one of their players was on drugs, who was to say how many of the others, who weren't tested, might have been? I spoke to Sparky about it, and he sounded pretty confident. 'We've got a good chance here,' he told me. He even went so far as to say, 'I'm very optimistic,' but perhaps he just wanted it that much. Certainly his distress was real enough when UEFA turned us down. He'd believed it might go our way. By contrast I had mixed feelings about the possibility of going through like that. I'd already dealt with my disappointment. My attitude was that we hadn't played well enough to get through, and I'm afraid to say that I never had any great faith in our chances of impressing anybody at UEFA headquarters.

As you can imagine, morale was pretty low at this stage, so it was a welcome lift when we beat Scotland 4–0 in a friendly in February, with Robbie Earnshaw scoring a hat-trick. By agreement between Sparky and the gaffer, I played just the first half. That result dug us out of the trough we were in after failing to qualify and was the beginning of a nice little run in which we beat Hungary and Canada and drew with Norway. For the 2006 World Cup qualifiers we were drawn in a group that had everyone talking about the old Home Internationals. We'd be playing England again for the first time for over twenty years, as well as Northern Ireland, Poland, Austria and Azerbaijan.

The game in Azerbaijan in September 2004 was the fifth anniversary of Sparky's appointment as manager. After what happened in Russia I was suspended for the first two games, and didn't make the trip, but I watched the game unfold on TV from the edge of my seat. Gary Speed scored first for us with a typical goal, arriving in the box late and volleying in a knockdown from John Hartson. I thought we'd be all right after that, but they equalized almost straight away with a long range free-kick. The shot was from 40 yards out, and from that distance you expect them to be saved. It wasn't. It was the first goal Wales had conceded in over five hours of play, and what a way to do it. Dropping two points over there was a galling start to another campaign.

Our second game was against Northern Ireland in Cardiff

five days later. Still suspended, I had to watch on the box again. The Italian referee lost it completely. Flashing red cards like a mad magician, he sent off three players in the first half-hour. Robbie Savage went after only nine minutes, for grabbing Michael Hughes, who he accused of trying to break his leg. Hughes went with him for the original foul. Then David Healy was the third to go, for a gesture he made to the crowd after scoring. That was Northern Ireland's second goal, Jeff Whitley had got their first, from 20 yards, after ten minutes. John Hartson and Robbie Earnshaw scored for us, but it was another bad result. We'd been looking for six points from those first two games. To get just two wasn't going to be good enough. We could only hope that the campaign would play out as a reverse of the Euro qualifiers and that we'd get stronger as we went on. The prospect of that took a hammer blow when, less than a week later, Mark Hughes was appointed manager of Blackburn Rovers. We were going to lose the man we thought could guide us to the World Cup. He agreed with Blackburn that he could stay in charge, on a part-time basis, for the next two qualifiers in October, but after that it would be bye-bye Sparky.

Even worse, the first of these was England at Old Trafford. This was the match everybody in Wales had been looking forward to, but now, with our manager on the way out and two poor performances in September, morale wasn't exactly sky high. If we'd won our first two games, as we'd expected to, it would have given us some leeway, but now we needed a big result against the strongest team in the group. I'd never played against England and, like all Welshmen, I was particularly keen to beat them. I'd also never played for anyone but the home team at Old Trafford, so experiencing it from the away perspective was going to be interesting. At least I'd be wearing red!

It was given a massive build-up, but the match itself was an anti-climax. In a footballing sense, we didn't turn up. We definitely missed Robbie Savage, who was suspended for his red card against the Irish. Without his competitive instinct we had no *hywl*, as the Welsh call sporting passion. Instead of getting stuck into them, we showed too much respect and never caused them the slightest trouble. I know from talking to the United lads in their team that England couldn't believe how easy they'd had it.

We were wrong-footed right from the start, when Alan Melville, our experienced centre-half, was injured during the warm-up and had to drop out. We were adjusting when England lined up with three strikers, Owen, Defoe and Rooney, which we hadn't expected and couldn't handle. We were never in it, they controlled and ran the game from start to finish. Neither Craig Bellamy nor I saw enough of the ball to cause any damage, we were defending nearly all the time. Gary Neville kept running past me and making me chase him, instead of the other way around. The only positive I could take from it was that I nutmegged Nev and also Nicky Butt. I wanted to give them stick afterwards, but how could I after our performance and the result?

The outcome was an enormous disappointment because we thought we could cause them problems. We knew their ability would stretch us, but we'd been confident that John Hartson would trouble their defenders in the air, and that my pace, and Bellamy's, would hurt them out wide. Sadly, the confidence was misplaced. Getting stick at corners from the Stretford end capped a miserable night's performance. When we played Poland in Cardiff the following Wednesday we were no better. It was Sparky's last game, and we wanted to give him a good send-off – nobody more than me – but a stomach bug had me confined to bed in the Vale of

Glamorgan Hotel from Sunday until Thursday, and I could only watch on television as it all unravelled.

The start was promising, Robbie Earnshaw opening the scoring with his ninth goal in seventeen internationals, but then the roof fell in. The Poles hit back with three in fifteen minutes and when John Hartson pulled one back, in added time, it was not much of a consolation. With two points from our first four games, we were merely making up the numbers. In the Euro 2004 campaign, we'd got off to a great start and had been unable to hang on in there at the end. Now we were out almost before we had begun, and the fall-out was pretty demoralizing. It wasn't only Sparky who went, there were others, including Gary Speed, our captain, who decided they'd had enough too. Speeds, with eighty-five caps behind him, had been brilliant for Wales, and Robbie Savage immediately called for him to be appointed manager, in partnership with Brian Flynn, but it wasn't to be.

There were some reservations when John Toshack took over because he had been pretty critical of a lot of the lads, myself included, while working as a pundit on radio and TV. He was on a lot, and always seemed to be having a go at someone, especially me, for the number of times I didn't play, or the way I played, and Sparky, for his results. With me it was always: 'Why is Giggs playing so much in the middle when he should be out wide, providing the crosses?' A lot of it didn't appear to be constructive criticism. When we got back in the dressing room after a game, the telly was on and there he'd be, slaughtering us. Emotions were high. The adrenaline was still running, and it didn't go down at all well. We called him every name under the sun, hurling abuse at the TV. Knowing the strength of feeling, it didn't surprise me when some of the older players decided they weren't going to play for John, and retired from international football. As Gary Speed was one of them, we needed a new captain. The choice boiled down to me or Robbie Savage. Sav and John didn't see eye to eye from the beginning, so he was out of the equation, and I was offered the job, despite the fact that I was very much a Sparky man. John told me he wanted me to play on until the 2008 European Championship, by which time I'd be thirty-four. To help me to do that, he said he'd leave me out of some friendly internationals or maybe just play me for half a game, on the understanding that I'd turn up for all the competitive ones. It all sounded reasonable enough until I began to wonder how effective a captain I'd be if I wasn't going to be there for half the games.

After that we didn't get off to a great start. I joined up with the squad in Cardiff for John's first match, against Hungary in February, but had to pull out the day before the game with the old hamstring trouble. Because I was injured, I didn't actually do any training, but I know that the lads who did weren't too keen on the new regime. Sav was particularly critical. In fairness, the result itself was a good one, a 2–0 win, but the problems between Sav and John came to a head before the World Cup resumption at home to Austria at the end of March. John phoned him to tell him he was leaving him out of the squad because he wanted to try other players. Sav told him to stuff it, he was retiring from international football anyway.

Sav phoned me straight afterwards to explain what had gone on. It was fair enough, he reckoned, not to be included in the team, but he didn't feel there was any question that he was good enough to be in the squad. I sympathized with him, but the only conclusion I could draw was that John had his own clear ideas about how the new midfield would operate. It was unfortunate for Sav, though. Wales haven't got enough quality players to be doing without the likes of Robbie Savage, so maybe we'll see him back in the near future.

One of the things Sav went on to say about John, in a newspaper article, was that his methods were 'stone age'. They *were* certainly very different from Sparky's, but every manager has his own way of doing things. Before Sparky took charge, the Welsh set-up was very amateurish. He'd experienced it as a player and, when he became manager, he wasted no time in overhauling it. He'd known nothing but the best at club level, and he tried to replicate everything he had been used to there for his country. Wales started preparing the Man United way. Straight away he introduced daily itineraries, which were pushed under our doors each day and told us exactly what we'd be doing, and he had us wearing blazers instead of tracksuits, so we looked the business. That sort of thing might appear insignificant, but it's about thoroughness, taking care of every detail. Players with top clubs take that sort of thing for granted, but Wales have to use people from outside the Premier League, and to see the professionalism Sparky expected from everybody helped them to make the big step up.

John is completely different, much more old school. The prepared itineraries fell by the wayside. Instead, he called us all into a room when we arrived at the hotel and told us what we'd be doing all week. That's it, from then on it was up to us to remember it. I'm not saying it's the wrong way, it's just his way. He was always going to need time to get to know how international management works. It was obviously very different in nature from the club jobs he'd had before, bringing with it its own particular challenges. It's not an everyday thing. Sometimes he has to go four or five months without seeing his players. It's tough trying to build a team under those conditions, and he is probably still getting used to that. He's also been forced to grapple with the fact that so many senior players have retired, and the need to have to bring through younger, less experienced replacements.

We played Austria in back-to-back qualifiers, in Cardiff and in Vienna, on 26 and 30 March, and lost them both, which had John under pressure from the start. For the first game, which was my fiftieth international, I was appointed captain on a permanent basis. Unfortunately, we lost 2–0, but John changed the formation for the second game and we were much better out there. We were beaten again, 1–0, but we created enough chances to have won the game easily. We battered them, really; I was playing up front with Craig Bellamy, and we did everything but score. Their goal was a soft one that trickled through our 'keeper's legs. So although it was another bad result, the performance was encouraging. The overall position, on the other hand, was anything but. After six qualifying ties we were joint bottom of the group with Azerbaijan, on just two points.

A lot of people wondered if United would have released me for both games against Austria if they had still been in the Champions League and going for the title. I don't know the answer to that, but it became a major talking point when I came back from playing the full game in Vienna on the Wednesday and had to come off after only five minutes when United played Blackburn and drew 0–0 on the Saturday. The hamstring went the first time I made a run, which started the old club v. country thing again. I know the gaffer thought it was down to the travelling with Wales – getting back from Austria at four o'clock in the morning, and at Cardiff airport, not in Manchester. That's the problem: whenever I go away with Wales, I get back to Cardiff in the early hours and then have the long drive back to Manchester. I'm stuck on a plane for three or four hours, then drive for three hours to get maybe four hours in bed before I have to go in to United for a warm-down.

Obviously there is a lot of improvement needed, and having made me captain, John does discuss most things with me. He seems to have a lot of confidence in me, and feels that if I lead by example, I can lift the other players. When he wants to talk things over, or if something is bothering him, he comes to me and John Hartson – the senior pros. Friendlies will still be a bone of contention, but John, to his credit, said he'd deal with that situation match by match. He'll see who United are playing the weekend after internationals, and maybe only play me for half the game. He seems quite relaxed about it really, prepared to play me for forty-five minutes here, and ninety there. He knew we weren't going to qualify for the 2006 World Cup, so from the start he was building towards the 2008 European Championship, and with that in mind it wasn't vital that I played every game in 2005. Like the gaffer, he's willing to rest me occasionally and can see the benefits in it.

History Is Made

Arsenal had taken our title, so it was no surprise that big changes were made for the 1998–9 season. Choccy McClair had gone and now another old stalwart left. The arrival of Jaap Stam meant it was the end of the road for Gary Pallister, who was sold to Middlesbrough for £2m. Jaap wasn't the only major signing. Jesper Blomqvist, the Swedish winger who had played against us for Gothenburg, arrived from Parma for £4m, and just as the season started we signed Dwight Yorke from Aston Villa for a club record fee of £12.6m. In total, the gaffer had spent £27m, which was an impressive outlay in those pre-Abramovich days and the season ahead was a prospect to relish.

I'm not sure Becks saw it that way, though. The papers had given him terrible stick for getting sent off against Argentina at the '98 World Cup, and he seemed to be public enemy number one when the season got under way. People had burnt effigies of him and he was given police protection, just in case, on the day he returned to pre-season training. After the World Cup, he had tried to get away from it all on holiday, but he was accosted wherever he went, and in the end he was glad to be back within the security of the club and among people he knew and trusted, the players.

As we played the first away games, it immediately became clear just what a torrid time he was going to have to endure. Away supporters picked on him horribly, bringing his wife and family into it, and I think it's underestimated how well Becks stood up to that ordeal. Not only did he rise above the relentless, foul abuse, he played like a king that season. He showed tremendous strength of character, but he'd be the first to admit that he had a lot of help from his teammates and his manager – the people who mattered to him were all very supportive. He deserves full credit, though: he could have shrivelled under the treatment he received, but instead he rose to the challenge and became an even better player. Becks was the most high-profile target, but he wasn't the only one who came in for criticism at the start of that season. Jaap Stam had not had a particularly good World Cup with Holland, and a couple of mistakes in the Charity Shield, which we lost 3–0 to Arsenal, had a lot of people wondering whether the gaffer had signed an expensive dud. I wasn't one of them. I'd watched the World Cup, and was amazed when the Dutch marked two against two at the back – Jaap and De Boer had no cover. There were times when Jaap was on his own, and I don't care who you are, no team can afford to defend like that.

Because he needed a rest after the tournament, Jaap joined us for pre-season training a bit late, and it was against that background that he faced Nicolas Anelka in the Charity Shield and didn't play well. After that, he took a bit of stick, but the players had seen enough from him in training, and in our pre-season games, to realize how good he was. Just before he joined us, we'd seen pictures of him on the cover of a magazine, where he looked massive. I was sure that he was too big and muscular to be quick enough, but I was wrong about that. He was quick all right. After just a few games we knew we'd signed a great player. Once his pace took him into the channel ahead of an attacking player, they had no chance. He was so strong that it was always going to be a mismatch. Jaap would not be beaten.

There was a feeling within the club at the time that we

lacked a striker who could hold the ball up, turn and run at the opposition, and I know the gaffer tried to get Patrick Kluivert, who was the main man at AC Milan then. Kluivert wouldn't come, and it was then that we signed Dwight Yorke. He had a bit of everything – a cross between Teddy Sheringham and Andy Cole. The main thing was that he could turn his man on the edge of the penalty box and dribble past, which with Europe in mind is the extra dimension the gaffer was looking for. He had been giving the Champions League a lot of thought, because that was the big one we still had to win, and he'd come to the conclusion that we needed something extra there. Yorkey was to provide it up front, but that wasn't the only area where there was room for improvement. At Old Trafford, because of the gung-ho way we attacked in European games, we needed defenders who were quite happy defending one-on-one, but with Jaap joining Ronny Johnsen at the back, we felt we'd got that. We could play the way we wanted to play. Yorkey was also a lovely guy and we got on straight away. I'd met him a couple of times before he joined us, and I remember he came and sat with me before his first training session. He was an instant hit in the dressing room because of his friendly, easy-going manner. He was always smiling, always happy. The day after he arrived, United agreed to sell Ole Gunnar to Tottenham for £5.5m. I'm relieved that Ole turned down the move, but it puzzled me that we were willing to sell a player of his calibre in the first place. I can only think that the club was trying to do the right thing by Ole, and provide him with the opportunity to be a regular starter elsewhere. Ole's refusal was to prove a godsend.

We had to pre-qualify for the Champions League, which we did by beating the Polish champions, LKS Łódź, 2–0 on aggregate. I scored the first goal of that European campaign, after a quarter of an hour of the home leg. Then after that, we were drawn in what became known as the 'Group of Death', with Barcelona, Bayern Munich and Brondby.

In the Premiership, Yorkey scored twice on his home debut, Ole nailed the other two in a 4–1 win against Charlton, and we also beat Coventry 2–0 before our first major test that season, at home to Barça. I opened the scoring early on, climbing above Luis Enrique to head in a cross from Becks, and Paul Scholes made it 2–0 after twenty-five minutes, following up when an overhead kick from Yorkey bounced out off the crossbar. We'd started really well, but Barcelona's quality brought them back into the game. Rivaldo, who was brilliant that night, had a goal wrongly disallowed for offside, but Sonny Anderson scored two minutes into the second half and on the hour Jaap was harshly deemed to have fouled Rivaldo and Giovanni equalized with the penalty. It was a cracking game, and at 2–2 it was anybody's. Becks made it 3–2 to us with a lovely 25-yard free-kick, but Barça weren't finished, and another penalty, for a Nicky Butt handball, gave them a draw from a match neither team deserved to lose. That didn't mean we were particularly happy to have to settle for one – especially after being ahead for so much of the game.

That Sunday we had to go to Arsenal, where we were badly beaten, 3–0. I was up front with Yorkey, with Jesper Blomqvist on the left, but the game was played at the other end, where Tony Adams outjumped Jaap to head them into an early lead. Anelka made it 2–0 before half-time, and we were never in it. Nicky Butt was sent off for the second time in five days, for bringing down Vieira when he was bearing down on goal, and Ljungberg, on his home debut, coolly chipped Peter for the third. It was our fourth defeat on the bounce against Arsenal. Inevitably it gave rise to talk of them having the psychological edge. Not in my mind they didn't.

At the end of September it was Champions League time again, away to Bayern Munich, where we should have won, and would have done so but for a mistake by Peter Schmeichel, when he rushed out to claim a long throw, missed it and let in Elber to score. The match ended 2–2. Two draws then, and two Champions League games we could have won. At least we'd got a couple of away goals on the trip to Germany.

Going into October. The Cole–Yorke partnership had gelled nicely, and both scored in a 3–0 defeat of Southampton at The Dell, which put us second behind Villa. The two of them were full of goals as we hit top gear that month. After beating Wimbledon 5–1 we put six past Brondby, where I got the first two and at last the European campaign began to fire. I played on the right this time, with Jesper on the left. Wes Brown was just coming into the team then and he played at right-back. The gaffer said, 'Wes is having his first European game, make sure you help him out.' It was the other way around when Wes crossed for me to score the opening goal. My second was a header, from Jesper's cross. Brondby weren't a bad team at that time either. They had beaten Bayern Munich 2–1, but we just battered them. They can't have imagined it would be as bad in the second game, a fortnight later, but we beat them 5–0 at home, going 3–0 up after only sixteen minutes.

Towards the end of November we had the return game with Barcelona, and this one was even better than the first match. It started with a bang and then didn't let up for ninety minutes. Anderson scored in the first minute, which brought back memories of our nightmare in the Nou Camp in '94, but Peter made some good saves to keep us in it, and after twenty-five minutes Yorkey equalized after a good run by Jesper. Early in the second half Andy Cole put us in front, but Rivaldo made it 2–2 with a curling free-kick. Yorkey headed in a cross from Becks for 3–2, then Rivaldo scored with an overhead kick, and might have won it for them near the end when he hit the bar from twenty-five yards. 3–3 again. If we both got to the final, at least we'd know the score!

At the end of November, John Gregory's Villa were still on top of the league, one point ahead of us with fourteen games played. Our old mate Dion Dublin had scored seven goals for them in his last three matches. It was now that Blackburn, looking for a manager to replace Roy Hodgson, made an official approach for Brian Kidd, who left us at the beginning of December. There had been talk of him going before, to Everton, and I'd sensed that Kiddo wanted to be his own man, rather than a number two. He probably felt that if he turned down Blackburn, he might not get another chance. So I wasn't surprised, but I was disappointed, when he left. We'd always enjoyed a really good relationship and I liked the way he worked. I made a point of speaking to him before he left, saying goodbye and wishing him well.

The following week we had the return with Bayern, at home. I beat Thomas Strunz to set up a goal for Roy Keane, but Hasan Salihamidzic equalized on a night when Stefan Effenberg lived up to his big reputation in midfield. We thought we'd need to win to get into the quarter-finals, and the 1–1 draw we managed wouldn't have been good enough but for favourable results elsewhere, which put us through as one of the two best runners-up.

Our less than surefooted progress in the Champions League was reflected domestically. In the Premiership we were still struggling to overtake Villa, and two points from our next three games didn't do much to help us. Against Middlesbrough at home we were dreadful, 3–0 down in an hour before Butt and Scholes pulled us back to 3–2 but that made it six matches in a row without a win, and we were down to third. It certainly didn't look like it had the makings of an historic season at this stage.

It wasn't until Boxing Day that we finally started to roll, keeping our first clean sheet for two months in beating Nottingham Forest 3–0 at home. Certainly Forest were poor – they hadn't won in the league for sixteen games – but we took them apart. Ronny Johnsen scored the first two goals, one of them after I'd had a header saved, and I got the third with a chip over Dave Beasant.

At the time there was a lot of talk about the 'decline' of Peter Schmeichel, who had made it known that he planned to leave us at the end of the season. This sort of story tends to take on a life of its own. Peter *had* made more mistakes than usual, but now I felt he was back to his best, and after the clean sheet against Forest he did it again, in much more difficult circumstances, away to Chelsea, who were second in the table. Chelsea were on top throughout the first half and attacked us in waves, but Peter was in dominant, morale-breaking form, and made some outstanding saves, chiefly from Zola. We were better in the second half, after Teddy Sheringham had come on for Scholesy, but we were relieved to come away with a point. We had Peter to thank.

By the end of January we went top of the table for the first time after Yorkey got an eighty-ninth-minute winner at Charlton. Steve McClaren arrived from Derby as the gaffer's new number two at the beginning of February. He was different in style from Kiddo, who was a lot more outgoing and liked joining in the banter with the lads. He was more comfortable than Steve in the players' company partly because he'd been around the club a long time. Steve was more serious, but he was all right. And where it mattered, he delivered. He took us on to the next level of professionalism, introducing all the latest ideas. For the first time it was laid down exactly what we would be doing throughout each week. We had an itinerary which told us everything, and we thought that was brilliant. Like soldiers, players like to be told what to do.

Mind you, we didn't always obey orders. On a pre-season trip to Australia, in 2000, Steve was in charge because the gaffer had stayed at home. One night in Melbourne he told us we could go out, but that we had to be back in our hotel, the Crown, by one a.m. Teddy Sheringham, Dwight Yorke and Mark Bosnich went out in one group. The three of them together looked quite a cocktail, and I couldn't help thinking it was safer to break away from them as they tended to attract trouble – well, Yorkey and Bozzy did anyway – so I went to a club with Nicky Butt. It got to about 2.30 in the morning, and we were in a corner of this club, chatting, when the owner, who knew who we were, came over to us. 'Is that your boss who has just walked in?' he asked, pointing to the other side of the room. It was Steve, with the goal-keeping coach, Tony Coton. *Shit!* They'd got wind of the fact that some players were out breaking the curfew, and Steve, in charge for the first time, had set out to catch the culprits. Butty and I exchanged glances and made up our minds. 'Have you got a back door?' I asked the owner, and he quickly ushered us out through the fire exit to safety. Or so we thought. We were underground, lost in a maze of concrete corridors. The two of us had been wandering around for about ten minutes and were starting to wonder whether we'd ever see daylight when we saw this security guard running towards us. He didn't look like he'd come to help. 'Got them!' he shouted into his walky-talky. He grabbed us and slammed us both up against the wall. 'What the hell are you doing down here?' he snarled at us. 'We're with Man United, we're footballers,' I tried to explain but it didn't register. 'Who the fuck are Man United?' Time for some fast talking. Eventually, we managed to calm him down and explain that United were a 'soccer' team, that we were players and that we were only down in his underground tunnels because his boss had sent us there. He finally spoke to the nightclub owner and let us go. We'd taken a wrong turn, but he showed us the way. Twenty minutes after escaping from the club, I opened a door marked 'Fire Exit' and there was Steve, walking towards us. I jumped straight back and closed the door. I didn't think he'd clocked us. At least he didn't come barrelling through the door to find us! We waited in silence for five minutes then sneaked away back to the hotel without being seen. A close shave.

We weren't the only ones who'd had a late night, and training the next morning, in the Australian heat, was nobody's idea of fun. We'd done a run and some stretches, then Steve said, 'Right, come on, we'll have another jog.' So we're running again and we can hear this strange noise, like distant thunder. It was Yorkey. He was hidden behind a bush, fast asleep and snoring his head off. What made the sight of him even funnier was that he'd obviously been trying to do a thigh stretch when he nodded off, because he was still in the stretch position. It took Steve ages to wake him, and he had a right go at him, but Yorkey wasn't bothered in the slightest. Halfway through his bollocking he went back to sleep!

Steve was nobody's fool, though – far from it. He was a deep thinker who knew everything about everybody – what they'd done in the last game, who needed running in training and who didn't – and the lads really took to him. I didn't have the benefit of working with him right from the start. He was appointed in the first week of February 1999, and started just two days after my hamstring had gone yet again during a 1–0 win at home to Derby. I wish I could say I was missed, but in our next match, with Jesper Blomqvist deputizing, the lads annihilated Nottingham Forest, who were bottom of the table, 8–1 at their place. Yorke and Cole got two apiece, but the highlight of the afternoon was Ole's appearance as substitute. He didn't get on until the seventy-second minute, but then scored four in the last ten minutes! Ron Atkinson, Forest's manager at the time, was never one to be lost for words, and he summed it up perfectly. 'Good job they didn't put Solskjaer on earlier,' he said after the game, 'or we'd really have been in trouble!'

I was missing again when we beat Fulham 1–0 in the fifth round of the FA Cup, but back as substitute at least when Arsenal came to Old Trafford and drew 1–1. It was a big game – winning it the previous season had enabled them to go on and win the title – but we were the better team this time, and would have won it had Yorkey not missed a penalty. Or if Tony Adams hadn't played out of his skin. He was outstanding.

I was in from the start away to Coventry, and scored the winner late on, from a Becks cross. Unbeaten in February and having scored fourteen times in the process, we went into the quarter-finals of the Champions League, against Inter Milan, in reassuring form. Inter were the team we'd wanted to avoid, but it was becoming clear that if we were going to win the European Cup, we'd have to do it the hard way. The first leg was at home. Before these big European matches, everyone plays mind games. There always seems to be one player who comes out with a wind-up, and it was Diego Simeone this time. His history with Becks meant he had to be the one. The day before the game Simeone made his play when he admitted to the press that he had deliberately play-acted to get Becks sent off when England played Argentina in the World Cup the previous year. He wasn't exactly Becks' favourite player, but ultimately I think it worked to our advantage. We won 2–0 with two headers from Yorkey, and both goals came from Beckham crosses. So Becks had the last laugh, but the result doesn't tell the whole story. Even without Ronaldo, who was injured, Inter had dangerous attackers in Zamorano, Djorkaeff and Roberto Baggio, and both Peter Schmeichel and Henning Berg, who cleared one off the line, were brilliant in denying them the away goal that would have made the return leg in the San Siro much more difficult. On a personal note, my enjoyment was marred when Javier Zanetti broke my nose with an elbow – something AC Milan also did to me in March 2005. Nice people, the Milanese. And people talk about me going to play over there!

That put me out of the FA Cup sixth-round tie against Chelsea which ended 0–0. Despite being all over them, we only drew. I was back for the replay, at Stamford Bridge. We took the lead after only four minutes, through Yorkey, then weathered the storm when they hit back, with Peter making a vital save from Zola. Around the hour mark Yorkey got his second, with a lovely chip on the run, and that was that. We were through to the semis.

We were unchanged for the trip to Newcastle, where Andy loved scoring twice against his old club to take us four points clear of Arsenal at the top of the league. Although we knew Andy enjoyed that, I don't think we heard him say so. That wasn't his way. To be honest he didn't say much at all! And some read too much into that. People who don't know him sometimes find his manner difficult, but he's a good lad. He didn't say much in his few months at United, but once you got to know him, he really opened up. The thing about him was that if he took a dislike to you, that was the end of it. He just wouldn't speak to you again, or even acknowledge you! There was no beating about the bush with him. It happened with him and Teddy. They seemed to get on all right at first, as two Londoners, but then they fell out over an incident in a game and never saw eye to eye after that. The rest of us just left them to it, safe in the knowledge that it never affected the way the two of them played together. The gaffer wouldn't have stood for that.

The Newcastle result left us unbeaten in fourteen matches as we went into the return leg against Inter, in Milan. The gaffer now says that this match was the biggest step forward the team had taken under his management. Ronaldo was fit to play this time, so we used Ronny Johnsen alongside Roy in centre midfield to deny him the space to run at us.

The French referee refused them what looked very much like a penalty when Peter threw himself in front of Zamorano. That was a real piece of luck, and we were fortunate again when Zanetti shot against a post. Peter then made a great reflex save from Ronaldo, who was otherwise very subdued, and was substituted on the hour. His replacement, Ventola, scored three minutes later, and the San Siro exploded into life as Inter went for the second goal they needed to equalize on aggregate. It was very much 'game on', and in the sort of hostile atmosphere you only get on the Continent, the tie became a real test of our discipline and composure. Ze Elias somehow missed a sitter, then the gaffer took off Ronny Johnsen and sent on Paul Scholes, which proved to be a masterstroke. With two minutes of normal time remaining, Paul scored coolly from 8 yards, and it was game, set and match. That massive stadium was half-empty before the final whistle. We were in the semi-finals of the Champions League for the second time in three years and also top of the Premiership and in the last four in the FA Cup. Suddenly people were talking about 'the treble'.

A 3–1 win at home to Everton ensured we stayed unbeaten again throughout March, and were four points clear at the top of the league with thirty matches played. We'd had six games in eighteen days, but the squad was big enough to cope with that. The players the gaffer had brought in at the start of the season were crucial, ensuring that fatigue was never a factor.

We were unbeaten in twenty matches going into the first leg of our Champions League semi-final against Juventus, which was at home. We knew it was going to be difficult, and in the end we were relieved to come out of it with a 1–1 draw. Whatever Eric might have to say about water-carriers, the reality was that in Deschamps, Zidane and Davids they had the best midfield of any club side in the world. For the first hour the three of them ran the game, keeping us well and truly on the rack. Antonio Conte gave them the lead after twenty-five minutes, from a Davids cross, and at half-time the gaffer had his work cut out to get us back into it. He singled out me and Becks, the two wide men, for particular attention. He ripped into us for getting forward too much, leaving Roy Keane and Paul Scholes outnumbered and overrun by their three in midfield. He said we hadn't done as we were told, that we hadn't been in the game and that it wasn't good enough. He was right. The two of us went out determined to make amends. In the second half Becks was to hang back more and tuck in, leaving me to push on. The pattern started to change just after the hour, when I had a decent shot saved and so did Keaney. Teddy came on to replace Dwight Yorke, who had been very quiet, and had the ball in the net with a header after eighty-six minutes, only to be flagged offside. It looked like we were going to lose, which would have left us with an impossible task in Turin, but in the ninetieth minute Teddy went up with their 'keeper and the ball fell nicely for me to smack into the roof of the net from 5 yards. It was a crucial goal – even the gaffer had to forgive me for my performance in the first half! The fans weren't happy with 1–1 at home, and it had left us with a lot to do in the second leg, but scoring a late goal meant that the psychological advantage lay with us. It was our opponents who'd had an away victory snatched from their grasp. We were confident we would score out there and go through.

Next up, four days later, was another 'easy' game: an FA Cup semi-final against our strongest rivals, Arsenal, at Villa Park. After our European exertions we wanted it settled in the ninety minutes, so of course it went to extra time and a replay. In the first match, which was goalless, Roy Keane had the ball in the net, but what we all thought was a perfectly good goal was ruled out by David Elleray because Yorkey was allegedly offside. There was a row about it at the time, and we felt robbed of a result, but in the end I suppose I should be grateful. If it hadn't been for Elleray's decision there'd have been no replay and I'd never have had the chance to score my best goal ever, and the one I'd like to be remembered by.

The gaffer left me out of the starting line-up, explaining that he wanted to 'freshen up' the team. The others 'rested' were Cole, Yorke and Denis Irwin, with Blomqvist in for me, Phil Neville for Denis and Sheringham and Solskjaer the strikers. The match was an absolute epic, unlikely to be forgotten by anyone who took part, or by those who witnessed it, either in person on on television. It had every emotion you can experience in football. We started well, and Becks put us ahead after seventeen minutes with one of his 20-yarders, from a lay-off by his cockney mate, Teddy. We should have scored more in the first half, when we were on top, but failed to take our chances, and then Arsenal started to hit back. Midway through the second half they had a lucky break when a shot from Bergkamp that was heading straight for Peter was deflected past him by Jaap Stam. They were lifted by the goal, and thought they had us when Roy Keane was sent off, four minutes later, for his second yellow card. Our luck seemed to be out when Mr Elleray awarded them a penalty in the ninetieth minute, for Phil Neville's foul on Ray Parlour. Now, Peter Schmeichel was a marvellous 'keeper – the best in the world – but he was *hopeless* at penalties. I'd never seen him save one, but what is it they say: cometh the hour, cometh the man? Peter saved brilliantly from Bergkamp, and you felt the impact of that ripple through the whole team. We were all inspired by it.

I'd come on as sub and touched the ball four or five times before that goal and given it away every time. I was thinking, 'I'm having a nightmare here, I can't pass the ball so I'll have to be more direct.' I'd got on after about an hour, in place of Jesper, so I was feeling reasonably fresh going into extra time, and that served me in good stead when I fastened on to a loose pass from Vieira, ten yards or so inside our own half. I'm told that the gaffer was on his feet, screaming for me to run at Lee Dixon, but in all the din I wasn't aware of that. It would be nice to say that I had it all in my head, what I was going to do, but it doesn't happen like that. It unfolds too quickly to think. Instead, instinct and feel take over. It seemed to pan out in slow motion. When Vieira tried to get back at me I just dipped my shoulder and went past him, then others came and went the same way until I was in the box. Dixon and Adams tried to get to me, but I got away from them, and then I'm up against David Seaman. Now I did pause for a millisecond and thought, 'Just hit it.' And I did, firing the ball up past the England goalkeeper and into the roof of the net. It was the kind of amazing finish you dream about. Who'd have believed it, the way I was playing?

It was either brilliant management or a fantastic coincidence. But I suppose we should give the gaffer the benefit of the doubt. Between the first game against Arsenal and the replay, he called me into his office to remind me that it was my pace and direct running at defenders that made me the player I was. He does it maybe once a season, just makes a point to remind me of my strengths. When I look at videos of me when I was nineteen or twenty I think I look like a headless chicken, running and running with no real purpose. Partly because of that I was trying to add more to my game, but in doing so I lost sight of my strongest assets. I went too far towards becoming a pass and move midfielder, and stopped dribbling and beating players as much as I ought to have been. In becoming too safety-first and less inclined to run directly at the opposition I was in danger of becoming an average midfielder instead of a match-winning winger. That is how the gaffer sees me, and he just wanted to make sure I knew it!

In his own autobiography, he wrote: 'The real Ryan Giggs should step forward more often.' I'm not sure what he means by that, but if he means that I should score more goals like that one, it's easier said than done! I suspect it's just that he thinks I should try not to overcomplicate my game, and that by concentrating on what I'm good at I'm a better, more instinctive player. It's not a confidence thing, though, not at all, it's got more to do with my injuries. The hamstring problems have stopped me being the player I was between seventeen and twenty, because I've been forced to play within myself. If I'm really honest with myself, I don't think I've sprinted *flat out* for ten years. In the back of my mind I'm frightened of the damage I might do to the hamstrings if I really let myself go. I was fortunate that during the FA Cup replay *nearly* flat out was good enough!

There was champagne in the dressing room after that win, but we didn't have long to savour the moment. We now faced an even bigger semi-final, away to Juventus. I say we, but I wasn't involved. I was gutted at having to miss the game with an ankle injury I'd picked up in the Arsenal replay. I travelled with the lads and watched from the directors' box at the Stadio delle Alpi, which was a strange experience. From where I was sitting it seemed that Cole and Yorke were winning every header and getting to all the flick-ons, and that we were getting into their back four so easily, but the score told a different story. It was Juventus who scored two early goals, through Filippo Inzaghi. They were 2–0 up after just eleven minutes. We were in deep trouble, but the gaffer had said all along that we'd need to score twice, so that situation hadn't changed. It may sound as if I'm talking with the benefit of hindsight, but I have to say I always thought we were going to score the goals we needed and, despite the terrible start to the game. For some reason I was never that worried.

My confidence should, perhaps, have been dented when Roy Keane was booked. It meant that he would miss the final, should we get there in similar circumstances to Paul Gascoigne's at the 1990 World Cup. Gazza had buckled and cried on the pitch, but the devastating blow had a dramatically different effect on our captain. Roy reacted as if the semi was now his final. He has never played better, he just rolled his sleeves and turned the tie around through sheer force of personality. It was an awesome display. He put us back in contention with a headed goal from a Becks corner midway through the first half, and another header, this time from Yorkey, had us level after thirty-four minutes. At 2–2 the away goals rule had us halfway to the final, and both Yorke and Irwin hit the woodwork before Andy got the winner, six minutes from the end. It was a magnificent result, and it even got to the gaffer. He said after the game that the second half was the best forty-five minutes he had seen from any United team, and that wasn't the kind of praise he'd give lightly. The downside was that Keane and Scholes had both been booked for the second time in the competition and would be ruled out of the final. And after all they'd done to get us. You wouldn't wish it on your worst enemy.

At around this time, in what was to be the most successful season any English club had ever had, it was revealed publicly that Chelsea's annual wage bill was higher than ours and that Alex Ferguson wasn't the best-paid manager in the country. I couldn't understand that, given that he was the most successful. I don't think the players were all that bothered, especially at that stage in the season. I know a lot are motivated by money, but with one or two exceptions I haven't come across many while I've been at United. *All* footballers at our level get good money anyway and we're more interested in winning trophies than whether so-and-so at another club may be earning a few grand more. We all knew we could probably get slightly better deals elsewhere, but with United we had the best of both worlds: we were well paid and more importantly we were winning things all the time. Obviously you've got to look after yourself and your family, but a few quid either way doesn't make that much difference when you're getting tens of thousands every week.

At the end of April it was Arsenal, not Chelsea, who had us worried, winning successive matches 5–1 against Wimbledon and 6–1 at Middlesbrough, with Kanu and Anelka among the goals. Going into May they were a point ahead of us, although we at least had the cushion of a game in hand. We beat Villa 2–1 at home, but then managed only a draw at Liverpool after being 2–0 up. Jamie Redknapp brought them back into it after seventy minutes with a dodgy penalty, and five minutes later Denis Irwin was sent off when he was yellow-carded for the second time, for allegedly kicking the ball away when the referee blew his whistle. Down to ten men, we thought we had held out, but then Incey, of all people, got an eighty-ninth-minute equalizer. The gaffer really loved that! He was furious with us for dropping two points, but he was incandescent with rage about the ref, David Elleray, who had never been top of his list of favourite refs. He had a point. It was a ridiculous sending-off. Referees should consider who they are dealing with. Some of our players would show dissent, try to have the last word or make their feelings obvious, but Denis wasn't one of them. He'd *never* do anything like that, he was too disciplined and too professional. He was simply passing the ball just as Elleray blew his whistle, not petulantly kicking it away. It wasn't Elleray's finest decision and was particularly frustating because it meant that Denis would be suspended and miss the FA Cup final because of it. The gaffer always had a bit of a thing about Elleray and I wasn't too keen on him either after he had a little dig at me in print. He announced that I was moody and that he could tell what I was going to be like by whether I'd had a shave or not. If I hadn't, I'd be angry and difficult to deal with, if I was clean-shaven I'd be nice and calm. What?!! It was a load of rubbish. On one occasion, as we were lining up in the tunnel to play Chelsea at Stamford Bridge he turned to me and said, 'Oh, you've had a shave today, you look a lot better like that.' I suppose he was just trying to be friendly, but it sounded patronizing. 'Mind your own business, Mr Chips,' I thought. 'You may be a school-master at Harrow, but I'm not one of your snotty kids.'

Oddly enough, though, it wasn't only Elleray who took his cue from the state of my chin. If I came in for a match clean-shaven, the gaffer would always start reading into it. 'You were out last night, weren't you?' he'd ask me. I'd deny it, but there was no putting him off his theory. 'Yes you were,' he'd carry on, like a lawyer producing a piece of evidence. 'You've had a shave, that's a giveaway. I can always tell.' Then he'd look pleased with himself! I couldn't win with him – if I was clean-shaven I'd been up to no good and if I was unshaven it would be: 'Get a shave – and get a haircut as well.' I never did, of course, but he liked to *think* he could make me!

We'd slipped three points behind Arsenal, and desperately needed to win our next game, at Middlesbrough, but it looked like being one of those days when Teddy Sheringham had a goal disallowed for offside – wrongly, as the television replays proved. But in first-half stoppage time Yorkey headed in for a vital 1–0 which put us back on top on goals scored (we were level with Arsenal on seventy-five points with an identical goal difference). The question now was: who would blink first? And it was Arsenal. They had won fifteen and drawn the other four of their last nineteen league games when they went to Leeds on 11 May and came

The Welsh managers: Bobby
Gould, Terry Yorath, Mark
Hughes and John Toshack

Playing for Wales in 1993

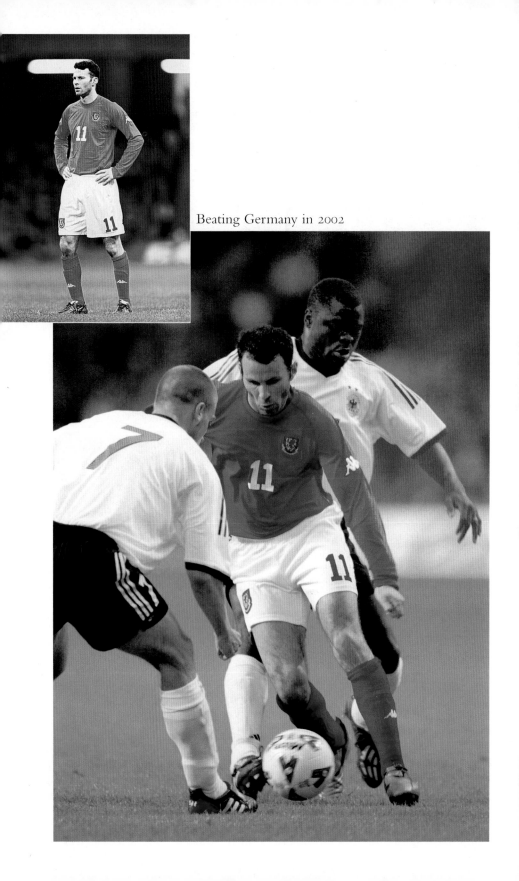

Beating Germany in 2002

Beating Italy in the Euro 2004 qualifiers

Celebrating our fourth goal against Azerbaijan in a Euro 2004 qualifier at the Millennium Stadium

A rare run-in with the ref during a tense game against the Russians in Moscow

Wales miss out again

The Russians celebrate during the return leg. My body language tells you all you need to know about how I felt

A strange feeling – playing against Nev and Becks at Old Trafford

Time off during the FIFA World Cup Championships in Rio, January 2000

25 February 2001

In action against Southampton.
We won the game and the
championship

United clinch their seventh title
in nine seasons with a win
against Coventry

Thanking the supporters with my sister Bethany, at my testimonial against Celtic in 2001

The testimonial team photo

unstuck at last, Jimmy-Floyd Hasselbaink getting the only goal in the eighty-sixth minute.

It was just the break we needed. We now had it in our power to kill off our great rivals twenty-four hours later, on a fateful night at Blackburn. They needed to beat us if they were going to stay up. Our old mate Kiddo was their manager, but he and the gaffer were no longer close. The situation made for a highly charged night. There was a lot riding on it for all concerned.

It was our sixtieth match that season, played in five different countries. Some of the lads were feeling the pace a bit, but for once the breaks I'd had with injuries counted in my favour and I still felt pretty fresh. It made no difference to us. The game was a grind. Both sides needed to win, but neither was good enough on the night, and it ended with a miserable goalless draw. They played with only one man up, which seemed a strange thing to do when they needed all three points if they were to survive.

It was a great shame that the gaffer and Kiddo had fallen out after being friends for so long. I was particularly sad to see him go. I liked Kiddo a lot and, like many of our players, I owed him a great deal for all the encouragement and support he gave me when I was starting out in the game. I don't know all the ins and outs of what went on between the two of them, but I have to say I'm surprised it became a feud. Others might tell you different, but from personal experience, I don't think the gaffer is one to hold a grudge. We've had some massive arguments, but the next day he's always been big enough to shake hands and get on with things. Rows, however heated, have been quickly forgotten.

The result at Ewood Park left us needing to win our last game, at home to Tottenham, to be sure of the title. Arsenal, still in contention, were also at home, to Villa. It all came down to the last match and the climax to the season was unbelievably tense. For the first time for years, I felt nervous before the game. I knew I wasn't the only one either. It was a match we all knew we were capable of winning, and should win, but you can't escape the feeling that anything can happen in a football match. And it did. Midway through the first half Les Ferdinand put Spurs in front. To their credit, they had come to try to win, not just defend, and there was real anxiety in the ground until just before half-time, when Becks equalized with an angled shot. Andy Cole put us 2–1 up early in the second half, but we missed a few chances to make the game safe and relieve some of the tension. That wasn't helped by the news that Arsenal were ahead against Villa. One slip, and a Spurs equalizer would cost us the championship. But it didn't happen. We managed to hold on to our lead to extend our unbeaten run to thirty-one matches. The 'Theatre of Dreams' exploded into party mode.

And so did the players. We celebrated at Henrys, a pub in Manchester, but the evening turned sour for Roy Keane. A girl came over and gave him a lot of hassle. He tried to be patient but at one stage I think she even kicked him. Anyway, it all went off, and the next thing we knew, the press and the police turned up at the same time – someone in her party had obviously called them both. Poor old Roy spent the night in the cells and the papers had a field day. For a time, there was doubt whether he would play in the Cup final, where we were up against Ruud Gullit's Newcastle.

He did in the end, but only briefly as it turned out. He was injured early on in a clash with Gary Speed and had to be substituted after only ten minutes. It wasn't one of the better finals. Teddy Sheringham, on for Roy, scored in the eleventh minute, and after that it was pretty much routine. Teddy made the second goal for Scholesy, early in the second half, and Newcastle just weren't good enough to threaten the second leg of our treble. Something none of us had dared believe could happen was now very much on.

The celebrations that night were low-key. The Big One, the European Cup final, was only four days away. From Wembley we moved to Bisham Abbey to start intensive preparations for the final, which included watching a condensed, forty-minute video of our two previous Champions League games against our opponents in the final, Bayern Munich. This was analysed and picked apart. Patterns of play and strengths and weaknesses were identified and tactics developed to cope. On the Monday we flew to the venue, Barcelona, on Concorde. I don't like flying at all, but this was different. It was incredible once we were in the air. I usually hate take-offs, and Concorde took off faster than normal planes. We seemed to get into the air really quickly and then almost stop. There was a sudden change of engine noise, as if they'd shut the jets down, and I thought we were going to fall out of the sky! Once I got over that panic, I started to relax and get into it. I couldn't take my eyes off the speedo in front of my seat, which said we were doing twice the speed of sound, an awesome thought. Even Dennis Bergkamp might have enjoyed it!

Our base in Spain was outside Barcelona, at a lovely hotel in Sitges. The players got twenty-four tickets each, which sounds like a lot, but only just covered all the people I was trying to cater for.

The gaffer had some difficult decisions to make. We were without Keane and Scholes, both suspended, so what was he to do in midfield? He thought of moving me into the centre with Nicky Butt, but opted to use Becks there, with me in his normal role, on the right, and Blomqvist in my usual position, on the left. The thinking was that we needed someone to control the game from the middle, and not allow Effenberg to do it for them. That would have been Roy's job, and without him the gaffer thought Becks was best suited to it. Despite raised eyebrows from some commentators, I was comfortable on the right. I'd played there quite often before, so that wasn't a problem for me.

It was a nice, romantic coincidence that the match was played on what would have been Sir Matt Busby's ninetieth birthday. An omen perhaps, but not one which helped settle us down. We were all a bit edgy – even for players who had won so much, the European Cup final was something new, and the biggest night we'd known. That was the reason, I think, that we never approached the quality of performance we'd produced in getting there. We were too inhibited. I hate to say it, but the occasion got to us a bit. And it all became even more fraught when Mario Basler gave them the lead with a free-kick after only six minutes. After that, the game settled into a fairly predictable pattern – we did most of the attacking and they were content to defend their lead in numbers and attack only on the break. Their defenders did a good job on Yorke and Cole, who were shut out. The pattern of the game needed to be broken, and midway through the second half the gaffer sent on Teddy Sheringham, in place of Blomqvist. Ted's cleverness caused them new problems, and we began to make headway, but still couldn't make a breakthrough. And worse, the Germans were still creating chances of their own. Scholl hit a post and Jancker rattled the crossbar, before the fourth official displayed a board indicating that there would be three minutes of stoppage time. With the score still 1–0 to them the outcome seemed settled. We'd lost it. Even the gaffer admitted he was rehearsing his loser's speech. I know I thought we were done for.

What happened next was bewildering, even to those taking part. Going into added time, we had a corner, and Peter Schmeichel, intent on some last-gasp heroics in his last game for us, charged forward. There was no longer anything to lose. The big Dane's presence in the penalty area undoubtedly distracted the Bayern defenders when the corner from Becks arced over into the box. The ball deflected out to me, on the edge of the area. I swung at it with my right foot, only to watch a horrible miscue head wide before Teddy stuck out a boot and diverted it into the net from 6 yards out.

The unbelievable relief was exhilarating. The thought of extra time was just beginning to sink in when Ole Gunnar Solskjaer's selfless running won us another corner. Again Becks took it. This time he picked the near post, where he found Teddy waiting. Teddy headed it on for Ole to nudge in. It was jaw-dropping. We'd been dead and buried. Seconds later the final whistle brought pandemonium. I've never known anything like the emotion that spilled out in that moment, and I never will again. All around us distraught Germans wondered how it had all gone up in smoke. For once everyone, including the gaffer, wanted to do interviews. Usually they were a chore, but not this time. We all wanted to talk about what had happened – the magnitude of what we'd achieved. We'd made history, and it was time to get something on record for posterity.

After that night's eventful celebrations, we finally got back to Manchester and did the open-top bus parade from the airport to Old Trafford. I'll never forget turning down Deansgate and finding it blocked with fans. All the streets were packed. We've had one or two celebrations like that, but this time the atmosphere was really special. There was an intensity about the whole thing, only heightened perhaps, by the last-gasp manner of the victory.

People have asked me if that was the monkey off our back, if we felt we were finally free of all the comparisons with the Best, Law, Charlton team, but I didn't think of it like that. For me, the big feeling of relief came when we won the league for the first time, and I'm sure comparisons with 1968 meant more to the gaffer than they did to the players. I know he was very keen to emulate Sir Matt by winning the European Cup, that was his greatest challenge.

If you want to analyse what the different teams did, I suppose you'd have to say our class of '99 surpassed that of '68 by doing the treble. It wasn't only me who thought so, the Queen agreed. The gaffer was knighted in her birthday honours!

The only people who seemed to have their doubts were the PFA (the Professional Football Association) and the football writers, both of whom made David Ginola the Footballer of the Year. I can only think that there were so many United players in the running that the split vote let Ginola in. To be fair, I would have found it impossible to single out any one of our players. It could have been Peter Schmeichel or Roy Keane just as easily as anyone else. But Ginola? I don't think so.

Finally, we have to come to my mate Tony Camilleri, and his is a sorry story. He took his wife to the game and she hated it, and spent the second half nagging him to leave early. Eventually, sick of the earache, he gave in and they left ten minutes before the end. Tony has never forgiven her – still hammers her about it today. He's never lived it down!

'Easy, Easy'

Having won the lot, how do you improve on it? The gaffer was determined to try, and there were four new faces in the squad for the millennium season. Peter Schmeichel had gone, to Sporting Lisbon, and we had two new 'keepers: Mark Bosnich from Aston Villa and Massimo Taibi from Venezia. The other newcomers were Mikael Silvestre, who chose to join us ahead of Liverpool from Inter Milan, and Quinton Fortune from Atletico Madrid.

There was controversy before the next season started when we were told we wouldn't be competing in the FA Cup. United were criticized for not taking part but it wasn't up to us. It was explained that the FA wanted us to go to Brazil in January for the Club World Championship because they felt it would help England's bid to stage the 2006 World Cup, which of course went to Germany in the end. The players weren't happy about the decision – we all wanted to play in the FA Cup. We couldn't understand why the club couldn't do what they'd started doing in the League Cup, and field the reserves in the third round. After all, that was all we would miss by taking part in the Rio tournament.

After all the pre-season debate about the rights and wrongs of the decision, it was good to get back to the football. After a 1–1 draw at Everton on the opening day, we seemed to carry on where we'd left off the previous season, with Cole and Yorke again prolific in a run of six straight wins in the league. We beat Sheffield Wednesday 4–0 and Newcastle 5–1, with Andy getting four of them against his old club. The best results, though, were away wins at Arsenal and Liverpool, which showed we were very much on the right track. Roy Keane scored twice at Highbury, where Arsenal's 2–1 defeat was their first at home in the league for nearly two years. Very satisfying.

Bozzy started the season in goal, but was injured in the third game and replaced by Raimond Van der Gouw. The Dutchman played in the next three in the Premiership and the September Champions League ties that marked the beginning of our defence of the European Cup. A disappointing 0–0 draw at home to Zagreb, who were managed by Ossie Ardiles, wasn't the best way to begin, but things picked up nicely, with a 3–0 victory in Graz and the 2–1 defeat of Marseille at home.

With Bosnich injured, our other keeper, Massimo Taibi, received a knock to his confidence in his debut in a 3–2 win at Anfield. He let in another three when we drew 3–3 at home to Southampton, and in that game there was no doubt that two of the goals were directly down to his mistakes. The gaffer stood by him, but when he let in five at Chelsea at the beginning of October the writing was on the wall. Sadly, everybody could see he was struggling, and he never seemed to recover from that poor start. That was the last we saw of Massimo in the first team. Losing 5–0 at Stamford Bridge was a real shaker. It was a disaster from the start, with Gus Poyet scoring in the first minute before Nicky Butt got red-carded midway through the first half. I wasn't playing in that one, but I was back for the Champions League tie away to Marseille in mid-October. We lost that, then four days later we were beaten again, 3–1 at Tottenham, which put us down to fourth in the table. It was early days, but it didn't feel good enough. Bozzy was fit and back in goal now and doing OK. He was an athletic guy and a good shot-stopper, but his kicking was a major weakness. I don't think he ever had the faintest idea where the ball was going when he booted it. And if he didn't, what chance did his teammates have? Our goalkeeping coach, Tony Coton, tried to remedy the problem, but Bozzy was pretty stubborn. A typical Aussie with attitude in spades, I'm not sure that he listened to anyone.

We managed to see off Zagreb and Sturm Graz to win our Champions League group, but the second stage got off to a terrible start, when we lost 2–0 away to Fiorentina. That was before the Italian club's financial troubles, and they had a good side then. Batistuta, who was at his peak, and Balbo scored the goals, and Rui Costa gave us problems in midfield too.

We all cared passionately about the Champions League and bad results hurt. The same wasn't really true of the upcoming Club Championship in Brazil or the FIFA world championship in November. Despite that, we won in Tokyo, beating Palmeiras of Brazil, to become the first British club to be FIFA Transcontinental champions. Roy Keane scored the goal and I won a car from the sponsors as man of the match. At the presentation they asked me if I wanted the car, a Toyota Celica, or the money equivalent. It was easy. I quickly said I'd have the money, but the looks I got from every direction told me that was the wrong answer, so I quickly changed my mind, deciding that I really wanted a Toyota Celica after all. It cost me a small fortune to transport the car home. Then I had to pay duty on it. I didn't even need it – I had a car – so I gave it to my brother Rhodri. It's the most expensive award I've ever won!

By Christmas we were well set. Top of the table after a burst of six successive wins, and going strong in the Champions League after beating Valencia. But it wasn't results that were making headlines at the end of the year, it was nationality, when Chelsea made history by starting their league game against Southampton without a single British player in their team. I wouldn't say I was surprised, it wasn't something that suddenly happened overnight, Chelsea had been heading in that direction for some time under Vialli, but it's not something I could ever see happening at United. Our crowd like to identify with the local lads in the team, and the club takes great pride in bringing through players like me, the Neville brothers, Nicky Butt and Paul Scholes. The gaffer's also brought the best young English talent into the side in players like Rio Ferdinand and Wayne Rooney.

At the beginning of January we had to fly out to Rio for the World Club Championship. We'd been warned about it, but the heat still took us by surprise, it was unbearable. To try and avoid it we were getting up at seven in the morning to train at eight, before the sun was at its strongest. It hardly helped. The temperature is shown on the lampposts out there, and even when we were setting out it was already 35 degrees C. On the way back from training it was pushing past 40. We had to finish by ten, it was just too hot. There was still lots to enjoy about the trip. It was good to see Rio and to play in the famous Maracanã Stadium, and our hotel, on Ipanema Beach, was lovely, but the weather was no good for football – not for us, at least. The other teams, from Mexico, Brazil and Australia, were used to it, so we were at a definite disadvantage. Our first game, against Necaxa, of Mexico, became overheated in more ways than one when Keaney was red-carded and the gaffer was sent from the bench for protesting too loudly. For what it was worth, which in our eyes wasn't a lot, we drew 1–1. Our second game just two days later was against the local team, Vasco da Gama. They were a good side and took it very seriously. We, by contrast, were pretty knackered and didn't. It showed in the scoreline. We lost 3–1. For our last match, against South Melbourne, the gaffer only played the reserves. They won 2–0, but the football didn't amount to much, and for a couple of our games there was hardly anyone there. The organization was a shambles, they played matches one after the other, and half-way through our game the crowd for the next one would start turning up. But while the whole exercise was a waste of time, it's hard to complain too much. We had a brilliant opportunity to relax in the sun, which all of us enjoyed.

Somebody even arranged a hang-gliding trip, which definitely wouldn't have been allowed if the gaffer had found out about it. If anybody had picked up a serious injury that way, our insurance wouldn't have covered it. I was up for it along with Keaney, Butty and Coley. Keaney and Butty went on ahead. I looked at Coley. 'Right, are we going then?' I asked. He just shook his head. 'I'm not going, man.' 'Why not?' I asked. He'd seemed so keen on the idea. He shook his head again. 'Giggsy, look at the date – it's Friday the 13th, man. I'm not going.'

It put the wind up me, so I didn't go either! By this stage, though, it was too late to stop Keaney and Butty. They were on their way. Coley and I went out by the pool instead. We were lying there with the other players and the coaching staff when there was all this shouting from up in the sky, and a couple of hang-gliders went over. It was them. The gaffer was out there, on a sunlounger. 'Gaffer, they're our lads,' somebody told him, looking for a reaction. He thought it was a wind-up. 'That's none of my players,' he said. 'They know better than that. They wouldn't dare.' Meanwhile, the two hang-gliders were circling, but so high that nobody could see who it was. I'm sure the gaffer discovered the truth afterwards, but at the time he wouldn't admit that his players would do such a thing. And Keaney and Butty definitely weren't going to confess.

We were out of the country for less than a fortnight, but the trip meant we hadn't played a league match for a month. We were fortunate that none of our rivals was able to take advantage, and we went to the top of the league again as soon as we came back. Then, though, there was an incident at the end of January that attracted a load of bad publicity and did the club no favours at all.

We were playing Middlesbrough at home. It was an explosive game throughout. Incey was back at our place for the first time as a Middlesbrough player, and the crowd booed him every time he touched the ball, which was a shame. I couldn't help but get wound up by that. The treatment two other old boys got was completely the opposite. Bryan Robson and Gary Pallister were cheered like returning heroes, which of course they were. The penalty that caused the trouble came about twenty minutes from the end – not long after Christian Ziege had been sent off for a foul on Becks. Juninho fell under a challenge from Jaap and Andy D'Urso pointed to the spot, for the first penalty any visiting team had been given at Old Trafford in more than six years. The lads went mad, and half a dozen of us chased him to the touchline. The game was held up while he tried to restore order, booking Roy Keane for dissent. When Juninho finally took the penalty, Bozzy saved it, and we went on to win 1–0 when Mark Schwarzer, his Australian rival, fumbled a shot from Becks over his own line. The papers said we acted like a pack of wolves, and the pictures they showed on television were really embarrassing. Roy Keane and Jaap Stam were screaming in D'Urso's face and it looked awful. I have to admit I was in there somewhere as well. There was me, Keane, Butt, Stam and a couple more.

The gaffer read us the riot act over our behaviour. He understood our frustration, but he knew that sort of reaction could only harm us long term. 'You've all got to calm down,' he said. 'I don't want to see anything like that ever again. It's wrong, and it will only turn all the referees against you.'

The result did us no harm at all, of course, taking us back to the top of the table, ahead of Leeds, and six points clear in early February. It was at this time that the first cracks in the relationship between the gaffer and Becks started to show. Towards the end of February we had a top-of-the-table clash with Leeds at Elland Road, and there was a big row between the two of them at the training ground. Becks' celebrity status was growing all the time, and it was clear that it was starting to get up the gaffer's nose. The newspapers seemed to be becoming obsessed with the real and perceived differences between them. So when Becks was left out of the team at Leeds, the headline-writers went to town. The result hardly got noticed in the fevered debate over his absence, but we won the game 1–0, with Andy Cole's 100th goal for the club.

I liked Andy as a player. He had his critics, but he was a goalscorer, pure and simple. He wasn't versatile in any way, you couldn't play him on the right wing or wide on the left, or in midfield, but what he was good at was running in behind defenders and stretching the opposition, which gave me room. I think he was a victim of his own success in getting into great positions all the time. His instincts brought him so many chances that he was always going to miss a few, but his record for us was excellent, and all the lads really rated him. He didn't only do it for us either, his goals-per-game ratio with Newcastle was phenomenal, and he hasn't done badly at Fulham either. But all the talk after the Leeds game was not of Coley but of the big row and whether Becks would be fined. We didn't know it at the time, but the falling-out was going to become permanent.

Becks was back in the side when we resumed the Champions League campaign at home to Bordeaux in March. I scored just before half-time and Teddy Sheringham got our second late on for a comfortable 2–0 win. A week later we beat them 2–1 in France, with a late winner from Ole Gunnar, and we went on to win the group. That meant we avoided Barcelona and Bayern Munich at the knockout stage. The downside was that we got Real Madrid.

Near the end of March we went seven points clear at the top of the Premiership with a 4–0 win at Bradford, and when second-placed Leeds lost 2–1 at Leicester the following day their manager, David O'Leary, conceded that the title was ours. His own team promptly took their lead from his defeatist attitude and lost their next three without scoring a goal. Belief is infectious, and so is its absence.

At the beginning of April, we all thought we came away with a decent result at the Bernabéu, when Bozzy's man-of-the-match performance brought us a goalless draw in our first leg against Real. Despite that dodgy kicking, you had to admit that Bozzy would get to shots you thought he couldn't possibly reach. He was our star man on a few occasions that season.

While the lads had been pretty happy, the gaffer was anything but. He said 0–0 was no kind of result, we needed to score, and he was absolutely right, of course. Their players weren't the sort to come to Old Trafford and be intimidated. And when we faced them for the return leg Real went 3–0 up, with an own-goal from Roy Keane and two in two minutes from Raúl, before Becks pulled one back well into the second half. It was too late by then, and a penalty from Paul Scholes after eighty-eight minutes meant nothing really.

Steve McManaman played for them, and Geremi and Anelka got on as substitutes, but the players who impressed me most were Redondo, who was superb in central midfield, and Casillas, then just eighteen, who had a tremendous game in goal.

We were out of the Champions League, but running away with the Premiership. Just three days after the defeat by Real we won the title for the sixth time in eight seasons, with four games to spare. We won each of our last eleven matches, and in the end we were champions by eighteen points, from Arsenal, which was a staggering margin. It all seemed easier than ever. We'd done the treble the previous year, so our confidence was sky-high. The gaffer had brought in players who had made the squad even stronger, and there was nobody to touch us. It probably helped us in the championship that we hadn't entered the FA Cup and that the reserves had gone out of the League Cup at the first stage. Also, our break in the sun in Brazil meant we were fresher than the rest when it mattered.

Typical of our strength in depth was our four top strikers, any one of whom would have walked into any other team in the league. So I couldn't see how we needed another one, but it was now that the gaffer agreed a British record fee of £18.5m with PSV Eindhoven for Ruud Van Nistelrooy. We all thought, 'What do we need him for?' but then we asked Jaap, who was pretty clear about it. He was the new Van Basten, he said. The move didn't come off then because he ruptured his cruciate ligaments during a fitness test, but going for Ruud showed once again that the gaffer was never happy to let things stand still. He was always looking for ways to improve what was already the best team in the country.

We received the Premiership trophy on 6 May, after

beating Spurs 3–1, but we were upstaged by Monsieur Cantona. Eric turned up to see us and was given a prolonged standing ovation by his old fan club. Before the game he came into the dressing room to see his old teammates, and to introduce himself to the players who had joined since he left. It was always good to see him. He'd been to a few of our Champions League games, but apart from that he never kept in touch with anybody. He'd just turn up out of the blue, that was Eric's way.

Keaney was voted Footballer of the Year by the players and the press. I wouldn't necessarily say that was his best season, because he was brilliant in the treble year, but at around that time he was definitely at his peak and full of confidence. He was fantastic that season.

Manchester United were honoured collectively, when we were named World Team of the Year, ahead of the Australian winners of the Rugby World Cup. The presentation was made in Monaco, and I went to the ceremony with my girlfriend, Emma Gardner, who was my best mate's sister. We went with Ronny Johnsen and his wife and the gaffer and Mrs, now Lady, Ferguson. I didn't really want to go, but there were internationals being played at the time, others couldn't make it and I drew the short straw, or so I thought. As it turned out, I loved every minute. We flew out by private jet, went to the presentation in the afternoon, and then on to a glittering 'do' they had in the evening. It was like the Oscars for sports people. All my heroes were there in one place. I was sat next to ex-Miami Dolphins quarter-back Dan Marino.

Me and Emma were on the front row with Sylvester Stallone, Nelson Mandela and Naomi Campbell. Apart from them, nearly all my sporting heroes were there: Viv Richards, Daley Thompson, Ed Moses, Ian Botham, Seb Coe – every sporting legend you could think of. The only one who disappointed me was Coe. When I walked past he made some smart-ass comment about footballers. I can't remember exactly what he said, but it was something about the way I was dressed. It was such a shame, as from when I was a boy I vividly remember the excitement that surrounded his duels with Steve Ovett. I felt very let down.

Fergie's Finest?

During the summer of 2000, the gaffer had another go at replacing Peter Schmeichel. The previous season Mark Bosnich, Raimond Van der Gouw and Massimo Taibi had all been used without really making the 'keeper's spot their own, and now he brought in Fabien Barthez from Monaco. Taibi had been written off after just four games in the Premier League, and was sold back to Italy, to Reggina, for £2.5m in July. With Bozzy, the problem wasn't his ability so much as his determination to do things his way. He had his own programme that he followed in the gym and his own pre-match warm-up. He wouldn't change either of them for anyone and that definitely rubbed people up the wrong way. Peter Schmeichel was a hard act to follow. You need stability in goal, and we've really missed that. The teams that have been really successful – us with Peter, Arsenal with Seaman and Liverpool with Grobbelaar – have all had it, and we needed to find it again. We all hoped that Barthez would be the answer.

There were also significant changes at Arsenal that summer, with Petit and Overmars both going to Barcelona and Pires joining from Marseille. For a winger, Pires has turned out to be some goalscorer, but it took him a little while to get used to the tempo of English football. We were all a bit surprised that Arsenal let Petit and Overmars go. Both had been such big players for them – in '98 they were brilliant – and at United we all thought the team would be weaker without them. We lost the Charity Shield to Chelsea, then somebody made the mistake of having us play Man City in Denis Irwin's testimonial match. When these two teams meet it is never charitable or friendly, and this was no exception. George Weah got stuck into Denis after about two minutes, and injured him quite badly, and after that it all kicked off. Put it this way, I don't think the two clubs would consider meeting in a testimonial again.

The league got off to a sluggish start too, when we drew two of our first three games, but then we hit form in style by thrashing Bradford 6–0. It was at this point that Henning Berg left us after three years, going back to Blackburn. Henning was underestimated; he was a difficult defender to play against. He didn't make many mistakes, but unfortunately those he did make tended to be in big games, and got a lot of publicity. In reality he was a good, consistent defender. By sod's law Jaap Stam picked up an Achilles injury less than two weeks after Henning left, but Wes Brown came in and impressed in the four months Jaap was sidelined.

In the Champions League we started impressively, beating Anderlecht 5–1 at home, with Andy Cole getting a hat-trick and equalling Denis Law's club record of seventeen European goals. A week later we drew 0–0 away to Dinamo Kiev in an unremarkable match.

Towards the end of September we dropped two points at home in a 3–3 draw with Chelsea, but not for the first time the headlines were made by events off the pitch when Dwight Yorke reacted to being left out of the team by storming out of Old Trafford. The truth was that Yorkey had been gradually falling out of favour. I think this was about the time when he started seeing Jordan, and that sort of high-profile relationship attracted the sort of publicity he could have done without. He was on a slippery slope and it didn't help him that Teddy was having a great season. By November he had thirteen goals already, which was some going for him. It couldn't have happened at a worse time for Yorkey.

With a difficult away match at Arsenal the following weekend, a number of the senior players were rested for the Champions League tie against PSV in Eindhoven. But they were strong that night, and we came away with a 3–1 defeat. Ironically, it didn't even help us at Highbury, where we lost 1–0, for our first league defeat in eight months. It was no consolation whatsoever that the winner, by Thierry Henry, was one of the goals of the season, a spectacular volley. On top of Premiership and Champions League duties, there were also competitive games for Wales to consider. In the middle of October 2000 I joined up with the Welsh team for a World Cup qualifier against Poland in Warsaw. The match was hardly memorable, we drew 0–0, but while I was away the police were called because of an incident that happened at my new home, in a place called Blackrod, near Chorley in Lancashire. My girlfriend, Emma, was at home when she thought she heard someone on the roof and dialled 999. She was particularly spooked because of the remoteness of the house. It was ironic, really, as I'd moved there because of that, in order to try to get some privacy. The small estate I'd been living on in Worsley, much as I enjoyed it there, was a bit of a goldfish bowl. A small minority of fans followed me everywhere, and the house in Worsley just offered no escape: it was too easy to find.

The place at Blackrod, which was two miles from Bolton's Reebok Stadium, went from one extreme to the other. It was an old place right out in the sticks, with no neighbours. I didn't find it myself, but phoned five or six estate agents, told them what I was looking for and my price range, which was about £750,000, and they did the rest. I was lucky, they found me a great spot, and I loved it. Nobody was caught that night when I was in Warsaw, but some strange things happened around that time. A man calling himself Mr Williams rang BT saying he had bought the house from me and wanted a new phone number. At the time, it was quite easy, all you had to do was to give them your name, address and phone number and you could change the billing. It puzzled me when I got a couple of bills in this 'Mr Williams" name, but the police told me it was quite a common trick. I didn't dwell on it too much, but Emma was quite worried and distressed about it, especially as with me playing games around the country and abroad, she was quite often by herself.

I'd known Emma for years before she moved in – she was the sister of one of my best mates, David – and we were good friends long before we got together. At the time I had two Boxer dogs, and it was because of them, really, that our relationship began. Emma was doing a degree specializing in animal behaviour, and so whenever I was away she would stay at my house and look after the dogs. I think she loved them as much as I did! Over a period we became closer and closer, and then we started going out. She moved in and did a great job of decorating Blackrod in her own style. It really felt like home and we enjoyed our time there.

Back in the Champions League, we made amends for the Eindhoven result by beating PSV 3–1 at home but lost at Anderlecht 2–1. At this stage we were neck and neck with Arsenal in the league, on twenty-one points, and when we battered Southampton 5–0 at the end of October, they went and did the same to Manchester City. It didn't look as if we were going to run away with the title this time. Arsenal were in good nick and were determined not to let us have it so easy again.

In Europe we struggled to beat Kiev 1–0 at home, and they missed what should have been a tap-in late on, which would have put us out. This was the game when Keaney sounded off about the 'prawn sandwich brigade', who, he said, were ruining the atmosphere at Old Trafford. I knew exactly what he meant. After the club built the new North Stand, the old volume just wasn't there any more. When the fans expected us to steamroller the opposition and we didn't, the crowd just went dead. Maybe they expect it from us now, and don't feel the same responsibility to lift us with their noise. So Keaney, typically, had his say. Of course, it was a gift for the other lads, and he got a lot of stick over it. He must have got sick of hearing that he was just a prawn in the game!

Deep down though, we all knew it just showed how much he cared. His performances on the pitch reflected it too, and in mid-November that was recognized when he was nominated for European Footballer of the Year. But it wasn't just Roy. Our success the previous season was acknowledged by the fact that me, Jaap Stam, Paul Scholes and David Beckham were all nominated too. It was a great boost going into the second stage of the Champions League, where we were grouped with Sturm Graz, Valencia and Panathinaikos. We got off to a flying start, beating the Greeks 3–1 at home, with Paul Scholes getting a couple, and won 2–0 in Graz, where I got the second.

It wasn't all plain sailing, though. In the league we could only draw 3–3 with Charlton, when I hit the crossbar from the half-way line. I was gutted when that didn't go in! At least Ole knocked in the rebound. We always seem to have good games at Charlton. They're not ultra-defensive against us, they like to play football and it's always pretty open. It's a place I like to play. Alan Curbishley is a good manager as his record at Charlton makes clear. After that 3–3 we lost 1–0 at home to Liverpool, to a Danny Murphy free-kick. That was an especially galling result as it was our first defeat at Old Trafford for two years.

Despite all our nominations, it was Luis Figo who was chosen European Footballer of the Year. Personally, I thought he should have won it the year before, when it went to Rivaldo. We played against Figo and Barcelona in our treble season, when I didn't know much about him, but I can recall looking at him and thinking, 'You're some player.' After that I always followed his progress, and for the next couple of years I thought he was the best player in the world, so there was no real gripe with him scooping the prize. He'd earned it.

Just before Christmas, when we beat Ipswich to go eight points clear in the league, the gaffer came out and said this was the best team he'd ever had. It was quite a statement, coming just two years after our historic treble, but it was nothing compared to what followed it: he announced that he was going to retire in eighteen months' time. Nobody believed him, of course. The lads who had been with him at the club for any length of time couldn't imagine the training ground without him there, day in, day out. He was still first in every morning and last out every night. There was no way he could live without it.

In January Bozzy left for Chelsea, and it was hardly a surprise to see him go. He'd been out of the picture all season, training with the reserves. I'd known him on and off since I was seventeen, and he'd always been strange, always a bit different. It was typically daft when he gave that Nazi salute at Tottenham. He never changed at all in that respect. It wasn't a case of him becoming Billy Big-Time – he was always very loud and very opinionated, and very stubborn. It was a combination that was sure to set the gaffer's teeth on edge.

After missing the FA Cup the previous season, we didn't linger long this time, West Ham put us out in the fourth round with a goal from Paolo Di Canio. A lot of people loved that, taking great pleasure in saying we got what we deserved because we'd devalued the tournament when we chose not to take part in it. As if we'd had any choice!

At the beginning of February we beat Everton 1–0 to move fifteen points clear of Arsenal, and the championship looked to have turned into a one-horse race again. As if to rub it in, we battered them 6–1 at home, with Yorkey, who was temporarily back in favour, getting a hat-trick. I was annoyed to be in bed with the flu for that one. In the Champions League things weren't so easy, and we were held to three successive draws, at home and away by Valencia and by Panathinaikos in Athens, before booking our place in the quarter-finals with a 3–0 win at home to Sturm Graz.

Around now the official club magazine surveyed the fans to pick their 'Greatest United Player Of all Time'. In order, the top four were Eric Cantona, George Best, Ryan Giggs and Bobby Charlton. No complaints at all, it was a fantastic compliment and an honour to be in that company, but I didn't take much notice. I saw something similar about the great comedians the other day, and Tommy Cooper didn't get a look-in, which only goes to show how little store you can set by them! It's all about eras, isn't it? I'm not sure who votes in magazine surveys, but I suspect it's mostly young people, who won't have seen Best or Charlton play. They vote according to the evidence of their own eyes, and the best, most charismatic player in their time was Eric.

The following week our goalkeeping problem surfaced again and we 'hired' Andy Goram, from Motherwell, for three months for a fee of £100,000. He was a real character, what you might call a social animal. He played just the two games towards the end of that season but he still made an impression on everyone. We provided the opposition in a testimonial for Tommy Boyd, the Celtic defender, and that gave us an excuse for a good night out with Andy afterwards. He was a funny lad, great company.

At the end of March Liverpool beat us 2–0 at Anfield, to complete the home and away double over United for the first time in twenty-two years, Gerrard and Fowler scoring. Liverpool had a good record against us, but it was still a bit of a shaker, as they were going through a bad spell at the time, and had won only one of their previous six league games. We had an even bigger shock a few days later when Bayern Munich came to Old Trafford for the first leg of our Champions League quarter-final and won 1–0, with a late goal by Sergio. An away goal down, we knew we faced a hell of a task in the return.

Obviously that was a big disappointment, but we weren't down for long as eleven days later, on 14 April, we clinched our seventh title in nine seasons with a 4–2 win at home to Coventry. Yorkey got the first two goals and I weighed in with the third as we won the league with five games to spare. We were out on our own, in more ways than one. There seemed to be some substance to the gaffer's claim that it was the best team he'd ever had.

And yet that didn't stop us going out of Europe. The defeat at home had left us with too much to do in Munich, and losing again, this time 2–1, put us out 3–1 on aggregate. I got our goal over there, but it came too late to affect the outcome. The thing most people remember about that game is the hoaxer who got on our pre-match team photo, standing next to Andy Cole. I saw him, but didn't give it much thought, as I assumed it had to be a charity thing. He came from north Manchester and some of the lads knew him. It wasn't just us, he's pulled that sort of stunt quite a few times, masquerading as a member of the England cricket team, coming on to the court at Wimbledon. He's well known for it now. Perhaps he should try boxing next!

The title was already won when Keaney was sent off for that notorious, over-the-top challenge on Haaland in the Manchester derby at Old Trafford. It *was* a terrible tackle, all the more so because we'd won the league and there was nothing at stake. There was no love lost between the two of them. Roy was to pay for that tackle many times over. Teddy Sheringham was a double Footballer of the Year winner that season. Both the players and the football writers gave him the nod, and deservedly so. He'd had a difficult start with us, trying to fill Eric's boots, but now, at thirty-five, he'd really come into his own. I loved playing with him and he was great for our defenders. They could clear the ball up to him from anywhere and know it would stick. He'd win most of his headers, or could bring it down on his chest as well as being better than anyone else at bringing others into the play. He did a great job for England too, and I think they probably left him out too early.

With Teddy doing so well for us, it was a bit of a surprise when the gaffer went ahead and signed Ruud Van Nistelrooy, now fit again, for £19m. I was certainly puzzled by the fact that our best player that season was being replaced. No doubt Teddy's age was the reason, but I don't think that it mattered as much for him as it might have done with certain other players. Teddy hadn't lost his pace – he was never quick, that wasn't what his game was all about. As he'd shown that season, the better the players he had around him, the better he became. I was going to miss him because I'd always enjoyed it when we played together.

The problem was that Teddy had been offered a deal to rejoin Tottenham that he couldn't refuse. If we'd even been able to give him a new two-year contract I'm sure he would have stayed, but the club would only commit to another twelve months. Unsurprisingly, he took the three years on offer at Spurs. As things turned out, the gaffer's faith in Ruud was repaid in full. Sir Alex had decided to change the way we played in Europe; he felt we'd become too predictable, and Ruud was brought in with that in mind.

We'd won the league by ten points, from Arsenal. And yet at the end of another great season there were serious concerns about the future of the management. The gaffer was in dispute with the club over pay, and announced that he would 'sever links' in twelve months' time. With Sir Alex announcing his intention to leave, Steve McLaren wasn't sure about his own prospects either. Then, in June, Steve McClaren left to replace Bryan Robson as manager at Middlesbrough. We heard he'd been told he wasn't going to get the number one job, so Middlesbrough was obviously a good chance for him. It was a big blow for us, though. Steve was undoubtedly one of the reasons we'd been so successful. He was a modernizer, very up to date with the latest ideas and methods. I really enjoyed his training, which was always innovative, and he brought in a sports psychologist, Bill Beswick, who I liked a lot. I never went to see him on a one-to-one basis, but I thought his ideas were good, and a few of the lads felt they benefited from individual sessions with him. Steve McLaren, the man who hired him, would be missed.

Arsenal at the Double

In April 2001 I had signed a new five-year contract, and confidently expected United to continue to be the dominant force in English football throughout the entire length of it. Unfortunately I was wrong, and the 2001–2 season marked the beginning of a worrying decline. It was made even more baffling when you considered the quality of the players brought in.

Freedom of contract and Bosman deals were worrying all the big clubs, and United were keen to get us all committed long term. So just after I did, Paul Scholes signed for six years, Nicky Butt for five and Wes Brown for four. Then even the gaffer, who had talked a lot about leaving, reversed his public decision to hang up his tracksuit and signed on for another five years. The fans, as ever, were far more interested in exciting new faces. Two new signings in particular fired everyone's imagination. Ruud Van Nistelrooy, who we had tried to sign a year earlier, was on his way to Old Trafford at last, and Juan Sebastian Verón, the Argentinian playmaker, joined from Lazio for £28m. It sent out a strong message of intent to our rivals, and yet they were pushing the boat out, too. Arsenal paid £25m in total for Richard Wright, Giovanni Van Bronckhorst and Francis Jeffers, as well as picking up Sol Campbell from Spurs on what was probably the most expensive 'free' transfer of all time! Meanwhile Chelsea forked out big money for Frank Lampard, Emmanuel Petit and Bolo Zenden. But with Ruud and

'Seba' strengthening an already championship-winning team, we thought we'd take some stopping.

Of all the signings that were made by others that summer, I have to say Lampard is the one who has surprised me most. I had always regarded him as a good, energetic midfielder, but the way he has come on since then has been hugely impressive. It helps, of course, being among better players, but Frank has got bigger, stronger and more confident. He's become a top central midfielder now and deserves great credit for the transformation. I used to think he needed a holding midfielder, like Claude Makelele, to play with him, but he has proved beyond a doubt that he can also operate with another goalscorer alongside him.

Back in the summer of 2001, though, I thought Jeffers, who went to Arsenal, might prove to be the better signing. At the time, people were saying he'd be even better than Michael Owen, and he does have loads of natural ability, but for some reason we've not seen as much of him as we might have done since he joined Arsenal. Sol Campbell has obviously done better for them. He's a good defender, strong and quick, and I know our gaffer was keen on him at that time. To my mind, though, Sol isn't a United player. I suppose that's easy to say now, with the benefit of hindsight and at the time I would have loved him to come. But looking back, we got Rio Ferdinand instead, and he most definitely fits the bill at Old Trafford. Rio is a classy, all-round footballer – more than just a defender.

When Seba Verón arrived he looked fantastic. He had unbelievable ability and is one of the best players I've ever seen. His passing was an absolute joy, and we're all still scratching our heads trying to work out why he wasn't a fabulous success. I think finding the best position for him was a large part of the problem. I *played* with him and I couldn't tell you what his best position was. It didn't work when we played him in the centre with Keane, he didn't like it out wide, and we weren't using a system where he could play in the hole, behind the main striker or strikers. He also suffered a few injuries, which held him back, and it didn't help that he couldn't speak any English, and needed a translator the whole time. How can you make friends and settle in when you can't communicate properly? I took him for a couple of nights out, but it was hopeless. We tried and both waved our arms at each other a bit, but I ended up talking to the interpreter all night!

Ruud couldn't have been more different. Like most Dutchmen, he spoke perfect English, and the lads took to him right from the start. It helped that he opened up with a hat-trick in a pre-season game against the Malaysian national team. If you're going to score goals like that, everybody is going to love you. I realized at once that if I put the ball in the right spot, he'd finish every time. He is deadly in and around the six-yard box, but it's not just there that he scores. If you ping it to him on the edge of the penalty area he'll turn and do his stuff. I've never known a striker take such a high percentage of his chances.

Talk of another signing just before the season proper started turned out to be just that – talk – when Arsène Wenger accused the gaffer of tapping up Patrick Vieira. The papers had a field day with that. The gaffer forcibly denied it and I didn't doubt him, but stories like that, however untrue, seem to have a life of their own – and during the off-season it's often much worse. Without any football being played the backpages often contain rumour and speculation, much of it groundless.

Before the season kicked off, Celtic came to Old Trafford

to play in my testimonial. We lost 4–3 in front of a crowd of 67,000, which was a marvellous turn-out. I'd wondered if anybody would even turn up for the game. I thought I might be seriously embarrassed with a gate of 3,000, but Celtic bought 15,000 tickets before they went on general sale, then said, 'If you've got any more we can sell them – it doesn't matter how many!' When the tickets went on the open market, my feelings about the game changed completely. The game sold out within a week. United fans had voted with their feet and I felt a little humbled to have even doubted it. Their support had been a feature throughout my career. Now they came through for me again and I was indebted to them. Touched.

Liverpool beat us in the Charity Shield, as it was still called then, but much more significant turned out to be the serialization of Jaap Stam's autobiography in the *Daily Mirror* the following day. In the book, Jaap spoke of a secret meeting that had been arranged with the gaffer. None of the rest of us knew the ins and outs of it, but we could hardly believe the speed of what happened next. Jaap was dropped for our 2–2 draw at Blackburn and was sold to Lazio less than a fortnight later. Only six months earlier Jaap had signed a five-year contract, and now, one week into the new season, our key defender was gone. I had been shocked by the newspaper headlines, but the gaffer had wanted to sign Laurent Blanc for a long time, so this was his chance.

What happened was a great pity really, because Jaap was a good player who had done well for us. There were never any goodbyes or anything, he was just gone. The gaffer had made it very clear who was boss, and Blanc joined us a couple of days later. Aged thirty-five, he still had huge presence, and although he'd never been blessed with raw pace, like Teddy, he relied on a sharp footballing brain to gain that extra yard. The Premiership was a lot faster than the other leagues he'd played in, and he found it hard to adapt. Where he did make a positive impression was in the way he looked after his body. He lived an athlete's life and he thought deeply about the game, which could be a French habit! As a pro he was an outstanding example to us all.

We started the season well enough, beating Fulham and Everton convincingly at home and drawing away to Blackburn and Aston Villa, but in the middle of September we lost 4–3 at Newcastle, which left us fifth in the table. I scored one of our goals, but more significant was Keaney getting sent off. He was suspended as a result, which was always a blow to the team's morale and performance. We went on to lose two more games in his absence.

In the Champions League we were grouped with Deportivo La Coruña, Lille and Olympiakos, and opened up with a 1–0 win at home to Lille, which was not as straightforward as it might sound. Becks scored in the ninetieth minute to avoid what could have been a costly draw. The following week we lost 2–1 in La Coruña in frustrating circumstances. Paul Scholes had given us the lead after forty minutes, and we looked set for a great result until Walter Pandiani, the striker who later joined Birmingham, and Noureddine Naybet, the defender who went to Spurs, scored in the eighty-sixth and eighty-ninth minutes. The turnaround was a sickener, but they were a good team, and we had some cracking games against them. They were a side who passed the opposition to death – fantastic to watch, not so good to play against. Every player had the confidence to want the ball and to use it well. The other striking feature was that they all seemed to be thirty-plus. Donato was thirty-eight, Mauro Silva thirty-three, and Fran, on the left wing, was thirty-two. But their age didn't matter, because they played to their strengths, passing the ball accurately and keeping it, not chasing it and tiring themselves out. Juan Valeron was their best player on the night, he was brilliant in midfield, and Diego Tristan caused us problems up front.

In Europe, the gaffer told us he wanted us to play a bit more like them. He felt European games were won in midfield, by players like Verón, Keane, Beckham and Scholes. When it comes to keeping the ball, there are few better in the world than those four, and that's what Sir Alex was looking to improve at that time. He wanted us to play not so much at full throttle, but to absorb pressure then counter-attack. In the Premier League it wasn't so serious when we lost possession because we knew we'd always get it back. There was a classic example of that just four days after the game in La Coruña, when we went to Tottenham and were 3–0 down at half-time and fought back to win 5–3. I didn't play, I was at home, injured, and I turned the telly off in disgust when it was 3–0. Then a mate phoned me and said it was 3–3. The turnaround was unbelievable – the gaffer called it our best-ever away performance. It was something, but I thought that was a bit over the top. We won the European Cup away from home!

The following week I was elsewhere again, with Wales, when Becks had one of his best games for England at Old Trafford. I was suspended, so I couldn't actually play in Cardiff, but I watched on TV, flicking between the two matches. Becks ran the game against Greece to almost single-handedly earn England a place at the World Cup. He was absolutely everywhere, covering every blade of grass. It's the mark of a great player that when the pressure is on you deliver. And he did that day. He got a lot of free-kicks that day. I kept thinking, 'He's going to score with one of these, he must.' You can't give Becks five or six pots at goal from virtually the same spot, as they did, and get away with it. He left it late, but he did it in the end.

He scored again a few days later when we beat Olympiakos 2–0 in the Champions League. That too was a good performance – the Greeks are always hard to beat out there, and it was their first home defeat in the competition for fourteen games. Verón played well that night, and was really looking the part at this stage. He liked to feel the sun on his back, and the good weather and firm pitches seemed to bring the best out of him. It's easy to forget now that he got off to a great start with us – so much so that he was named Premiership Player of the Month for September.

The return against Deportivo, in mid-October, was a real shock to the system. Ruud scored twice but we still lost 3–2, after conceding two really soft goals. It was a cracking game and we played well, but they were a very good side, top of La Liga at the time. The bottom line was that we couldn't give away goals and hope for Champions League success.

Three days later we were beaten 2–1 at home by Bolton, which was the start of a terrible run in the league. We lost five and won only one of seven games, and had dropped to ninth in the table by early December. There was relief from the Premiership in the Champions League, when we beat Olympiakos 3–0 at Old Trafford, but even that wasn't as easy as it sounds. The first goal, from Ole Gunnar Solskjaer, didn't come until the eightieth minute, I got the second after eighty-eight and Ruud made it three with seconds to go. That victory booked our place in the second phase.

In November Liverpool beat us 3–1 at Anfield, with Michael Owen scoring twice. This was around the time he was named European Footballer of the Year, and his pace was a real problem for our defence. He hangs on the shoulder of defenders, and you always have to be wary of him.

Even when he's not doing anything, defenders are uncomfortable with him around. He forces them to do things in a hurry, which means they make more mistakes. Laurent Blanc was left out that day, probably because the gaffer didn't think he could handle Michael's speed off the mark.

We had another nightmare as we went down 3–1 at Arsenal, and bad became worse at the start of December, when we lost successive home games to Chelsea and West Ham. With Jaap gone we were having a terrible time defensively and we even tried to shore things up when Keaney played centre-half at Chelsea. We finally stopped the rot a couple of weeks later when, never a team to do things by halves, we hammered Derby 5–0. And that began a run of eight successive wins in the league. By mid-January we were top of the table.

The gaffer's accent on midfield play meant we were using only one striker up front, which was Ruud. As a result Andy Cole wasn't getting a game and he wasn't prepared to accept that. He just wasn't happy with being a substitute all the time. It might have been different if Ruud had been injured, which would have given him a chance, but that never happened, and when he fell behind Ole in the pecking order, he felt it was time to go. Displaying a typical striker's self-belief, he thought he was still good enough to be starting, and he wasn't the type to take things quietly. He let the gaffer know exactly what his feelings were in no uncertain terms.

I roomed with him for years, and I know him better than most. He is a very proud man, and you could tell a lot from his body language. If he wasn't happy, he wasn't the type to hide it well. He was a top player, a top goalscorer and I was sorry, but unsurprised, to see him move on. We replaced him in January with Diego Forlan. He was a lovely lad, who got off to a slow start with us. He looked like a goalscorer in training, he had a good shot with both feet, and in practice he scored all sorts of goals, but it just didn't happen for him on the pitch as quickly as he would have liked, and when a striker doesn't score for the length of time he didn't, it ruins his confidence. Among the fans, it all became a joke. And that, of course, only made things worse for Diego.

Fortunately, Ruud was on fire. It was a fantastic start, especially when you remember that he had missed the previous season with that bad knee injury. Coming to a new club, there was a huge amount of pressure on him to perform, but he thrived on it. He's so strong, mentally, he just thinks he's going to score all the time, and that season, that's exactly what he did. He had scored twenty-one times by the middle of January. And when we beat Blackburn 2–1 in January for our eighth win on the trot, he set a Premier League record by scoring in eight successive games. The two sequences were anything but a coincidence.

By this stage we were top of the league, but our great run came to an end when we lost 1–0 at home to Liverpool. Danny Murphy got the goal – for some reason he did it time and again against us. I don't know why he managed to cause us so much grief, I've never regarded him as anything other than a tidy midfield player, but why he always used to sink us is mystifying. In the next match, Middlesbrough knocked us out of the FA Cup in the fourth round, and the mood at the club hardly improved when the head of security at Old Trafford, Ned Kelly, was suspended for alleged ticket touting. Ned was a very popular figure in the dressing room, the lads put a great deal of trust in him. If you ever needed anything sorted out, Ned was the man to go to. Consider it done, seemed to be the watchword. Whenever the players went on a night out, Ned would always be there with one of his security men. He'd charge the club for that, not us. It was part of his job to look after us – act as a minder, if you like. He was a confident bloke and funny with it. He got on well with the lads and he was pally with the manager. He was ex-SAS, too, and one year he organized a day out at Stirling Lines, their headquarters, down in Hereford. We all went on that one. He was a rough, tough sort, but that was his job. We all liked him and it was sad he went the way he did.

Of course, the season rolled on without him, and for the second time that season we came out of a dip with a bit of style, winning 2–0 at Charlton to go back to the top of the table, ahead of Liverpool. We then put five past Nantes in the Champions League. Before that game, a statue of Denis Law was unveiled at Old Trafford. The Law Man, European Footballer of the Year in 1964, is obviously a legend after what he did for, and achieved with, the club. I think he was Sir Alex's hero, you could see it in the gaffer's face. But the younger players and fans don't really know that much about him, which is a great pity. He was a top player – you can tell that from his goalscoring record, but I'm not sure some of the younger players would recognize him. You wonder sometimes what it takes to leave your mark. I didn't see him play, of course, and I find it strange that we often get old clips of Bobby Charlton or George Best on the telly, but never seem to see anything of Denis. And if they do show him, it's usually that goal for City that put United down!

In March the gaffer put an end to the speculation about his future by signing on for three more years, and Keaney, after widely reported negotiations, got a new, four-year contract that made him the club's top-paid player. There was no jealousy from the rest of us, we all knew he was worth every penny.

A goalless draw at home to Bayern Munich and a 3–0 victory over Boavista in Portugal saw us safely through to the last eight of the Champions League as unbeaten group winners, level on points with Bayern, but top because of our better head-to-head record. After that, it was a bit of a come-down to lose 1–0 at home to Middlesbrough, which enabled Liverpool – and Danny Murphy – to take over as league leaders. Alen Boksic got the goal early on. We'd come up against him playing for Juventus when he was at his peak, and he was brilliant then, but he was on his last legs now. 'Boro looked like it might be his last club.

I was intrigued by another big-name player coming to the end of his career. Matt le Tissier announced his retirement at the end of March, after sixteen years and 209 goals for Southampton. Like me, he was a one-club man, and perhaps we should applaud his loyalty, but I couldn't help wonder what he might have achieved elsewhere. At one stage, in the mid-nineties, he was linked with all the big teams, but he chose to stay put. Fair enough, that was his decision, but you have to ask questions about his ambition. Didn't he want to play at the very top? Could he have hacked it? We'll never know. He had outstanding ability – great feet and marvellous close control. He could pass and cross the ball as well as anyone in the game, and scored some stunning, memorable goals. The one thing lacking really was pace. He didn't do it often against us – although I do remember him chipping big Peter Schmeichel the day they beat us 6–3 down there . . .

After the defeat by 'Boro, we bounced back with four straight wins in the league. That had us running second in the table, still in with every chance of our fourth successive title.

In the quarter-finals of the Champions League, we came

up against familiar opposition in Deportivo, who had beaten us twice before, but this time we had no trouble with them. David Beckham scored a great goal, pinging it in from 30 yards, as we won the first leg 2–0 in Spain to make the return a formality. At home we beat them 3–2, Ole Gunnar Solskjaer scoring twice before I got our third.

The more significant development that night was the loss of Becks, with a broken bone in his foot – the now-famous metatarsal – caused by a bad tackle from Aldo Pedro Duscher. With the World Cup just around the corner, the timing couldn't have been worse for him. For a big tournament like that you need to be right physically, you need to have played all the games and have done all the fitness work with the others, which he hadn't. Playing in the heat in Japan, against the best in the world, was a big ask – too big – when he was nowhere near 100 per cent. If the injury had happened just a couple of weeks earlier, we'd have probably seen the real Becks in Japan. As it was, he was a shadow of the player he'd been in the qualifier against Greece.

Becks' fractured foot and the knowledge that he would miss the championship run-in left nobody in the mood to celebrate the Deportivo result. We needed all our best players at a time when Arsenal were going from strength to strength. By mid-April they had taken over at the top of the league after eight straight wins, and now they beat Middlesbrough 1–0 at Old Trafford in the semis to book their place in the FA Cup final. The double was on for them.

Thierry Henry was their star man – he scored twenty-four times in the Premiership that season – but it was still Ruud Van Nistelrooy, despite stiff competition from the Arsenal striker who was named PFA Player of the Year.

In the Champions League, we suddenly seemed to be

jinxed. In the first leg of our semi-final, against Bayer Leverkusen, we led twice, but could only draw 2–2 at home, and we lost Gary Neville after a quarter of an hour with exactly the same injury as Becks. The odds against two players from the same team breaking metatarsals in the space of a fortnight must be huge. With Becks' own recovery marginal, Gary had no chance of recovering in time to go to the World Cup with England. I've known Gaz a long time, and he was absolutely destroyed that he'd not be on the plane to the Far East. From United's point of view, it meant that another key player was out of the run-in. Despite that, we were still winning, beating Leeds, Leicester, Chelsea and Ipswich in quick succession, but so were Arsenal, which meant we could make no inroads into *their* lead. By the end of April they had reeled off eleven league wins on the trot. Then they beat Chelsea 2–0 in the Cup final to tee up the double. I watched the game on TV. Ray Parlour played particularly well, and even scored a good goal. I always had a high regard for him as a player. For someone like me, he was a nightmare to play against. He was usually on the right, and he would always be helping his full-back, up and down the line all day with that high-performance engine he had. He was an opponent we had proper respect for.

Already Cup-winners, Arsenal came to Old Trafford on 8 May needing only a draw to be sure of the title, and the double, with a game to spare. We were determined not to let them do it at our place, but they were in championship form, as they had been for a long time and we couldn't stop them. They won 1–0, with a goal from Sylvain Wiltord. That result, coupled with Liverpool thrashing Ipswich 5–0, meant we finished third. After the campaigns of recent years, it felt like a failure, and the mood at the club was grim.

It was a hard thing for us to admit, but Arsenal deserved

their success that season. There was a stage, after Christmas, when I really thought we were better than them. We went on a great run – twelve wins in thirteen league games – but we couldn't keep it up. We had a few injuries, but even before we lost Gaz and Becks we weren't hitting the same high notes as they were. Championships are all about peaking at the right time, and they were brilliant when it mattered. From our point of view, losing 1–0 at home to Middlesbrough in March was the killer.

Going out of the Champions League with a 1–1 draw at Leverkusen in the second leg meant that we ended the season empty-handed for only the third time in thirteen years. It wasn't anywhere near good enough; we'd fallen well below the standards we had set ourselves, and the gaffer and Keaney both let us know it. The difference was that the gaffer kept his criticisms behind closed doors – they were no less forceful for that. He is not one to slag off his players in public, he reserved that treatment for the media, and I can remember him having a right go at them at a press conference for the stick they'd given Seba Verón for most of the season, even though it was clear that Seba hadn't maintained his fantastic start. The thing was that, when you saw the ability Seba had in training, you just *had* to play him.

Roy had no such reservations. He would never back off when he thought something needed saying, and he accused certain players of not pulling their weight. He may have been right, but I think he says things like that as much to motivate himself as others, out of frustration and a need to feel that he was doing *something*, rather than a desire to slaughter his mates. The senior players, who were used to it, just thought, 'Here he goes again.' It was the younger ones who took most notice. Although perhaps it was them for whom it was intended.

We were all as disappointed as Roy at not winning anything. When that happens you go through all the games in your head, thinking of where you could have picked up more points, or where you might have done better, either individually or as a team. That's all you can do. In the final analysis we had to give credit to Arsenal that year. At the key times, their form was better than ours.

Keaney was still going on about it when he left with the Irish team for the World Cup. As the gaffer had pointed out, he could start a fight in an empty room, and he was in the kind of frame of mind to fall out with anybody. He soon did. He got a lot of stick for his row with Mick McCarthy, but I could understand where he was coming from when he let rip about the facilities, the food and the whole approach to the tournament. I was in the same boat with Wales. At Man United we were used to the best, and when we'd go away with our national teams it suffered a lot by comparison. Keaney told me that he thought a lot of people in the Irish camp were going to the World Cup just to take part. In contrast, he was going there to win it as part of a strong team that had put out the Dutch to even qualify. I'm sorry to say that he made my holiday, as I watched the drama unfold on the telly. There was Keaney scowling at the airport. There was McCarthy at the press conference, looking like he'd seen a ghost. There was Keaney back home walking the dog. Great entertainment.

That's More Like It

Sir Alex was always going to move heaven and earth to get us back to where he felt we belonged, and in July 2002 he persuaded the board to pay Leeds a club record £30m for Rio Ferdinand. We needed a lift after ending the previous season empty-handed, and there's nothing like a big signing to get everybody going. Rio had just had an outstanding World Cup for England. We'd known what a good player he was even before that and had always seen him as what we call a United player. He had that special something. There's nobody else in the Premier League quite like him. He's tall, super-fit and strong, but he's got much more than that. He's so good on the ball that he could play in almost any position. He's a real all-round footballer.

When he signed for us, Arsène Wenger chipped in to say that we'd paid £10m over the odds. It was probably just another attempt to wind up the gaffer, but I don't think Wenger would say that now, at least not with any conviction. Always superb, Rio has definitely improved since he's been at Old Trafford. Another significant, but less expensive and high-profile, new recruit was Carlos Queiroz as the new assistant manager. Steve McClaren hadn't been replaced on a permanent basis the previous season, and now the job went to the man who had managed Portugal and South Africa and was credited with discovering Luis Figo and Rui Costa when he coached Portugal to successive World Youth Championships in 1989 and 1991.

Carlos speaks five or six languages, and, with tremendous

experience in European football, his coaching credentials are second to none. The gaffer immediately entrusted him with large amounts of responsibility. He'd train us, prepare us for games, organize the team and decide the things we needed to work on. Some said he had too much influence, but I don't agree. He impressed me from the start.

In July Laurent Blanc signed a new one-year deal. He was thirty-six and faced a real challenge from Rio. We had Wes Brown doing well, John O'Shea coming through and Mikael Silvestre, but they were used a lot at full-back in those days, and David May was on the way out. It looked like we still needed Laurent in the middle. The cupboard was a little bare in the centre-back department.

In the summer of 2002 two good players had left us. Denis Irwin, after twelve years and 527 appearances, moved on to Wolves, and Dwight Yorke joined his old strike partner Andy Cole at Blackburn for £2m. Denis was nearly thirty-seven, but he hadn't had many injuries and was still very fit. He wasn't quite ready to retire, and we all wished him well. Yorkey was a bit different. He was still only thirty, but he'd lost his way since our treble season, when he was unquestionably brilliant. From scoring twenty goals in thirty-two league appearances in 1999–2000, he fell away to nine the following season, and in 2001–2 it was just *one* in ten games. I don't know if he lost his appetite for the game, but his social life, with Jordan and others, definitely wasn't to the gaffer's liking, and once he found himself out of favour, there was no way back. He was a big personality, though, and his presence would be missed in the dressing room.

Because we'd finished only third the previous season, we were involved in the qualifying rounds of the Champions League, where we were drawn against a team that sounded like a good-scoring Scrabble hand, Zalaegerszeg, of Hungary. There were a few jokes about that, but there was nothing to laugh about in Budapest. They beat us 1–0. We hadn't, perhaps, given them the respect they deserved. We didn't make the same mistake on the return. We made short work of them at home, beating them 5–0 to get into the Champions League proper.

When the league season started, I scored my 100th goal for the club in a 2–2 draw at Chelsea, before an explosive match at Sunderland. This brought Roy Keane and ex-Ireland teammate Jason McAteer up against each other. Jason, a mate of Mick McCarthy's, had criticized Roy for some of the things he'd said about the Irish set-up in his newly published autobiography. Roy, of course, took exception to that, and we went into the game at the Stadium of Light half expecting something to happen. We weren't disappointed. I got our goal in a 1–1 draw, but the result was incidental. What everybody will remember is Roy getting sent off. McAteer had needled him throughout the game, mentioning the book and making a gesture that suggested Roy was all mouth. Roy had had enough and stuck his elbow in McAteer's face, who went down like a sack of potatoes. Out came the red card. I think the gaffer, like the rest of us, knew some sort of clash was inevitable. He didn't even bother having a go at Roy about it in the dressing room afterwards. He probably took the view that we were going to lose him anyway, because Roy was already booked in for a hip operation that kept him out for three months. The problem had first occurred the previous season, but he had put off surgery to play in the World Cup, which was a bit ironic.

With Keaney now out, long-term, we lost successive league games at home to Bolton and away to Leeds, which left us with eight points from a possible eighteen. Ninth in the table, we'd made our worst-ever start in the Premiership. We needed to improve quickly, and we did. At the first group stage in the Champions League we beat Maccabi Haifa 5–2 at home. I got the first goal, after ten minutes, then got taken off early in the second half. I think the gaffer wanted to boost Diego's confidence, and he did get our fifth goal – with an eighty-ninth-minute penalty. In our second game in the group, a week later, we won 2–1 away to Bayer Leverkusen, with Ruud scoring twice, then in the Premiership we beat Charlton 3–1 at the Valley, where I got my third goal in eight league matches. I got two more against Olympiakos at home, which gave me five for the season by 1 October – good going for me, despite the team's slow start to the season.

Our 4–0 victory over Olympiakos was United's 100th in European competition, but I don't remember any great celebration of the milestone. Much more of a fuss was made when Diego finally scored in the Premiership, in his *twenty-third* game. It was a useful goal, too – a late equalizer at home to Aston Villa. In celebrating he took his shirt off and swung it round and round over his head, but then he found he couldn't get it back on, he kept getting caught up in the lining. Just when he thought he'd be in the clear, he got more stick than ever from the lads over that.

My 500th appearance for United at Fulham in mid-October was completely upstaged by events back in the north-west on the same day. Wayne Rooney was making a mark of his own at Goodison Park, and this was the day he really forced people to sit up and take notice by beating Arsenal's David Seaman with a fantastic shot to give Everton a 2–1 win against the champions.

In early November we qualified for the Champions League knock-out stages and were going well in the league.

We were up to third place when we went to play Manchester City in their new stadium. We hadn't lost in the derby for thirteen years, but all good runs have to come to an end, and they stuffed us 3–1 that day. Shaun Goater still dines out on that one – he scored twice.

Becks missed the derby game, having broken a rib in the previous game, against Southampton. An injury to David Beckham would usually be relied upon to dominate the headlines for days, if not weeks. On this occasion, however, the speculation about his recovery was brushed aside by a story about one of our old mates, Mark Bosnich. Now at Chelsea, Bozzy had tested positive for cocaine, though he denied having taken the drug. The Australian 'keeper had always been a bit different from the rest of us, but it still took me by surprise when this happened.

My own problems were of an entirely different nature, but that autumn was turning into a difficult period for me, too. My early season form had gradually deserted me, and for the first, and I hope last, time in my career the United fans turned on me. We had a few injuries and I had to play every game, but, to be honest, I wasn't making my presence felt. I wasn't playing at all well. With Keaney out, I was wearing the captain's armband, and although we weren't losing many, we were drawing games that we should have been winning. I wasn't contributing like I wanted to, and it didn't take the gaffer long to pick up on it. 'You're not looking confident,' he told me. 'What's wrong?' I told him I was finding it hard to cope with the grind of playing every game. For one reason or another – often injuries – I normally had a greater chance to recover between games.

The stick I was getting from the stands wasn't helping either. Things came to a head in January, when we played Blackburn at home in the first leg of the Worthington Cup semi-finals. I was substituted with about twenty minutes to go, and a section of the crowd booed me as I came off. The papers and the radio phone-ins picked up on it, making a lot of the fact that I wasn't playing well, and the gaffer left me out of the team for four games. 'He's not the player he was,' people were saying. I never doubted my ability, though. But while I was sure it was just temporary, it was a pretty horrible time. Looking back, I think my problem was that the relentless schedule affected my game, then because of that my confidence took a dip. And once that happens, it just seems to feed itself. The gaffer recalled me for the second leg of the semi-final against Blackburn. He must have known something I didn't, because my form started to come back. We won the game 3–1 and from then until the end of the season I played as well as I've ever done. Throughout it all the fans I met out and about in Manchester were all very good to me. People would come up to me in the street or in the shops: 'We're all behind you,' they'd assure me. 'Don't listen to any of the crap, or take notice of what's in the papers. We all love you.' It happened more than you might imagine and its effect on my self-confidence was real. It definitely helped me rediscover my self-belief and form, and I'm grateful to every one of them who took the trouble to have a word.

At the second group stage in the Champions League we started away to Basle and won 3–1. Ruud scored twice, and now had eighteen goals in nineteen appearances in the competition. He was a huge threat, whoever we played, and every team seemed to take special precautions to try to deal with him. Not that it did them much good.

At the beginning of December we had a memorable victory at Anfield – memorable because Diego Forlan became the unlikeliest of legends in the fans' eyes. He'd had a dreadful run but with a little help from Jerzy Dudek suddenly he was a hero. Liverpool had come out on top in the four previous games between us and were second in the table at the time, having won seven on the bounce in the league between the middle of September and early November, so the result was a particularly good one for us, moving us up to fourth. The football was pretty scrappy, and it looked very much like a 0–0 until about twenty minutes into the second half, when Dudek let a gentle backheader from Jamie Carragher slip through his hands and then through his legs. It offered Diego a tap-in. Two or three minutes later I set him up with another chance, and that was that. An instant hero!

The result gave us the confidence to beat Arsenal, who were top, 2–0 in our next game, Seba and Scholesy scoring. It was niggly stuff, as it so often is when the two sides meet, and Martin Keown, who always seemed to get himself particularly worked up, was later charged with improper conduct and fined by the FA after an incident which left Ruud sprawling on the floor. Bad-tempered or not, it was a big result for us, all the more so because it was the first time Arsenal had failed to score in fifty-six matches. Our defence was solid again, after conceding too often the previous season, and the gaffer told everyone that we were back to our best. As if to prove it, we saw off Deportivo 2–0 in the Champions League, with Ruud getting both, and a 3–0 win at home to West Ham lifted us to second in the table.

Just before Christmas Roy Keane returned after his hip operation, which should have been a boost, but instead his return coincided with successive away defeats at Blackburn and Middlesbrough. It was a wake-up call that launched an unstoppable run of form. We weren't beaten again in the league all season. It wasn't just the league either. Having won nothing the previous year, we were taking every competition seriously this time, especially as the victory over Blackburn had put us in the final of the Worthington Cup. There was progress in the FA Cup, too, and I scored a couple when we steam-rolled West Ham 6–0 in the fourth round.

In January Paul Scholes scored in every game we played, and was named Player of the Month. Everybody knows what a good player he is, and I'm not surprised Sven-Göran Eriksson has tried to persuade him to change his mind about retiring from international football. He won't. He has always scored more than his fair share of goals for United, but then the gaffer knows where to play him to get the best out of him. Eriksson was using him as an orthodox left-side midfielder, which he isn't. United sometimes play him on the left, but always with the licence to come in off the line and get forward, which is a freedom he didn't have with England. They were too rigid, they shackled him and lost him. Their loss was our gain.

By the beginning of February we were on one of those charges which used to burn off all our rivals, and had six wins on the trot. But what is it they say about pride coming before a fall? Our run in the league ended when City held us 1–1 in the derby at Old Trafford, and the next week we went out of the FA Cup in the fifth round, beaten 2–0 at home in a typically stormy scrap with the dreaded Arsenal. But crashing out of the Cup wasn't the big story that weekend, it just provoked it. In the changing room after the game the gaffer was furious about our poor performance, and laid into a few of us, before he turned his attention to Becks. They'd had a few major run-ins before this, and the relationship was strained. The gaffer was livid over how we'd thrown away the match. He said Becks was at fault for Arsenal's second goal by not staying with a runner. But Becks didn't just sit there and take it. He had a go right back at him. It only made the situation worse. The gaffer angrily kicked out at a boot which was on the floor in front of him (I still don't know whose it was). I flinched. For a split-second I thought I was in the firing line. I always got changed alongside Becks, and I was standing right next to him. But it flew straight at Becks' head. At first I didn't realize it had hit him. Then I looked round and saw blood on his face. It had caught him just above the eye, causing a cut that needed butterfly-stitching. Everybody went into freeze-frame for a split-second, we couldn't believe what had happened. It was a total freak, the gaffer couldn't have repeated it if he'd tried a hundred times. He was as shocked as the rest of us, but only momentarily. And now it was Becks' turn to go ballistic. He swore that he 'was fucking bleeding' and lunged at the gaffer. Before he got there I grabbed him quickly, but I couldn't hold him, he was so angry. Gary Neville and Ruud jumped in to help while he fought to get free of us.

I've never known it to get that bad before, but with the adrenaline running after a bad result, angry confrontations do happen in the dressing room in the heat of the moment. *I've* thrown things before. When the gaffer bollocked me at half-time against Juventus I threw my drink into the boot sling in anger. He didn't take kindly to having his trousers and shoes splashed with Ribena. He brought me off and fined me!

It's no secret that passions run high with the gaffer. Football means that much to him. And with fiery, competitive characters in the changing room, there will always be sharp differences of opinion. But he always knows where to draw the line – even that night at Sharpey's house when he threw everyone out. The incident with Becks was just an accident, and the row that caused it just a footballing row. End of story. Or it should have been.

Four days after Arsenal, it was still all over the front pages. We had a huge Champions League match at home to Juventus, and there was a big debate over whether Becks would be in the side. Even the players weren't sure, but he was in the end and played a major part in a good performance which brought us a much-needed 2–1 win. We got off to a flyer when Wes Brown scored after only three minutes, and Ruud added the second late on before Pavel Nedved pulled one back for them in the ninetieth minute.

A week later it was clear that the Beckham incident had caused no damage to our collective morale when we had one of the most impressive results in the club's long European history. Travelling to Turin to play Juve again, we turned them over 3–0 in the famous Stadio delle Alpi. We were already certain to qualify for the last eight, and the gaffer decided to rest a few of us before the Worthington Cup final the next weekend. I was one of those stood down, along with Ruud, Paul Scholes and Mikael Silvestre. I was pretty disappointed to have to start such an attractive match on the bench. Fortunately – at least from my perspective – I didn't have long to think about it. I was on after eight minutes, when Diego Forlan was injured, scored the first goal after fifteen, the second after forty-one and was pulled off again, after a kick on the knee, just after half-time. Eventful or what?

The bruised knee prevented me from training before the Worthington final, which was against Liverpool. I had a fitness test on the Saturday – the day before the game – when it didn't feel too good, but the gaffer wanted me to give it a go, so I played. We lost 2–0, with Dudek in outstanding form for them this time, but there were no flying boots in the dressing room. Losing to Liverpool is always a pain, but the gaffer was quite happy to turn his attention elsewhere.

He wanted to win the league again, and in March we went on another run of five straight wins, scoring goals for fun. On 22 March we beat Fulham 3–0 at home, before hitting top gear in our next two matches when we defeated Liverpool 4–0 and Newcastle 6–2 to go top for the first time. Arsenal, our main rivals for the title, as usual, lost 2–0 at Blackburn – their first loss for thirteen games – on the day we won at Aston Villa. The slip prompted a memorable reaction from the gaffer. It was, for Arsène Wenger and his team, 'squeeze your bum time', by which I presume he just meant it was nail-bitingly close!

In the quarter-finals of the Champions League we were drawn against Real Madrid, and that was definitely bad news. In the first leg, in the Bernabéu, their front men were too good for us. At 3–0 Ruud pulled one back, and we took some comfort from the thought that the away goal could make all the difference when we got them back to our place. That belief became even stronger when, before the return, we put in two good performances in the league that kept our confidence high. In mid-April we went to Arsenal, who were three points behind us in the table, but with a game in hand, and drew 2–2. It was the usual blood-and-thunder scrap, with Ruud giving us the lead and Henry scoring twice in the second half to put them 2–1 up, before I clawed back an equalizer. As ever in matches between us, the main talking point afterwards was not the result or the quality of the football played but a contentious incident – in this case Sol Campbell's sending-off for thrusting his arm into Ole Gunnar's face. In all honesty, it wasn't much of a foul, but contact was made, so you couldn't really fault the referee. Not that it stopped Arsène Wenger, of course. He made a lot of fuss, but all that achieved was to further stoke up the animosity between the two teams. As if that was necessary!

We moved on to beat Blackburn 3–1 at home, maintaining our lead at the top of the table, before Real came to Old Trafford for the Big One. We went into the second leg unbeaten in fifteen league matches, and in top form, but the gaffer sprang a major surprise on us, as well as them, by bringing back Seba Verón, who had been out injured for seven weeks, and started with Becks to the bench. The decision was pored over endlessly by the papers.

It was a great match, real thrill-a-minute stuff, but trailing 3–1 from the first leg, we needed to score first to have a chance. Instead, Ronaldo sprinted free to extend their lead after twelve minutes, and we were never going through after that. We now needed three just to take it into extra time. Ruud, the leading scorer in the Champions League that season, gave us some cause for hope just before the interval, with his twelfth goal in the competition, but it didn't last. Ronaldo struck again, from a Roberto Carlos cross, five minutes into the second half, and their second away goal meant we needed to score five to progress.

At least we gave the fans a match to remember. We pulled one back immediately, when Seba's scuffed shot was turned into his own net by Helguera, and then it took a brilliant performance by Casillas in the Real goal to prevent a dramatic turnaround. We were working up a real head of steam, but then Ronaldo again brought us to a halt. The Brazilian was at his unstoppable best that night and beat Fabien Barthez from more than 20 yards to complete a stunning hat-trick.

After sixty-three minutes, the gaffer brought on Becks in place of Seba. Determined to show that he should never have been left out, Becks scored with one of those stunning free-kicks of his to level it up on the night, then followed up a shot from Ruud, which Casillas was unable to hold, to give us the consolation of a 4–3 win. But the reality was that we'd always been two goals short of what we needed, and went out 6–5 on aggregate.

Going out of Europe was depressing, but at least we still had the league to play for, and the weekend did wonders for our morale, when Arsenal blew a two-goal lead to draw 2–2 at Bolton. We were playing the next day. As we set off for Tottenham on the team coach we listened to the radio commentary on the Bolton game. As the final whistle blew the coach erupted in loud whoops and cheers in celebration of Arsenal's misfortune. We took full advantage twenty-four hours later, beating Spurs 2–0 and bringing the title within touching distance. We won 4–1 at home to Charlton the following week, and were champions on the Sunday, when Arsenal lost 3–2 at home to Leeds, who were battling relegation at the time. Arsenal, we felt, had cracked under a period of sustained pressure from us.

We'd won the league for the eighth time in eleven years, which said a lot for our quality, but it seemed to get right up Arsène Wenger's nose. His reaction was to claim that Arsenal, not United, were the best side in the country. No wonder there's so much feeling between the two clubs. The best team wins the championship, it's as easy as that. Much more sensibly, Bobby Charlton said that because of his record, Alex Ferguson now had to be rated the club's best-ever manager, ahead of Matt Busby. It was a big call, but if anyone was qualified to make it, it was Sir Bobby. The manager's association, the LMA, voted David Moyes manager of the year, narrowly pipping the gaffer at the post. Moyes had done well reviving Everton, but they had won nothing and finished just seventh in the league and we beat them 2–1 at their place in our final game. It left us unbeaten in our last eighteen Premiership matches, fifteen of them won. Champions by five points from Arsenal, we'd played some marvellous attacking football. Ruud had scored forty-four goals in all competitions and Scholesy twenty. Even yours truly managed fifteen. Domestically, at any rate, it had been a vintage season.

But June saw two highly significant departures, when Becks finally moved to Real Madrid, for £25m, to be followed a week later by Carlos Queiroz, who also departed for the Bernabéu, to be head coach. In the dressing room, we were all a bit concerned that we'd lost one of our best players, but at the time the relationship between Becks and the gaffer was so strained, non-existent really, that we realized the split was best for everyone. The manner of his departure was sad, and none of us wanted to see someone of that quality go, but on the other hand Becks is a mate of mine and he was going to a great club. *'Good luck to him,'* I thought.

Fatherhood

I got together with Stacey late in 2002, and we moved into the apartment in Manchester in March 2003. At the start, things were difficult for us, because Emma and Stacey had been good friends, and Stacey's last boyfriend, Dave Gardner, knew and got on well with a few of the United players. It shouldn't have been a problem with Emma, because I'd split from her nearly a year before I moved in with Stacey. In Dave's case, he was friendly with Becks and was best man at Phil Neville's wedding. He was mates with both of them, and a couple of papers carried stories that my relationship with Stacey had split the dressing room, and that Becks and Phil weren't talking to me. The suggestion was that Stacey and Dave hadn't finished when I came on the scene, and that I'd broken them up. It was a load of crap. They split before I got involved, and the aggro that was reported simply never happened. Becks and Phil were never upset. Stacey was going out with one of my mates, they finished, and that's when we got together. It should have been straightforward, but of course it wasn't. It was complicated by the fact that Emma miscarried our baby just before we split. It happened quite early in the pregnancy, at the time of the first scan. She went to the hospital with my mum, and I was waiting at her house, to see how everything went. I was looking out of the window as they came up the drive and I could see from their faces that it wasn't good news. It was horrendous for Emma, and it hit me hard, too, because it was totally unexpected. The baby wasn't planned, but we were still excited about becoming parents. We'd been getting everything ready, and now it wasn't to be. I was glad my mum was with us – especially for Emma's sake.

Neither Emma nor I coped with the situation very well, and the relationship went downhill fast after the loss of the baby. To be brutally honest, it probably would have happened anyway. I'd known Emma for a long time, we'd always been friends, but at the back of my mind I knew she wasn't the one for me. The pregnancy hadn't been planned, but, for a brief while, the expectation of a baby became the glue that held us together. The loss hastened the end of our relationship. The memory of Emma's miscarriage was hard to shake when Stacey fell pregnant in the second half of 2002. So when Stacey went into labour ten weeks early, my worst fears came flooding back. Looking back at the way it happened still seems a bit surreal. We were in the apartment, we'd just moved in, and the birth was supposedly ten weeks away. It was eleven o'clock at night and we were going to bed. Stacey went to the toilet, and when she came back into the bedroom she looked shocked. 'My waters have broken,' she said. I panicked a bit, then rang my mum, who is a nurse, and she said, 'Ring the hospital.' I did that and was told to bring Stacey in straightaway. So I took her to our nearest hospital, the Hope in Salford. Stacey's mum and dad met us there, with my mum, who obviously knew what was what.

It was all a bit overwhelming, and they had to give Stacey a steroid injection because with her waters gone she was open to infection, which is obviously dangerous for the baby. They kept her in hospital for ten days because they didn't want the baby to arrive for as long as possible. Apparently it's in the last nine weeks that the lungs grow, and they wanted to give it as long as possible. It was a very worrying time for both of us, but the doctors reassured us, saying it was OK, and that babies were born healthy after twenty-six weeks. They were brilliant at the hospital. But when Libby was born, how premature she was really hit home hard. She was so small, just 3 lb 6 oz. It was such a relief when she came out crying really loudly because that told the doctors that her lungs were working just fine. She still had to be kept in special care for over three weeks, which was difficult for Stacey. She was released from hospital a couple of days after the birth, but Libby had to stay, so we could only visit all the time. I'd go before training every day, then back again afterwards. It was the year we caught Arsenal to win the championship, and in April big games were coming thick and fast. Two days after Libby was born, we played New-castle away. I even scored and yet my appearance on the pitch was deceptive, because that was the worst time for me. My daughter was still in the incubator, with jaundice. She looked so small and vulnerable that it was sometimes impossible to tear myself away. It was even worse for poor Stacey. Things have changed completely at the hospital since, and the system now is far less stressful. A new wing has been built, which I was privileged to be invited to open, and, crucially, there's a special care unit where parents can stay. Each of the rooms is equipped with a TV on which you can monitor your baby in the incubator on CCTV. It's marvellous. Despite our desire to take Libby home, we kept her in hospital a week longer than we needed to. If we'd taken her home we would still have had to feed her through the nose, and we didn't want that for fear of doing something wrong.

Eventually, becoming a father quietened me down and made me more responsible. I think that happens naturally. For the first six months, though, babies just lie there and don't really do anything! During that time I was still inclined to go out and let off steam. I needed that release occasionally because I was taking it in turns with Stacey to get up every four hours at night to feed Libby, which meant I was getting *much* less sleep than I was used to, and I was having to play twice a week as well. From the time Libby was two, though, I wanted nothing more than to stay in and be with her. Babies are just so interesting at that age. To be honest, I now prefer staying in with her to going out! We were also lucky in that a lot of our friends had children at around the same time. We've got a neighbour with a girl just a few months older than Libby, and there's four or five other couples we know with children of a similar age.

If I socialize with the other players now, it's usually on a prearranged group night. That's still something we all do every six months or so. You're obliged to go on those because they are seen as team-bonding exercises. But I don't behave like a single man any more – you won't see me out with the younger members of the team these days!

I'm probably well out of that scene, because my problem was always that I never knew when to go home. Whenever I went out I'd always be the last to leave, because I was scared I'd miss something. When I was younger I used to be out and about all the time, and it did get me into a few scrapes, but as a young lad you can get away with abusing your body because your natural fitness and powers of recovery are at their peak. When you get to thirty you feel it a lot more. I hardly ever stay out late now, just for fear of how bad I'm going to feel the next day more than anything else. A two-year-old doesn't leave you alone just because you're nursing a hangover. When I was younger I used to be very different. We'd all have a few beers, then start mixing our drinks – something I wouldn't even *consider* now. I look back on it and think, 'What on earth were you doing?' It makes no sense any more. I go out for a good meal and a nice bottle of wine and try to appreciate the finer things a bit more.

Not Our Year

On 1 July 2003 everybody at Old Trafford was more interested in David Beckham's transfer to Real Madrid – he had his medical that day – than something going on in London, which proved to be much more significant. At the same time that Becks was proving his fitness in the full glare of the television lights, Roman Abramovich was buying Chelsea, at an estimated cost of £150m. At United, we thought nothing of it, it didn't register at all. It all seemed to happen very quickly, and nobody had any idea how much money he was going to invest, let alone what his motives were. As we understood it, Chelsea were flat broke until he came along, but it didn't appear to be doing them any harm. In fact, just the opposite seemed to be the case. Because they had no money Claudio Ranieri stopped tinkering, stopped bringing in five or six new players at once, and finally gave his team the chance to gel. Forced to stick with what he had, he found some sort of continuity, and 2002–3 was one of Chelsea's better seasons. Now, however, it was all change again.

I tried to be sanguine about Becks' departure. He's a great player and had been a fixture in the dressing room for a long time. We'd miss him personally and I had always enjoyed playing with him; but now he was gone. As far as I was concerned, there was little to be gained by dwelling on it or even thinking about it. I was far more bothered that Patrick Vieira had agreed a new contract with Arsenal. I was hoping he'd go to Real, too! That way we wouldn't have to cope with him any more.

I've spoken with Becks a few times since he left, but usually when I was with Gary Neville. Nev and Becks are best mates, and in constant contact. At that time Nev and I lived in the same apartment block in Central Manchester and drove to training, or home games, together, sharing the driving. So if the two amigos were talking on their mobiles, I'd have a word. It was always good to catch up with him.

The other drama that July surrounded the gaffer's attempt to sign Ronaldinho, from Paris St Germain. He offered £19m for the Brazilian who had wrecked England's World Cup. For a week or two it seemed he might be coming, and the players all certainly thought he was. He'd visited Manchester for a look around, and the papers were saying he was close to signing. But, as we know, you can't believe everything you read. After a week or so of will-he-won't-he?, Ronaldinho opted for the Nou Camp. At the time I thought it seemed a bit of a gamble. All right, he'd done well at the World Cup, but we hadn't really noticed him at PSG, who were not among the European elite. I don't think anyone really knew for sure then how good he was going to be, and maybe he wouldn't have done as well in England as he did at Barcelona. What I will say is that I would have liked to find out! He has come on tremendously well, and there's no doubt that he's a brilliant player now.

I felt much greater disappointment when Damien Duff, who the gaffer wanted to sign from Blackburn, went instead to Chelsea for £17m. I thought we should have got Duff, who I really admire as a player. It didn't bother me in the slightest that he plays in my position. I can play on the right as well as the left, and so can he, so where's the problem? I believe signing him would definitely have improved the team. We'd also been in for Harry Kewell, who preferred to go to Liverpool, and all these knock-backs did start to make me wonder what was going on.

Until the last couple of seasons any player, given the choice, would always sign for United, but that's not the case any more, and the club has to ask itself why. Obviously I'm biased and I think *everyone* should sign for United. We are a bigger club than Chelsea, with a proud history of winning trophies. So with the possible exception of the London location, it *has* to be the money that is attracting good players there. Should we be paying more, in terms of transfer fees and wages? Maybe – the fans would certainly say so.

In the case of Kewell, and perhaps Duff, too, there is another factor to consider. Some potential signings just don't fancy the competition. Would either of those two get in the team ahead of me? Maybe, maybe not, but what is certain is that I'd have given them a real battle. It shouldn't be an issue, really. Good players have to trust in their own ability and back themselves. You've got to question a player who doesn't.

We did manage to make a couple of signings in July. The first was Tim Howard, the American goalkeeper, who cost £2.3m, and the second Eric Djemba Djemba, who came from Nantes for £3.5m. Tim had come on a visit the previous season, to have a look around with a view to joining us later, so we met him then. As a player, I rate him. But it's been hard for our 'keepers since Peter Schmeichel, because they are always going to be compared with him, and the trouble is he may well have been the best ever! Peter's legacy is a heavy burden for all his successors, who as a result, tend to find all their mistakes magnified in a way that doesn't happen at other clubs. I think Tim can be a quality 'keeper.

My family. Aunt Stacey, Mum, Grandad, me, Nan and Aunt Hayley

With Rhodri and Bethany

With Mum, Rhodri and the Premiership trophy

My family. With Stacey and
our daughter Libby

Fatherhood: with Libby

The Gaffer with his
Number Two, Carlos
Queiroz, in 2002

Equalizing against Chelsea at Stamford Bridge in 2002

Eight titles, eight bottles. The Gaffer and I are the only ones who have been involved in all of them

Winning the title for the eighth time in 2003

Tempers fray against Arsenal

Playing Rangers at Ibrox in the 2003
Champions League. The noise was incredible

In Red Square for Wales's Euro 2004 qualifier against Russia

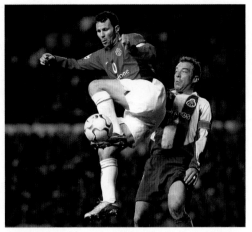

Battling against José Mourinho's FC Porto team in the 2003–4 Champions League. They went on to win it

Winning the 2004 FA Cup final to finish the season on a high

Scoring against Newcastle in April 2005

The new generation. Wayne Rooney scores his first goal for United

In full flight

In pre-season we went to America for two-and-a-half weeks. We had a week just training at the Nike complex in Portland, then played a couple of matches. We beat Celtic 4–0 in Seattle and Juventus 4–1 in New York's Giants Stadium in front of a 79,000 crowd. I scored two but Seba Verón was the man of the match. From New York we flew straight to Lisbon to play a friendly to open Sporting's new stadium, and Djemba Djemba, who had just signed, joined up with us there. *None* of us knew anything about him when he arrived, but first impressions were pretty favourable. He seemed ideally equipped to sit in front of the back four and play the holding role, winning the ball and then keeping things nice and simple – that's what he was bought for. Unfortunately, the poor guy had a terrible first season. He had to play in the African Nations Cup, which took him away for two months, and when he *was* with us he picked up a couple of injuries, which meant he never had a decent run of games to settle in.

Jet-lagged, we lost 3–1 in Lisbon on a day that was more memorable for Joe Cole joining Chelsea from West Ham. The gaffer had loved young Joe and wanted to sign him from way back. I've always thought he was talented and I think José Mourinho has brought discipline and responsibility to his game. The Chelsea system suits him, too. He's allowed to switch positions with Duff or Robben and to go and do pretty much what he wants when they are on the attack. Inevitably, Seba Verón's departure to Stamford Bridge for £12.5m caused much more of a stir in the northwest. I wasn't surprised, because Seba wasn't happy, so he had to move on. Football-wise he was having a bad time, and knew he wasn't playing anywhere near as well as he could. Like Joe Cole, he's difficult to categorize when it comes to defining his best position, but United don't change their whole formation to accommodate one player. He was used to a free role.

I played against Seba when Wales played Argentina, and everything they did went through him, he ran the show. United don't do that, we don't play it all through one individual, and Seba wasn't suited to being just a cog in the machine. It was also common knowledge that we had our eyes on Cristiano Ronaldo. So when we signed Ronaldo from Sporting for virtually the same fee Chelsea had paid for Seba, it was pretty easy to do the maths! He arrived a little later than we would have liked, just four days before the start of the league season. The first time I'd seen anything of him was in our friendly in Lisbon, when all our lads were knackered and didn't fancy the game at all, having just flown in, jet-lagged, from New York. I felt sorry for John O'Shea, our left-back, who had the job of marking Ronaldo in a game in which he was desperately keen to impress to get his move. What struck me first of all about Cristiano was his physique, which was more twenty-eight than eighteen. He was tall and strong, very impressive to look at. As a footballer, I noticed he had lovely balance and quick feet. He did tend to overdo that step-over of his a bit, though. He's down to about ten a game now!

Our opening league match was at home to Bolton, and I scored twice as we beat them quite easily, 4–0. My first came from a free-kick, which was a rarity. Thanks to Mr Beckham, I hadn't taken one for years! It was a great start to the season for me, but the game is remembered for Ronaldo coming on for the last half-hour and dazzling a tired defence with a brilliant display of pace and skill.

Chelsea, who had won 2–1 at Liverpool, with Seba Verón getting their first goal, were still spending money like water.

After Seba, they bought Adrian Mutu from Parma for £15.8m, then, in quick succession, signed Hernan Crespo from Inter for £16.8m, Alexei Smertin from Bordeaux for £3.8m and Claude Makelele from Real Madrid for £13.9m. Abramovich had spent an amazing £106m on players, and by now we knew he meant business. Financially, nobody could live with them. The game had never seen anything like it.

Like a lot of South Americans, Crespo couldn't settle in England and quickly went on loan to Italy, where the culture is, I guess, a little more like what he was used to in Argentina, and Smertin is only a squad player, but Makelele has been a great signing. He is very important to the way they play, protecting the whole back four. If the right-back goes forward, he'll shift across to fill in. He makes sure they're never left exposed and keeps the pressure on the opposition by breaking up their moves. There are not many players around who can do that job – Keaney does it for us these days and Incey used to. It's a critical role, screening the defence. Makelele never gets out of his own half, and you won't find many players who are happy doing that, but he doesn't want to score goals or create chances, he just wants to break up the play and be a spoiler. Keane and Ince were slightly different, they were both box-to-box midfielders by nature who had to adapt. Makelele, though, was brought up doing it. It would be too boring for me, but he's outstanding. Few players do boring better!

Our second match was away to Newcastle, where we won 2–1 and had the gaffer red-carded for the bollocking he gave the officials when they failed to spot the most obvious foul on me. I was clean through when I touched the ball past Titus Bramble, and he just took me out. I was looking up from the ground thinking, 'He's got to go,' but the referee,

Uriah Rennie, didn't give anything. I couldn't believe it and neither could the gaffer. The linesman was right on the spot as well and did nothing, so Sir Alex went ballistic. He kicked a water bottle across the dug-out and had to be restrained from charging on to the pitch. The FA fined him £10,000 and banned him from the touchline for two matches for what he said to Rennie, But I understood the strength of his frustration. I thought it was a disgraceful decision. Even if the referee missed it, the linesman was right there. The row over that decision stole headlines that rightfully belonged to Ruud, whose goal at St James' Park meant he had now scored fifteen times in his last ten games.

We beat Wolves 1–0 to make it three successive wins, but then came unstuck at one of our least favourite places, Southampton, where James Beattie scored from a corner right at the death to give them a 1–0 win.

Chelsea continued to make the news, and did it again in September when Peter Kenyon, our chief executive at Old Trafford, agreed to join them. I didn't know Kenyon that well and hadn't had much to do with him. It was really only when negotiating for the players' pool that we'd had much contact. I helped to run that, along with Roy Keane and Gary Neville, and Kenyon was the one we dealt with over how much the players got from MUTV, magazines and other commercial contracts. He seemed OK to deal with, but it was Nev who really impressed. If we ever had to fight our corner, it would be Nev who did the haggling. He could be a real Arthur Scargill – and we were to see more of that when another incident rocked Old Trafford later in the season.

In the Champions League we started impressively, with a 5–0 win at home to Panathinaikos, but there still seemed to be more interest in Chelsea, who scored five of their own, away to Wolves. Then all hell broke loose. The next day we were at home to Arsenal. The result was unremarkable, a 0–0 draw, but if there were no goals there was no shortage of action in what became known as the 'Battle of Old Trafford'.

Arsenal came into the game stung by criticism after a 3–0 mauling from Inter Milan in the Champions League, and they were clearly determined to make amends at our expense. Arsène Wenger dropped Robert Pires and Sylvain Wiltord, recalled Ray Parlour and picked a team to play for the draw, and it always seemed likely that he was going to get it. By the standards set by these two teams, it was pretty ordinary stuff for the first eighty minutes, with a lot of midfield scrapping and very few chances created. I clipped a post early on with a 25-yard free-kick, and Ronaldo was always a problem for Ashley Cole, but not much was happening until Vieira, who had been booked after a foul on Quinton Fortune a couple of minutes earlier, was sent off for kicking out in retaliation after Ruud had fallen on him. Keaney, who perhaps surprisingly has a lot of time for the Frenchman, escorted him away, sympathetic towards a kindred spirit as Vieira protested over and over again that he had made no contact with Ruud, who had jumped away. It doesn't take much to start trouble between these two sides, and the fuse had been well and truly lit. Gary Neville and Freddy Ljungberg were soon involved in a heated row and the match was at boiling point in added time when Keown pushed over Diego Forlan for a penalty. Ruud stepped forward to take it, but was delayed by Lehmann, who approached him as he was preparing to take the kick. He had to place the ball on the spot three times. This blatant gamesmanship hardly helped Ruud, who had missed his previous two penalties, and when he was finally allowed to take this one, he blasted it against the crossbar.

The final whistle went almost immediately afterwards, and Arsenal's celebration of a result that kept them on top of the table was provocative in the extreme. They gloated and goaded us, *especially* Keown, who had a bit of history with Ruud. He ran up to Ruud with his arms flapping in a way that made sure he would hit him on the head. Lauren, Cole and Parlour then joined in, surrounding and jostling Ruud in an intimidating way. A few of us rushed across to protect him. That didn't really help, but Ruud had been on his own. Lauren and Parlour were pushing and shoving him, and I barged into Lauren to clear him out of the way. That was it. The final tally was six yellow cards plus Vieira's red.

The day after the game, the FA announced that there would be an inquiry, and forty-eight hours later they charged eight players with misconduct. There were six from Arsenal – Lehmann, Lauren, Cole, Keown, Vieira and Parlour – plus me and Ronaldo. It's an unfortunate but inescapable fact that there is too much animosity between the two teams – it goes *way* beyond the normal rivalry between first and second, which is where we were for so long. Every time we meet there's so much hype and build-up and so much at stake that it always becomes more than a football match. I don't think anybody really wants it to boil over, but it always seems to happen. There's been bad blood between the clubs since 1990, when both were docked points after a twenty-one-man brawl, and that feeling has been feeding off itself ever since.

For trying to help Ruud I was one of the players charged after this one. The case was heard after our game at Chelsea in November. We stayed over and I went with Ronaldo to the hearing at a hotel near Heathrow the following day. The disciplinary panel had a barrister on their side, the prosecution had a QC acting for the FA, and we had the club solicitor, Maurice Watkins, representing us. I pleaded my innocence and said it was heat-of-the-moment stuff, that players were brought up to protect their teammates, and that was all I had been doing. They listened to me, then turned their attention to Ronaldo and absolutely grilled the poor lad. He was eighteen, he'd only been in the country five minutes and couldn't speak English, he needed an interpreter. And to hear the going-over they gave him, you would have thought he was accused of murder. It was ridiculous, all he'd done was push an opponent. The FA fined me £7,500 for barging Lauren aside. I thought it was a joke, but I wasn't laughing. They'd punished six Arsenal players so they felt they had to do a couple of ours. I was sure it was that simple. To me it was disgraceful that any United players were punished alongside six Arsenal players.

I thought Keown was the worst culprit. He'd provoked the confrontation. He always seemed to be very intense and had a scary look about him – the only player who can go ninety minutes without blinking!

There was worse to come when, two weeks after the Arsenal match, Rio Ferdinand missed his drugs test. I knew something was wrong earlier than anybody else because I was tested that day too. The way the system worked then was that the testers would turn up at the training ground, unannounced, and lots would be drawn to decide who they wanted to see. The club doctor then came to the dressing room and said, 'Right, I need you, you and you for drugs tests.'

On this occasion me and Rio were two of the four players who drew the short straw. After training I got changed and went up to the doctor's office at Carrington. During the test the doctor asked me, 'Have you seen Rio?' I told him I hadn't, did the business and thought that was that. Then I heard on the radio that Rio had missed the test, and that there was going to be trouble over it. Now, of course, I wish I'd said to Rio, 'Come on, let's go and get these tests done,' but it didn't occur to me then. Why would it? I did the test, showered and dressed in my own time, had my lunch and went home. I never gave any thought to what anybody else was supposed to be doing.

I'm not going to defend Rio, he was in the wrong, but I *can* understand how it happened. I often forget things after training, when my mind is still full of football; I'm thinking through what I've just been doing, and weighing up what I've been told. You get completely preoccupied and wrapped up in the morning's work. I've forgotten all about interviews that have been arranged. There's so much happening at Carrington that it's easy for things to slip your mind. Inevitably the system has changed as a result of the case to make sure that absent-mindedness can't have such far-reaching repercussions. Now, the testers will wait for you by the side of the training pitch and follow you to the changing room. Someone will sit there in the corner and wait for you. If that system had been in place then, Rio would have been OK. People have said, 'You should never miss a drugs test, there's no excuse,' and yes, I suppose that's true. I hadn't needed to be reminded, but I *could* have made the same mistake. And if I had, it would have been no more sinister than when Rio messed up. Of course, it certainly didn't help his case when Rio was photographed out shopping in town when he should have been doing the test. But then as far as he was concerned, there was no reason he shouldn't be!

It became an even bigger talking point when the FA wouldn't let Sven-Göran Eriksson pick him for England's vital European Championship qualifier in Turkey. The gaffer and the directors made the point that the FA seemed to be pre-judging the issue, and that Rio should be allowed to play on until he was found guilty or otherwise.

I was away with Wales while all this was going on, but down in Cardiff we followed on TV and in the papers how the England players were threatening to strike and refuse to play in Istanbul if Rio wasn't reinstated in the squad. And Nev again showed that in another life he'd have been a good trade union boss, but Rio's fate was sealed as far as internationals were concerned and he was banned.

Back on the field there was a significant result in the league when Chelsea, who were unbeaten, lost for the first time, 2–1 at Arsenal. The same day we won 1–0 at Leeds, which kept us in second place, sandwiched between the two London teams.

In the Champions League, we had lost 2–1 away to Stuttgart, who were a good side at the time, but now we repaired the damage by beating Rangers 1–0 at Ibrox, with an early goal from Phil Neville. The atmosphere up there was amazing, I remember the hairs standing up on the back of my neck as we lined up for the handshakes before the kick-off. Even up in the directors' box they were leaping about like men possessed. We had a few hard-core fans there, but we couldn't hear them, the din the Scots made had the whole stadium jumping. After a good result like that, it was a bit of a shock when we lost at home to Fulham three days later. Louis Saha didn't score that day, but his pace gave our defenders a lot of problems, and it was on the back of that performance that the gaffer signed him shortly afterwards. It was a bad result – one that dropped us to third place, behind Arsenal and Chelsea – an indication of things to come.

In November our form picked up nicely, and we strung together three successive wins in the Premiership as well as beating Rangers 3–0 at home in the Champions League. I particularly enjoyed our 2–1 victory at Liverpool, where I scored twice in the second half. I played on the right that day, and I have to confess that one of my goals was a fluke cross that went in. I was looking for Ruud at the back post and everyone missed it, including Jerzy Dudek. It was what I call a good bad 'un. My second was a sidefoot job close in, and I embarrassed poor Dudek again, putting the ball through his legs. It's always nice to score, of course, but there's nowhere better for a United player to do it than at Anfield. Nutmegging the 'keeper's was the icing on the cake.

Arsenal were now unbeaten in their first thirteen league games, a record-breaking start to the season, and our attempt to keep up with them faltered when we lost 1–0 at Chelsea, to a Frank Lampard penalty. But the run-up to Christmas was a great time for us, we were playing really well and we thought we were going to come on strong and blow everyone away in the second half of the season. From 6 December through to 7 January we won six Premiership matches on the trot, as well as beating Stuttgart 2–0 at home in the Champions League. Against the Germans, Ruud scored his twenty-eighth goal in thirty European matches, to equal Denis Law's club record.

In mid-December, by winning the Manchester derby at our place, we went top for the first time. It didn't last long though. Arsenal took over twenty-four hours later. It was all pretty neck and neck, and Chelsea too were also very much in contention. But, looking back now, our title chances were dealt a fatal blow the following week, when Rio's ban was finally confirmed. He was going to be out for eight months. We thought he'd be suspended for the rest of the season, but then the FA added a bit on for good measure. Rio appealed immediately, and he was allowed to play on, pending the outcome, but we feared the worst when FIFA warned us not to take court action. The club reluctantly withdrew its appeal in the knowledge that Rio's situation might be made worse rather than better.

During the ban, the lads were sympathetic. You don't like to see any player train all week and not play on the Saturday, there's nothing worse than that. It's the same when people get injured. We felt the FA had made an example of Rio, but at least one good thing has come out of it, in that the system is now policed properly. There was never any suggestion whatsoever that Rio had taken drugs of any kind and personally, I don't think performance-enhancing drugs are used in football anyway. I don't see how anyone could do it. For a one-off race in athletics I can imagine it working, but over a whole football season you'd never get away with it.

The ban finally came into effect in mid-January, and from that moment on we never hit the top of the table again. Wes Brown was brought in for the second half of the season to partner Mikael Silvestre in central defence. With Rio's calming influence we'd been top of the league, we looked solid and we weren't letting many goals in. Now, straight-away, we conceded eight in the next three games.

The last time we were top was on 11 January, after a goalless draw at home to Newcastle, which left us one point ahead of Arsenal. I was injured in that game and missed the next two. The transfer window had opened, and after declaring his interest in Arjen Robben, then at PSV Eind-hoven, the gaffer signed Louis Saha from Fulham for £12m. I didn't know a lot about Robben at the time, so I talked to Ruud about him. 'What's he like?' I asked. 'Am I better than him or what?' I was joking, but at the same time I obviously had a vested interest. 'Of course you are, Ryan,' Ruud laughed, before becoming more serious. 'Arjen is a good player,' he told me, 'and we'd do well to get him.' I knew much more about Louis, who had always given us trouble, whether it was Jaap or Rio marking him. His pace and strength made him a handful, and he had a habit of doing well against us.

The other title contenders weren't going to be outdone, and Arsenal bought José Antonio Reyes, from Seville, for £17.6m, while Chelsea went for Scott Parker, at Charlton, who cost them another £10m.

The England players weren't letting the Rio Ferdinand situation drop, and in January Gary Neville was prominent when a delegation went to see the FA for what were described as 'clear-the-air' talks. For as long as I've known him, going right back to our youth-team days, Gaz has never been happy unless he's organizing something, and this was typical. To be fair, all teams need somebody like that, and there were others involved in the discussions about Rio. Nev has a reputation as the ring-leader, and he usually is, but this time there were others who spoke out, too.

Arsenal went top on 18 January, after a 2–0 win at Aston Villa, and stayed there for the rest of the season. Of their last sixteen league games, they won eleven and drew the rest. Nobody could get near them, and we laboured in their wake. In February we were 3–0 up at Everton and let them right back in it at 3–3 before Ruud got an eighty-ninth-minute winner, then we lost our next game 3–2 at home to Middlesbrough. We were leaking too many goals. Arsenal, on the other hand, were flying, and won 2–1 at Chelsea in the middle of a run of nine straight wins. At least we were going well in the FA Cup. We'd got past Aston Villa and Northampton in earlier rounds, and now we beat Man City 4–2 at home to go through to the last eight.

But in the Champions League it was a different story. We were drawn against José Mourinho's Porto in the first knockout round, and were happy enough after the first leg, where we lost 2–1, but got the important away goal, through Quinton Fortune. Benni McCarthy scored both theirs, with two headers. I couldn't help but think that Rio would probably have prevented both of them. We had so much confidence in him and were missing him badly. The gaffer had a fair bit to say afterwards about their diving and conning free-kicks out of the referee. He was angry with their play-acting, which got Roy Keane sent off, and banned for the return. Djemba Djemba played in his place, and we were on course for the quarter-finals when Paul Scholes put us 1–0 up after about half an hour. It stayed that way until the ninetieth minute, which meant we were going through on the away goals rule, but then right at the death Costinha scored, leaving us no time to come back at them, and we were out, 3–2 on aggregate. It was a real sickener. Having been confident of going through, it felt as if something had been torn from us. And, although we didn't know it at the time, we'd be seeing a lot more of their charismatic young manager in the following season.

Then, to rub salt in the wound, Arjen Robben signed for Chelsea for £13.5m at the beginning of March. 'Why is he signing for them,' I thought, 'and not for us?' As with Duff before him, it worried me that he'd be choosing Chelsea in preference to us. Robben had been to Manchester and had a good look round before making his mind up. He was shown around Carrington, which is as good a training ground as you'll find anywhere. I'm told that the place Chelsea were using at the time was poor by comparison, so it can't have been the facilities that persuaded him. I felt at the time that it *must* have been the money they were offering. United didn't have the unlimited resources Roman Abramovich was providing.

Putting the European setback behind us, we pulled ourselves together for two big games against Arsenal in quick succession. The first was in the league, at Highbury, where we ended their nine-match winning sequence with a 1–1 draw, and six days later we played them again, at Villa Park, in the semi-finals of the FA Cup and killed their chances of the double by winning 1–0. They had a great chance early on, but Roy Carroll made a top-class save. Then Scholesy scored after half an hour, and we were pretty solid after that.

The result should have lifted us in the league, but it didn't happen. We lost our next game 1–0 at Portsmouth, and were then beaten at home by Liverpool. Danny Murphy – him *again!* – got the only goal. It was his third at Old Trafford in four years. We'd hit a wall and the following day, 25 April, Arsenal gained the one point they needed to win the league when they drew 2–2 at Tottenham. They were champions with four games to spare, but what really stuck in the throat was that we hadn't even made a fight of it. Our form had collapsed, and a 1–0 defeat at Blackburn was our third in four matches.

Arsenal went on to complete the season unbeaten, which was a fantastic achievement. I've played in some marvellous United teams, but we've only come close to doing that. Henry, who had scored thirty goals in the league, was deservedly named Footballer of the Year by both the players and the football writers.

We finished third in the Premiership, a massive fifteen points behind Arsenal, and four behind Chelsea. Three defeats we had near the end meant the season just petered out as far as the league was concerned. I believe there's no getting away from the fact that, with Rio in the side, there was a real dominance about our defence which we lacked when he was absent. With Rio at the back we never looked like conceding goals. He's got such presence and composure. It spreads confidence throughout the team. His ban was a killer. I'm not saying we'd have won the league with him there, but I *know* we'd have at least given Arsenal a run for their money.

There was some consolation on offer in the FA Cup, where we met Millwall in the final. The way they got there disproved the old theory that you have to beat the best to get that far – they hadn't played a single Premier League team – and they were very ordinary. They had finished a modest tenth in the old First Division, and the final was one of the least exciting in recent memory. We won 3–0, and the outcome was never in doubt from the moment Ronaldo headed us in front. Ruud scored the other two, with Millwall never threatening to cause an upset. It seemed like they didn't know whether to have a go or not, and even though the final was no classic, it was still a great way to end the season. We could only look forward to the next season when, with Rio back on board, I thought we'd be back on form. I certainly hoped so.

Russian Revolution

Coming into 2004–5, I thought we were certain to improve on the previous season, which had been a major disappointment. In the past, when we'd had a dip in the league, we always came back strongly the next time, and I really thought that would happen again. I was expecting big things, especially after the signings we made.

The summer of 2004 saw a flurry of comings and goings. At the end of May Carlos Queiroz, who had left Real Madrid after one season, was reappointed as the gaffer's number two, in place of Walter Smith, who had left to become Scotland manager. At around the same time, we signed Alan Smith, the Leeds and England striker, for £7m and Gabriel Heinze, the Argentinian left-back, from Paris St Germain for £6.9m.

We needed Smithy because Ole Gunnar Solskjaer was still injured, and Diego Forlan was on his way out and moved to Villareal, in Spain, just as the new season started. That would have left us short of strikers.

Smith and Heinze are both good players, and I was pleased that we had them on board. They could only strengthen what was already a strong squad. I was confident that normal service would be resumed, and that we'd start the season well, but it didn't happen. Looking back, the preparation was far from ideal. We went to America again in pre-season, but we seemed to arrive piecemeal, with players coming out late after Euro 2004. Others were injured, and some even played with injuries. It didn't help, of course, that Rio couldn't play. He was still suspended. We couldn't afford that sort of patchy preparation, not with the programme we had at the start of the season. In the first eight days we played Arsenal in the Community Shield, Dinamo Bucharest in the qualifying stage of the Champions League and then at Chelsea on the Premiership's opening day, and we needed to be in good nick for that lot.

In America, the tournament organizers, a company called Champions World, weren't happy that big-name players like Ruud and Ronaldo were at home, resting, after playing in the European Championship. They wanted our first team, not the reserves, and the club was put under pressure to bring out the likes of Paul Scholes and Mikael Silvestre, which they did for our last game.

For United, the tournament was not the success it had been the previous summer, when we won every game. This time we were booed off the pitch after drawing 0–0 with Bayern Munich, then losing on penalties, in our first match, in Chicago. We played well against Milan, when Scholesy scored for us and Shevchenko equalized in injury time. Unfortunately we made a mess of the penalty shoot-out again and then we lost 2–1 to Celtic in Philadelphia. There were big crowds at the games, and they were taken more seriously than the old pre-season friendlies. It was good preparation, getting you right into the swing of things straightaway, but too many players were missing for us to get maximum benefit.

Usually, I don't take any notice of the Charity Shield, or Community Shield as it is called these days. If you look back at the results over the years, they are no guide to the sort of season you are going to have. In our treble year, for example, Arsenal beat us 2–1. This time, though, everybody at United took it seriously because it gave us a chance to prove that

Arsène Wenger's team, who had just gone through the season unbeaten, were not invincible after all. It was a bigger blow than it would normally have been, then, when we lost 3–1. We probably had the better of the first half, but then they killed us off with a couple of goals on the counter-attack, like they do. Smithy scored for us with a lovely dipping volley. For once, there was no aggro. It was one of the quieter games between the two sides.

Three days later, we played in Bucharest and won 2–1. We were 1–0 down and struggling a bit, but then I scored and an own-goal gave us the winner. It was quite comfortable in the end. The result was a particularly good one, because we were starting the season without some important players. We went to Chelsea for that first league game without nine members of the first-team squad. Missing were Ruud, who'd had a hernia operation, Gabriel Heinze and Cristiano Ronaldo, who were playing at the Olympics, Wes Brown, Phil Neville, Kleberson, Saha, Solskjaer and Fletcher. Keaney had to play centre-half, which of course left us below strength in midfield.

Chelsea didn't have those problems and took the lead after a quarter of an hour, when Drogba, who towered above our defenders, set up Gudjohnsen to score. We got a bollocking from the gaffer at half-time for failing to shackle Drogba.

We weren't bad, we gave them a good game, but I missed our best chance with about ten minutes left, when I grazed the post with a header. We were reasonably happy with the way we'd played, but the result was definitely a psychological blow. We'd been anxious to get off to a good start, especially against a team we knew would be title contenders, and instead we'd lost. Looking back now, it was a crucial game. If we'd won that, as we could have done, the whole season might have been a different story. At the time, though, we weren't too worried. It was only our first game, we always knew it was going to be a tough one, and we'd played quite well. There was nothing to be concerned about – yet.

We'd been keeping an eye on Chelsea's emergence as a real force for some time. For four or five years we'd been looking at the players they were signing, aware that they were getting stronger and more dangerous all the time. Now Roman Abramovich was there, with money to burn, we knew something was stirring down at Stamford Bridge.

Ken Bates used to talk about them being the Manchester United of the south, and we'd laugh, but now it really was starting to happen. They were the glamour club, causing interest and excitement with all their big stars and razz-matazz. With the money at their disposal, they could afford to go out and outbid anyone for the best players available, and we knew we had a real problem. Don't forget they were a good team even before Abramovich allowed them to spend over £200m in two years. Robben and Duff had given their attack real quality, and it was going to be tough for the rest of us right from the start.

To be honest, on that first day they weren't particularly good. The new team was still gelling, and while that process was going on they were set up defensively, looking to win 1–0, which they did a lot early on.

We won our first home game 2–1 against promoted Norwich, David Bellion and Smithy getting the goals, but much more exciting than that result was the news that we were trying to sign Wayne Rooney, from Everton. Wayne had caused a great stir with England at Euro 2004, and the news that we were prepared to pay £20m for him was a welcome indication that the club were prepared to rival Chelsea for the very best.

Before the transfer happened we played the return against Dinamo Bucharest and won easily, 3–0, for a 5–1 aggregate. Smithy scored twice in a match which saw the return of Ronaldo and Kleberson. With Ronaldo back, the gaffer gave me a rest after what had been a hard pre-season.

I was back for our second away game, at Blackburn, where Smithy was on target again in a 1–1 draw. Brad Friedel was brilliant that day, playing us on his own, but we knew this was the sort of fixture we ought to be winning. At least Alan was on fire, with five goals – some of them pretty spectacular – in his first six appearances. He knew there would be competition for places from Rooney and Ruud and wanted to make a quick impression. Playing on his own up front, with Scholesy just off him, he really enjoyed himself. He was determined to make the most of it while he had the role all to himself.

Successive draws, at home to Everton and away to Bolton, told us we were well short of the form we needed if we were to compete with Chelsea and Arsenal. Five points from our first four league games just wasn't good enough. I was disappointed and a bit worried. I knew we should be beating the likes of Everton at home. It was all right making excuses, saying we were missing Ruud, but we couldn't blame all our problems on that, not with Smithy doing as well as he was.

In the Champions League proper we were 2–0 down at half-time away to Olympique Lyon, and it took a bollocking from the gaffer to get us going. We were the better side, but we didn't defend well. The first goal we conceded was terrible: Cris, their Brazilian defender, was gifted a tap-in. Fortunately, Ruud was back by now, and he came to our rescue, scoring twice in the second half. His record in the Champions League is phenomenal, and with these two he'd broken Denis Law's record of twenty-eight European goals.

After the start we'd had, 2–2 was a decent result, and now things were looking up. Rio's suspension had finished at last, and by way of celebration we beat Liverpool 2–1 at home in the league, with Mikael Silvestre exposing their defensive shortcomings by scoring with two headers, from a free-kick and a corner. Seeing off the scousers always gives us a boost, and we won 1–0 at Tottenham in our next match, and then hammered Fenerbahce 6–2 at our place in the Champions League. That one will always be remembered as Wayne Rooney's match. Can there ever have been a more sensational debut? The gaffer wondered publicly beforehand whether it was 'fair on the lad' to plunge him straight in, and what an answer he got! Wayne announced himself with a fantastic hat-trick, all scored in the space of thirty-seven fabulous minutes.

When he arrived, he was still recovering from the broken foot that put him out of Euro 2004 just when England needed him most. He couldn't train with the rest of us, he just played the games. But as soon as he made his first appearance in the dressing room he was immediately one of the lads. Some people fit in straightaway, for others it takes time. Wayne was one of us from the first time we met him. He knew a lot of our England players already, which helped of course, but his bubbly character would make him a great mixer in any company.

His powerful physique and his confidence are the first things you notice about him. On the training pitch, the first thing that struck me about him was his ability to receive the ball with his back to goal and turn with it under control in one movement, no matter how hard it had been pinged at him. He turns so quickly and so easily, it obviously comes naturally to him. That's the mark of a top player.

Against Fenerbahce, I scored the opening goal with a

header early on, then Wayne took over. For his first he lifted the ball over the 'keeper and into the roof of the net with a nice, deft touch. The second he clattered in low, from 25 yards, and the third was a free-kick into the top corner. The power and accuracy of his shooting were awesome, and the fans really took him to their hearts that night. He was buzzing in the dressing room afterwards, getting the match ball signed by everybody, but the older lads, myself included, did our best not to let him get too carried away, and the gaffer certainly didn't make a fuss of him. He said, 'Well done, great goals' but that was it.

Is it a good thing to start as well as that? I suppose it must be, but there is a downside. When Cristiano made his debut, against Bolton, some of the things he did on the ball were unbelievable, but the crowds have expected him to do the same in every game since, which is unfair. Wayne now had to live with an even bigger burden of expectation. Because he made it look as easy, the fans were looking to him to get a hat-trick every week. That would be a problem for most players, but not him, he has been able to take it in his stride.

It was around this time, in October, that talks started about my new contract. I still had eighteen months to go on the existing one, so there was no hurry from my point of view, but the club wanted to sort out my future long term and approached my agent, Harry Swales. The thing became something of a saga, which was unfortunate, and I didn't get to sign until May, but it is club policy not to let contracts run down. That's because if a player is allowed to get into his final season he can refuse any offer that's made and effectively sell himself, on a Bosman free transfer. So it was in everyone's interests to get me tied up as quickly as possible.

278

People said I was playing for my contract, and I suppose it might have seemed that way, but the first meeting about it was in October, and I wasn't playing well then. It wasn't until Christmas time that I had a good run for about two months. In all honesty, I wasn't turning it on with a new deal in mind. You don't think about that when your existing contract still has eighteen months to run. I never thought, 'I've got to play well to get a new contract,' I don't think like that. And despite what kept apprearing in the press, there were only two meetings between Harry and the club in all. The stumbling block in the negotiations was the length of the contract. It is club policy to offer only twelve-month extensions to players over the age of thirty, which I was, but Harry maintained that I was worth an extra two years which, given that my existing contract had another year to run, meant I would be contracted for another three years in all. That would take me to the age of thirty-four, and the club's concerns on that score were the reason the thing dragged on so long. Eventually, in May, a compromise was reached, whereby for the last two years of the contract my wages will be geared to appearances and performance, which is fine by me.

It did drag on too long, but I like to think it was handled much better than Rio Ferdinand's contract talks. In April Rio's agent, Pini Zahavi, told the press that Rio was the best defender in the world, and that as such his pay should reflect that.

In fairness, nobody knew the details of the contract Rio was looking for. The way the fans looked at it, Rio was out for eight months, and the club were good to him, but this was a major deal for him, a commitment for five years. Again, the headlines ran and ran.

Back at the football, I thought the 6–2 against Fenerbahce

might be lift-off, but I was wrong. We could only draw our next two league games, at home to Middlesbrough and away to Birmingham, and in mid-October we were sixth in the table, already a daunting eleven points behind the leaders, Arsenal, who had started the season as they had finished the previous May. They were still unbeaten in the league, after seventeen months and forty-nine matches, when they came to Old Trafford on Sunday 24 October, for an extraordinary afternoon that the press came to call 'The Battle of the Buffet'.

We were near full strength at last, although Keaney was missing, and Phil Neville took his place in centre midfield. It's fair to say that we were really up for this one. The game at Old Trafford the previous season, when they'd behaved like idiots after getting a draw, was still fresh in the memory, and the two managers had stirred it up in the press, so all the ingredients were there for a real tear-up. They'd made a big thing about going fifty games undefeated, so we were all out to prevent that.

It is always going to be a real scrap when we meet them, because that's the way to play Arsenal – to get into them and tackle hard and deny them the time and space to get their passing game together. A lot of teams give them too much respect, but we'll never make that mistake. If you do that, they are good enough to take you apart. The gaffer told us to get among them from the off. A lot was made in the media of our treatment of Reyes – we were accused of singling him out for deliberate intimidation. I don't think we kicked him off the park, as Arsenal suggested, but he had been man of the match when they beat us in the Community Shield two months earlier, so what did they expect? Of course we paid him special attention. He's a good player and we had to stop him causing us the same problems all over again. He had got off to a great start in English football and was playing well, but the gaffer said he hadn't seen anyone give him a hard time, and told us to put as much pressure on him as possible. There were a few tackles that were a bit over the top, but there always will be when United and Arsenal clash. The worst one wasn't on Reyes, it was by Ruud on Ashley Cole. A typical centre-forward's tackle that got him banned for three matches for it.

The ill feeling that is always just below the surface showed itself in the first half, when Rio brought down Ljungberg as he sprinted towards our goal. Arsenal felt Rio should have been sent off, and you could see they were furious when the referee, Mike Riley, took a lenient view. We didn't allow them to play. We were more determined and yes, more physical. I have to admit we were lucky with the penalty, which was the turning point. It came in the seventy-second minute, when Wayne took a tumble as Sol Campbell moved in to challenge him. At the time I thought Sol had brought him down, but television replays proved he hadn't touched him. I think Wayne assumed he was going to get tackled and went over, and to be fair to the referee, it did look like a penalty from his angle. Ruud scored from the spot, making up for his miss the previous year, and one goal was always going to win it. Wayne got our second in added time 2–0.

The match should be remembered as the one that ended Arsenal's long unbeaten run, but for most people it sticks in the mind for something else. It all went off in the tunnel as we came off the pitch, well in front of me. I was one of the last off, and with a lot of bodies, including security men, blocking my view, I could only hear, rather than see what was going on. There was a lot of shouting from the Arsenal players about our physical approach and the dodgy penalty, and some of our lads were having a go back. In that overheated atmosphere it only needs one player to bump into another and a ruck starts. By the time I got to the dressing room it was clear something was wrong. There is food in both changing rooms after every game, and the Arsenal players seemed to have thrown most of theirs around. Sir Alex had been caught in the crossfire. Chuffed with the result, the gaffer was still smiling though!

We were on a high after that result, looking forward to going on a charge up the table, but it didn't happen. The following Saturday we lost 2–0 at Portsmouth, which I regard as our most disappointing result of the whole season. As the gaffer said afterwards, we should be going there and winning. He had a right go at us, saying nobody had played well, that we ought to be ashamed of ourselves, and that he was particularly disappointed with our finishing, which had been poor from the start of the season. Our decision-making was poor, he said. We were passing when we should be shooting and vice versa. Unfortunately, as we know now, it wasn't to get any better. Portsmouth was certainly a low point for me, I was dropped for the next four games. I didn't get the famous hairdryer treatment, my bollocking came later when he had a 'quiet word' with me, which was much worse.

We finally got it together in November, which was a great month. We played seven times, winning six and drawing the other one. The run started with a Champions League tie at home to Sparta Prague, which was my first game out of the side. Beforehand, the gaffer complained about our lack of goals. Ruud took this personally, and went out and scored all four in a 4–1 win. That made it thirty-five in thirty-six European appearances for United. I don't know why his record in Europe is so much better than it is in the Premiership, I wouldn't say he was better suited to Champions League football, it's just that every time he gets a chance in European competition he seems to put it away.

Our old mate Karel Poborsky, now playing back in Prague with Sparta, got sent off three minutes from the end for his second yellow card. He got a standing ovation for the first time at Old Trafford!

The gaffer hadn't said anything about dropping me, and I thought he was just resting me for Sparta Prague. Then he named his team for the next match, which was the derby at home to Man City, and I wasn't in it again. He called me into his office two hours before the game and said, 'I'm leaving you out.' I asked why, and he said, 'You're not playing as well as I think you should be.' I told him I thought I was doing all right, but he wasn't having it. There was a time when I would argue a lot over things like that, but over the years I've learned that he never changes his mind, so now I don't bother, I just concentrate on trying to prove him wrong. The reaction he got was probably the one he wanted. When I got back in the side, I made sure he couldn't leave me out again. I was annoyed at the time, and thought that there weren't many players who were at the top of their games, but looking back I suppose he was right, and I shouldn't have been thinking about how anyone else was playing, only about getting my own performance right.

I was on the bench for the derby but got on early and should have scored in a goalless draw, and then I missed the Carling Cup tie against Crystal Palace, which a mixture of reserves and first-team players won 2–0. I was among the subs for a 3–1 win at Newcastle, where Wayne scored twice, and finally got my place back at home to Charlton on 20 November. Determined to keep it, I scored our first goal in a 2–0 win.

We kept our run going in December, the month starting with another victory over Arsenal, in the Carling Cup. Both teams fielded young reserves and the only goal was scored by David Bellion, after just eighteen seconds, which was three seconds slower than the fastest ever scored for United, by yours truly back in 1995. A 3–0 win at home to Southampton maintained our progress in the Premiership, but then the gaffer opted to field a weakened team away to Fenerbahce in the Champions League and we lost 3–0 to opponents we'd beaten 6–2 in September. It meant we were runners-up in the group, and that we had a more difficult task in the first knockout round, where we had to play Milan. If we'd won our group it would have been Werder Bremen.

We had a good Christmas, beating Crystal Palace, Bolton and Aston Villa, and another good win, away to Middlesbrough on New Year's Day, took us into 2005 in optimistic mood, but still nine points behind the league leaders, Chelsea. At the Riverside I scored for the third game running, and the gaffer was as complimentary about my form as he had been critical after Portsmouth. At this stage we'd scored ten times in winning four games on the bounce, but all season our form came in fits and starts, and now we went three without scoring. A goalless draw at home to Spurs was a case of two points dropped, and to make matters worse my hamstring went and I missed the next three games.

In the first of these we had the embarrassment of failing to score against Exeter at Old Trafford in the third round of the FA Cup. It was pretty much a reserve team, but Tim Howard, Phil Neville, Wes Brown and Eric Djemba Djemba all played, and any eleven United put out ought to be good enough to see off non-league opposition without needing a replay. The gaffer definitely wasn't happy and had a fair bit to say about it, pointing out with his usual forcefulness that our lads hadn't created much, and that Exeter had had the better chances.

Our Carling Cup semi-final against Chelsea was next, with the first leg at Stamford Bridge. The gaffer was taking it more seriously at this stage, but still rested Rio and Keaney, with one eye on the league match away to Liverpool three days later. They were at full strength, but we played well, and were happy enough with a goalless draw. I was still out injured when we went to Anfield on the Saturday and beat the old enemy 1–0 and I was in the full first team that went to Exeter and applied ourselves properly to win the replay with goals from Ronaldo and Rooney.

The home leg of the semi-final against Chelsea was a major disappointment. We thought we'd done the hard part by holding them down there, but they came to our place and won 2–1. Their winner was a bit flukey. Frank Lampard opened the scoring after about half an hour, then we should have had a penalty when Wayne Bridge fouled Quinton Fortune inside the box. I equalized midway through the second half, getting in behind John Terry and volleying over Peter Cech's head. It could have gone either way then, and Damien Duff settled it with a free-kick from out near the left touchline which was meant as a cross, but went in at the far post. Tim Howard got a lot of stick for that goal, but Duff 'did' him with what I usually do in those situations – aim just inside the far post in the knowledge that the ball will go in if nobody gets a touch. If you do that, it's a difficult decision for the 'keeper, whether to come for the cross or not. If it goes in, they'll always get blamed.

Three days later we beat Middlesbrough 3–0 at home in the FA Cup, Wayne scoring twice, which set us up nicely for the return bout with Arsenal, at Highbury on 1 February. It was a grudge match for them, after what had happened at our place, and the trouble started before the game. As players came off the pitch in dribs and drabs after the warm-up, Vieira chased Gary Neville into the tunnel and pushed him, shouting that Nev had better not kick Reyes again, like he had at Old Trafford. When we all got back in the dressing room, Keaney heard what Vieira had done and we could see he was angry and going to do something about it. So as the teams lined up in the tunnel, waiting to go out for the game, Keaney looked Vieira in the eye and told him, 'If you want to pick on someone, make it me.' It's a small tunnel at Highbury and you wouldn't want it to kick off in there.

After all that, we were really up for it, and made it a good, fast game. It was rough and tough as well, of course, with the usual half a dozen bookings, including me for a late tackle on Ashley Cole, and Mikael Silvestre sent off midway through the second half for butting Ljungberg. Arsenal took the lead after eight minutes, when Vieira headed in powerfully from a corner taken by Henry. I equalized from 20 yards with a shot that took a deflection off Cole. I think it was going in anyway, but Cole's contact sent the 'keeper the wrong way. Bergkamp made it 2–1 to them by nut-megging Roy Carroll, then Wayne got booked, wrongly, and went berserk at the referee. He went to tackle Vieira, but pulled his leg out of the way at the last moment. Vieira went down, making out there was contact, and Wayne, who had done nothing, couldn't believe it when he got the yellow card. He went up to the ref and made his point. The papers had a right go at him the next day, for setting a bad example to youngsters everywhere. It seemed a bit hard on him to me.

To be fair, it was an aggressive game, played on the edge. There were a lot of tackles flying in and players trying to get opponents booked. It's easy to say players should watch their tempers and their behaviour, a lot harder actually to do it in the heat of the battle. There will be a referee somewhere who will make a a few headlines by sending someone off, but if you take the competitive spirit out of the game, what will you be left with? This season the gaffer has brought in a number of fiery characters to give us an edge. It was starting to look like the 1993–4 season, with similarly competitive players like Robbo, Sparky and Incey. Wayne was just the latest in a long line. Like Keaney, if you took the aggression out of his game, he'd be half the player.

I set up Ronaldo to make it 2–2, then did it again for him to put us in front for the first time. For the first one I was put through the middle and I was going to have a shot from 30 yards, but then I saw Ronaldo out of the corner of my eye. Lauren made my decision for me, really. He came to close me down and I 'megged him and found Ronaldo, who finished nicely. For the second Keaney put me through and I was racing with Vieira when I looked up and saw the 'keeper coming out. Again my decision had been made for me. I touched it past Almunia and crossed it. When I hit it, I thought the ball was going in, but it bobbled along the goalline for Ronaldo to tap it in at the far post.

Our fourth goal, for 4–2, was a lovely chip by John O'Shea, who is a better footballer than people think. The gaffer sees him as a midfielder, rather than a full-back or centre-half, where he has played most of his games for us. At one stage he was seen as the natural successor to Denis Irwin, at left-back, but then we signed Gabriel Heinze, which knocked John back a bit. He's a confident lad, but that hit him hard. Now he sees a future for himself in midfield, where he is good enough to contribute a few goals.

We won our next two games 2–0, at home to Birmingham

and away to Man City, which meant we had taken forty-two points from the last forty-eight available. That's championship form, and in any other year it would have taken us to the top of the table, but Chelsea were matching us win for win, and we were still nine points behind them. We played the Manchester derby on the Sunday, and the day before Chelsea had gone to Everton, which looked like a difficult game for them, and won 1–0. As the gaffer admitted at the time, that result was a real kick in the teeth for us. Everton were going well, looking for a Champions League place, and we really thought Chelsea might slip up at last. But any chance of that vanished when James Beattie was sent off early on.

We were actually playing better football than Chelsea at that stage in the season. They were content just to hang in there and pinch 1–0 wins, and I remember they scored two goals in four games around that time. For the derby, Ruud was out with Achilles trouble and my hamstring had started playing up in the Birmingham game the previous week. The gaffer put me on the bench, just in case, and Cristiano was among the subs, too. As it turned out, both of us were needed in the end. We went on after a dour, goalless first half, and I like to think we livened things up. We certainly gave the crowd something to shout about – I was wearing black tights to protect my hamstring! We won with Wayne's sixth goal in eight games and an own-goal from Richard Dunne.

After that, we went to Everton in the fifth round of the FA Cup. It was our third 2–0 win on the trot, and memorable mainly for the horrible reception Wayne got on his first trip back to Goodison. He expected some stick, of course, but what happened was well over the top. There was graffiti on the walls of the stadium, threatening his life, he was called 'Judas' and all sorts, and there was an unpleasant incident when he came off after the warm-up and a woman who was standing on the pitch, near the players' tunnel, said something really insulting. Wayne had a go back, and nobody could blame him.

The Everton fans' reaction was silly, I thought. All right, they didn't want him to leave, but he'd done well for them for a couple of years, and he'd hardly left them in the lurch. They got £30m for him, and by spending some of that money wisely they were able to strengthen their squad and have done well without Wayne.

It was a nasty atmosphere from start to finish – I'm told there were thirty-odd arrests. It's not usually like that when we go to Goodison, it was only Wayne going back that gave the occasion such an edge. Normally, we only get that hostility at Liverpool. This time, though, someone in the crowd threw a mobile phone at Wayne, and our goalkeeper, Roy Carroll, had his head cut open by a flying coin.

The Everton team were less of a worry than their supporters, and Cristiano made the first goal for Quinton Fortune, then scored the second himself after Nigel Martyn had spilled a free-kick from Paul Scholes.

Another impressive win – our fifth on the bounce – put us in good heart for the first knockout round of the Champions League, where we were up against the favourites, Milan, with the first leg at home. We knew Milan were very strong, but we'd lost only two of our previous twenty-seven games, so we approached the challenge in optimistic mood. We missed chances early on and they soon took charge in midfield, where Pirlo and Gattuso were outstanding. They played better than us, but we probably had more chances. Apart from Scholesy, who had two, Quinton might have scored, and Ruud came close too. What was so disappointing about losing was that the only goal, with about a quarter of an hour left, was an absolute gift. First of all Seedorf was allowed too much space and time 20 yards out, and then, when he had a shot, the ball flew straight at Roy Carroll, who failed to hold it, leaving Crespo with a tap in. At o–o we would have fancied ourselves in the San Siro, but with a goal to make up we knew it was going to be a hell of a task.

Alan Smith was on the bench a lot, behind Ruud and Wayne in the queue for starting places, but he still had an excellent first season, scoring some important goals. He's a really nice lad – not at all what you'd expect from the way he plays his football. He reminds me of Mark Hughes a bit in that. He's quiet and shy off the pitch and doesn't like doing interviews, but on the field he comes over all aggressive, and he's certainly not a shy boy there!

Looking back, I suppose we knew our last chance of overhauling Chelsea had gone when we dropped two points at Crystal Palace on 5 March. We played first and Chelsea kicked off at Norwich when we'd finished, so it was a chance to cut their lead and put some pressure on them. But we blew it. We didn't perform as we should have done, and managed only a goalless draw. Ruud had only just got back into the team after his injury was still getting back into his stride. I had a shot late on which looked as if it was going in until a late deflection took it over the bar.

The gaffer was disappointed with us afterwards. He told us we had started too slowly, that we never settled and picked up the tempo. He said we had to do better if we wanted to start winning things again. With the amount of possession we had, we should have won the game easily, but we didn't turn all our time on the ball into enough clear-cut chances. Our play in the final third of the pitch, and our final pass, let us down. We lacked a bit of composure. We were shooting when we should have passed and vice versa. They went down to ten men, which should have made it easier, but it doesn't always work out like that. They just took a winger off, put on an extra defender and kept everybody behind the ball. They settled for the draw, which I think they would have taken before the game.

We couldn't afford that slip because Chelsea had a run of easy games, playing Norwich, West Brom, Palace and Southampton, and we knew they weren't going to drop too many points there. So we needed to get as close to them as we could. Norwich actually took the lead against them that day, and if we'd won earlier, who knows what might have happened. It was hardly the ideal form to take with us into the return leg in Milan, but the gaffer was confident that we could score out there. On the day of the game, we were shown a video of the first leg, which gave us a more positive view of what had happened that night. We came off thinking we hadn't played well, but then we looked at the film of our good passages of play and saw that we had created three really good chances. After studying the video, we came out thinking we did all right. We knew we could play better than that, so maybe all was not lost after all.

After what had gone on at Palace, the gaffer stressed the need for a quick tempo. The game plan was to keep the ball and quieten the crowd for the first twenty minutes, then try to get on top in midfield through Keaney and Scholesy, with Wayne dropping in as well, and control the game. If we could do that, the gaffer said the pace we had from Ronaldo and me could cause them problems on the break. We did manage to do that a couple of times, but couldn't score. I still maintain that we are just as good as them, that there is nothing to choose between us really, other than the fact that they took their chances. It was as simple as that. It took us a while to get into our stride, but midway through the first half I had a chance and hit the post, shooting from left to right. If that had gone in, I'm sure it would have been very different. I did everything right, really, I shot across the 'keeper and couldn't have hit it any better, but it didn't go in. We weren't on the rack at any stage, and the goal they got at our place should have been prevented. Over the two games, they had four chances and we had six or seven.

Everyone was disappointed with himself that night, but while things like that hurt just as much when you get older, experience does teach you to deal with it better. You're still a bad loser, but you cope. If you analyse every performance individually, every player could have done better. As a team, we did all right, negating their system and looking dangerous at times, but it's the final ball that wins games, and that was where individuals were lacking. To be honest, there were no great deeds done this time. We didn't score in the home leg against Milan, we didn't score against Palace and we didn't score in the San Siro. We've got to look at that and ask whether we are creating enough and question individual decision-making.

The gaffer felt we'd complicated the game too much in the second half. They weren't dealing with crosses very well, and he thought we hadn't exploited that as we should have done. We were making too many passes instead of getting it out wide, crossing and attacking the ball. Everyone was very down, but by the time we got on the plane home it was a case of time moves on. We had an FA Cup tie away to Southampton in four days' time, we had to get Milan out of our heads and look forward to that.

I didn't play in that one, but the lads had no trouble without me. Southampton had caused us problems in the past, but not this time. We won 4–0 at St Mary's, and it could have been more. The new, bigger stadium is much more to our liking than The Dell, where we felt cramped and penned in, with the crowd on top of us.

The draw for the semi-finals, made the next day, kept us and Arsenal apart. We were paired with Newcastle, who were going well at the time, and Arsenal got Blackburn, whose results had been steadily improving under Sparky. They were in real danger of relegation when he took over, but he's organized the defence and packed the midfield with hustlers, as he had done with Wales. By doing that, he'd made them hard to play against.

Before the Newcastle tie, in Cardiff, we had three league games to play, and we were looking to put some sort of pressure on Chelsea, or at least get a grip on second place, ahead of Arsenal. It didn't happen. Instead, we went into a mini-crisis. We scraped a 1–0 win at home to Fulham, could only draw 0–0 with Blackburn at Old Trafford and then we lost 2–0 at Norwich, who were six points adrift at the bottom of the table. They'd lost five on the trot in the league, and hadn't kept a clean sheet for six months.

I missed that one, because of my hamstring trouble, and the gaffer rested Keaney, Ruud, Wayne Rooney and Ronaldo with one eye on the semi-final, which was eight days later. Nigel Worthington, the Norwich manager, said doing that showed an arrogant lack of respect for his team, and maybe it provided extra motivation for his players. Whatever the reason, they raised their game and we were unable to respond. It was not until the third minute of stoppage time that their 'keeper, Robert Green, had to make a save, so they were good value for their best result of the season.

We got loads of stick for that one. The gaffer was furious. It was real doom and gloom and the end of the world because it was Norwich, who had such a poor record. We were going through a sticky patch, and it just multiplied the feeling that we were really struggling. For the week afterwards, everyone was as miserable as sin. Ideally we'd have liked a game a couple of days later to get Norwich out of our system, but it was eight days before the semi-final, which was a long time to mull it over. The gaffer made it plain that he was looking for the right, angry reaction in training, and I think he got that. As a bonding exercise, he organized white-water rafting in north Wales. I didn't go because apart from my hamstring troubling me, I had a heavy cold, and a dip in a freezing river was the last thing I needed. It was only a day trip, after training on the Thursday. The papers made a lot of it, and especially the fact that they stopped for fish and chips on the way back, but a lot of teams do that sort of thing nowadays – paintballing and go-karting are quite common.

Between the two games, Keaney had his say, in the dressing room, in the papers and on TV. The gist of what he said was that all the players should be asking themselves if they were giving 100 per cent, because he wasn't sure that they were. As captain, he was entitled to put that question. Mentally, he comes from the same mould as the gaffer, and won't settle for anyone falling below the standards that have been set at the club over the years. If anybody does, he will let them know. I don't think any of the players was going out on the pitch with the intention of giving less than 100 per cent, but it is a fact that if they all do, we should be beating teams like Norwich. We didn't, we lost, and the captain has the right to ask why. He obviously thought something needed to be said to make sure we were all in the right frame of mind for the semi-final. When he said his piece in the dressing room, the gaffer just stood back and left him to it, probably agreeing with everything. But it wasn't just Keaney who spoke up – I had a few words myself, and so did Gary Neville. At times like that, the senior players should take a lead. The ones who have grown up at Man United know all about the standards expected and what it takes to win things, and ought to be passing that knowledge on to the younger lads coming through, or to players brought in from another club.

In terms of travelling, we treated the semi-final like any other away game. We flew down to Cardiff the previous day, while the Saturday semi was being played, and stayed at the hotel Wales use, the Vale of Glamorgan. Sparky had grabbed that for Blackburn, who checked out just before we arrived. My hamstring was improving every day, and I thought I'd be fit enough to play. The gaffer, though, had probably decided on his line-up on the Friday, although we didn't get to know it until the usual time, at the team meeting on the morning of the game. I'd trained on the Tuesday, but I was ill, and in bed all day on the Wednesday, and I didn't do much on the Thursday, because I was still feeling a bit rough. On the Friday and Saturday I felt OK and trained normally, but by then I think the manager had made up his mind about the team. When I spoke to him he said my recovery and preparation time had been a bit too short. I said, 'Yeah, but I feel good, and because it's the semi-final I think it's worth the risk,' and he told me he would think about it, and that I'd be one of the subs, at least.

After considering it, he said he didn't think it was worth the risk starting me, in case the injury flared up again, which could put me out of the final – if we got there. He'd been to the Millennium Stadium the previous week, to see his son, Darren, play for Wrexham in the LDV final, and thought the pitch would be too heavy for me.

Looking back, we had everything going for us as we went into the game. We'd just been beaten by Norwich, and were determined to make amends, while Newcastle had gone out of the UEFA Cup on the Thursday and were very down after that, and were also without important players like Lee Bowyer and Kieron Dyer, who were suspended. The decisive fact was that we played well. They couldn't get near Scholesy and Rooney in the first twenty minutes, Ronaldo had the beating of their left-back, Babayaro, and we seized the initiative right from the start and never lost it. We battered them really and could have won by a bigger margin than 4–1. They were never in it.

I felt sorry for Butty. He's an old mate, and normally I'd have made a point of speaking to him afterwards, but he was so down that I didn't think I should. Newcastle's season had gone down the pan in the space of four days. I tried to ring him later, but didn't get through.

In the dressing room in Cardiff, the champagne was out. We were in the FA Cup final, which is always a cause for celebration. When we got there the previous season I told myself to enjoy it because it could be my last time, now we were back again. We flew back to Manchester about seven o'clock that night. Someone suggested we should go for a drink, but we all went our separate ways. Some of the lads had wives and kids with them, I had a couple of mates. My mum hadn't come down this time, but my family from Cardiff were all there – ten or eleven of them.

As a team, we found ourselves in a déjà vu situation. Twelve months earlier we'd been out of it in the league and out of Europe, with only the FA Cup left to play for, and here we were again. The scenario was a bit of a downer, or at least it certainly was for me. Liverpool were seeing off Juventus in the Champions League and Chelsea were beating Bayern Munich, and we weren't involved, so just as I was starting to forget our defeat by Milan it was all brought back to me, and I found myself watching Liverpool and Chelsea on telly and thinking, 'How I wish I was playing in this game.' So then I had to get it out of my system all over again.

The semi-final win should have been just the tonic we needed, but three days later we went to Everton and lost again in the league, big Duncan Ferguson getting the only goal. We had now gone three games without scoring in the Premiership, and it was to be 24 April before any of our players got into double figures, which was a terrible statistic, given the attacking players we had at the club.

I felt sorry for Ruud because he'd been out injured a long time, and I could identify with his situation. When I started playing in the first team I had two or three seasons when I hardly missed a game. I was flying, but then I began to suffer with injuries and I knew what Ruud was going through. He found it took longer than he expected to get back into the swing of things.

Ruud is the ultimate professional, but he sees himself only as a goalscorer. If he's not scoring goals he feels he's not doing his job. If we come off having won 4–0 and he's not scored, he's not happy. He was like it during the 2004 Cup final. We were leading 1–0 at half-time, but if you looked at him in the dressing room you'd have thought we were 3–0 down. 'Ruud, you'll get your chances in the second half,' I told him, 'don't worry,' and of course he ended up scoring twice.

Chelsea won the league with three matches to spare, by beating Bolton 2–0 at the Reebok. The game was live on Sky TV, but we didn't see it. We were travelling down to London by train at the time, for our match away to Charlton the following day. When we arrived at the hotel I just caught the end of the match, but when I saw the score I switched the telly off straightaway. I couldn't bear seeing them celebrate. Don't get me wrong, I wasn't favouring Arsenal. It didn't matter to me who won the title if we didn't. That's what made the endplay unbearable – again it wasn't us who won it.

For a long time earlier in the season people said that it could be the title decider when Chelsea came to Old Trafford, but when they did, on 10 May, they were already champions, and the gaffer decided our players should form a guard of honour and clap them on to the pitch. It wasn't popular with some of the lads. I wasn't playing, which I wasn't happy about. When I asked the gaffer why, he just said he wanted to try Wayne Rooney on the left, and I sensed there and then that I wouldn't be starting the Cup final. At least missing the Chelsea game meant I didn't have to join in the honour guard thing. Chelsea had done it for us in 2002, and it was decided that we should reciprocate. I don't think you'd find us doing it for Arsenal, or if we did we'd give them all a slap, rather than a clap, as they ran out!

We didn't play badly, but they still beat us 3–1. They rested John Terry and Didier Drogba, both their full-backs were out and neither Arjen Robben nor Damien Duff played, but they played with the confidence of champions and kept the ball more than we did.

At the final whistle, we did the lap of honour that we do after the last home game every season, but we did it in a near-deserted stadium. The fans were understandably disappointed, and a lot of them didn't hang around to watch. We got the message and we'll move heaven and earth to avoid that experience again.

There was one more league match to play before the Cup final, away to Southampton, where we won 2–1. I was brought back to rest Ronaldo, and I suppose if I'd played out of my skin and scored a couple of goals I might have forced my way into the team for Cardiff, but to be honest I didn't stand out on the day. After the Chelsea game, I couldn't see the gaffer doing anything but playing Ronaldo and Rooney in the wide positions. He'd made his intentions clear. I could have played elsewhere, but Darren Fletcher was in, to strengthen the midfield, and that meant there was no room for me. Arsenal are very left-sided, and Fletcher was picked to provide insurance against that. I could understand that, and I thought it was right to play him on the right, but I believe I should have been in the team somewhere else.

I didn't go to the manager at any stage to ask if I'd be playing in Cardiff, that's not how it works at United. I carried on as normal, hoping I would be playing, but deep down, I knew I wouldn't be. Sometimes you can tell from training who's in and who's not. The first team often wear bibs when they play against the rest in practice, or the guys taking all the set pieces will know they're in. This time, though, there were none of those indications because the gaffer mixed it up more than usual, probably to keep us all sharp.

We trained at Carrington on the Wednesday, then flew down to Cardiff that afternoon. That gave us three nights in the hotel before the final, and a lot of time to think about what the team would be. There were three of us in limbo – me, Gary Neville and Alan Smith – all hoping to play but not really expecting to, and we spent a lot of time talking about our respective chances. Nev wasn't fully fit and Smudger knew Ruud would probably play instead. We didn't find out for certain until the morning of the game. There was this knock on the door of my hotel room at about 10.30, and I knew who it was straightaway. I could tell from the gaffer's face that it wasn't good news. He explained that it was a difficult situation, that he was having to leave out an experienced player who couldn't have given any more for the club. He said it was a hard decision for him to make, but he wasn't going to play me. There was no point in arguing with him, I've learned that over the years, but I told him I was upset, and didn't agree with what he was doing. I said I always played well against Arsenal, that obviously I wanted to play in the Cup final, and I felt I deserved to. That was it. There was no arguing, no shouting, I just put my point across and he said he understood how I felt. He was broadly sympathetic and accepted that I had a proven track record of playing well in big games, but the bottom line was that he thought he had to go with Fletcher, Rooney and Ronaldo. The last place had been between me and Ronaldo, and he felt Ronny was playing better than me at the time.

In the Millennium Stadium there are giant television screens at either end, and as I took my place on the bench, just before the kick-off, I remember glancing up and seeing this giant close up of me with a face like thunder. I'd been quite calm and focused on the team winning until I sat down. That's when it really hit me that I wasn't playing in the Cup final. It had never happened before, and it really got to me in that moment. To say I wasn't happy would be an understatement. I felt as I looked on that screen. Pissed off. It was the FA Cup final, and there'd have been something wrong with it if I wasn't.

Once the game started, I knew I had to be up for it, ready to go on if anybody was injured in the first few minutes, but I wasn't happy. It was the Cup final, it was against Arsenal. I'd been desperate to play and here I was, watching others. It kept coming back to me that my best game all season had been against Arsenal, at Highbury. The thought of what I could do against them made it all the more disappointing.

I have to be fair and admit that Rooney and Ronaldo were outstanding, going past Lauren and Ashley Cole virtually at will and creating chances. The amount of possession we had was unbelievable, and at half-time it was going so well that the gaffer just said, 'Keep getting the ball to Rooney and Ronaldo, let them do their stuff, and we'll be OK.'

Arsenal's team, and the way they played, surprised us. With Thierry Henry unfit, we thought they'd start with Robin Van Persie up front, but they went in with Dennis Bergkamp as the lone striker, which was a big ask for a thirty-six-year-old. I suppose they felt they had to try something a bit different because we'd beaten them three times earlier in the season.

For us, the chances kept coming, but none of them was taken. When it was still goalless with twenty minutes to go, I was dying to get on. Robert Pires was playing right midfield, and he's hardly the best defender around, so it was made for me, but I just seemed to spend most of the second half warming up. It's a strange feeling, sitting on the bench, waiting for your chance. First and foremost, you want your team to win, but you want to be part of it as well, and you know that's not going to happen if they're scoring four or five.

About five minutes from the end of normal time I was warming up behind the goal when Freddy Ljungberg somehow cleared Ruud's close-range header off the line, via the crossbar. How he kept that one out I'll never know, and the thought occurred then that maybe it wasn't going to be our day.

When the ninety minutes were up, I walked over to the centre circle to wish the lads luck for extra time, and the gaffer said, 'Get stripped, you're on.' A couple of my first touches were a bit slack. Getting on like that isn't easy, people expect you to be fresh and to make an impact against tired opponents, but it's hard to get into the match speed.

No matter how much warming-up you've done, it takes time to adjust. I did OK, I made a couple of runs in between Lauren and Touré, and Scholesy picked me out, but as soon as I'd done that Arsenal changed things and moved Vieira on to my side instead of Pires. He is obviously much better defensively, but he was tiring, and I still felt that if I got the ball, I could do some damage. Getting the ball was the problem. Arsenal were content just to keep possession and wait for penalties, so the tempo didn't suit the way I play. It was too stop-start.

I did manage to create a good chance for Ruud, but it didn't come off. The story of our season, really. In extra time Ronaldo and Rooney were tiring, understandably, so we weren't getting so much joy down the wings, but I still felt we could get the one goal which was always going to be enough. We didn't, of course, but when it went to penalties it was still fifty-fifty, still everything to play for.

We practise penalties quite often in training. Taking them is all about confidence, not how good a player is, or what position he plays. If you feel confident about it, you take one. The gaffer and Carlos Queiroz decided on the order, on the basis that you always put your best penalty-takers first. They asked the usual suspects if they fancied it, and got the replies they expected. I would have taken my turn, but there were others in front of me. Ruud will always be up for it, and he made it look easy. Lauren scored for 1–1, then Scholesy had his kick saved by Jens Lehmann. My old mate was devastated. I couldn't think of anything to say to him that would help.

I wasn't alone in being lost for words. We were all gutted, and the gaffer found it hard to come up with anything appropriate to say. I think losing hit the younger players hardest. The likes of Rooney, Ronaldo and Fletcher are

302

nowhere near as experienced as me, Keaney and Nev when it comes to dealing with disappointment, and it was up to us to help them cope. I went up to each of them in turn and said, 'Look, don't blame yourself, you couldn't have done any more, you were brilliant today. Shit happens.' They weren't in the mood to listen, they were so down, but you do everything you can to comfort your mates.

Personally I kept thinking it was all so different from twelve months earlier, when we were the ones doing the lap of honour. Now we had to stand there and watch Arsenal, our biggest rivals, cavorting around. We tried to tell ourselves that we were unlucky, that we'd been the better team, but it was no consolation really. Clutching at straws, I suppose the match should give us heart for next season, because we played well and were better than a good Arsenal team.

From the stadium we went straight back to our hotel, the Holland House, near Cardiff prison. Our best-ever party was after we'd lost the Cup final to Everton, back in 1995, and this one wasn't bad either. It sometimes works like that, with people thinking, 'Fuck it, let's have a great night, forget about it and just enjoy ourselves.' Nev organized a drink for the players and the staff only, on the first floor of the hotel. We had forty-five minutes together, as a team, before we went and joined the families. We chatted among ourselves, and tried to cheer ourselves up. Everybody kept telling one another, 'Right, we'll forget it and have a good night,' but in those circumstances you go from banter and forced laughter to awkward silence and then: 'How the hell did we lose that game?' You try to enjoy yourself, but the result keeps coming back to you.

Eventually we joined our families and guests for the real party. Stacey was there, along with my friend Stuart and his girlfriend. My mum was due to come but she was ill in bed with a chest infection and missed the final. I went to bed sometime between one-thirty and two a.m., but a few of the lads stayed out later.

We flew back to Manchester that lunchtime, by which time we all just wanted to get away on holiday and take a complete break from football. On the Monday I went to Marbella for a week with Stacey, leaving Mum to look after Libby. At Manchester airport we got in the lift and three scousers got in – they were on their way to the European Cup final, in Istanbul. They took great delight in telling me they were 'made up' when they saw us lose in Cardiff, so I said, 'I'll be made up when you get beaten on Wednesday.' There were three of them so I was praying the lift didn't get stuck!

Liverpool won in Istanbul, of course. After that, I didn't buy a paper for a week.

The Future

There was an obvious temptation to talk about the summer of 2005 as a watershed for Manchester United. The club had changed ownership, taken over by the Glazer family, from America, and players who had provided the backbone of the team for many years, such as myself, Roy Keane, Paul Scholes and Gary Neville, were now senior players.

But it would be stretching the point too far, though, to describe it as the end of an era. The gaffer is criticized only now because of the success he has had in the past. When people suggest it's time for a change, I always ask, 'Who are you going to bring in instead?' and the answers I get are unconvincing, to say the least. Sir Alex knows the club inside out, he knows the players better than they know themselves, he has bought with the future in mind and he wants to see the team through the present transition. He is still as vigorous and as passionate as ever, and I see no evidence that the fires that burn within him have dimmed in any way.

The players still want him in charge, providing all-important continuity and stability where it matters most. Everybody was disappointed with 2004–5, but it's not as if we haven't won anything for years. We were Premiership champions in 2003, won the FA Cup in 2004 and basically we're a young side who will learn and improve.

In my first full season, when we lost out on the title to Leeds, we came back stronger and won it the next time. Sometimes you need disappointments to spur you on to greater things, and I think that will be the case for young men like Rooney, Ronaldo, Ferdinand and Fletcher in 2005–6.

We have played a different style over the past couple of seasons. We've learned the hard way that against the top teams – the Milans, Arsenals and Chelseas – games are won in midfield, where keeping possession is the key. We've got the players to do that, but we're still learning and adapting to the new system, and while we do that consistency is proving elusive. That said, missing chances, hitting the post from 3 or 4 yards, isn't about tactics, it's about concentration. Truthfully, it's about players not doing their job properly.

Coming third in the Premiership for the third time in four seasons and ending 2004–5 empty-handed were unacceptable, showing how far we had fallen from our position as unarguably the best team in the country in the decade between 1993 and 2003, when we won the title on eight occasions. New ownership may be the spur we need to kick on, who knows?

With Malcolm Glazer, we have to wait and see. There's been a great deal of speculation about the future, and I sympathize with the fans' concern, but as a player I'm more interested in the manager I'm playing for, and the suggestions that the takeover saga affected the team's form in the second half of 2004–5 are well wide of the mark. When players go out on the pitch they're focused on football, not share prices. That said, it is a relief that the situation has finally been resolved. It wouldn't have done us any good to go into the new season under a cloud of uncertainty. If we're going to catch Chelsea, we need to be able to concentrate totally on football, with no off-the-field distractions.

It was obvious that something pretty big needed to be done to make up the ground lost to Chelsea and Arsenal. Chelsea were streets ahead of us in 2004–5, when they finished eighteen points better off and won the league with three matches to spare. Why? Because they had a bigger squad and played with more consistency. We thought they would have a blip at some stage, which would enable us to catch them, but they never did. The inevitable injuries and suspensions didn't bother them because they had so many good players. For example, when Arjen Robben was injured, Joe Cole came in and played brilliantly.

The gaffer acted quickly to remedy our most obvious weakness in June 2005 by signing Edwin Van der Saar, the vastly experienced Dutch goalkeeper, from Fulham. Stability at the back is an essential requirement for any team looking to challenge for honours, and in Cech, Chelsea had the same 'keeper all season.

Just as important as any reinforcements is the need for key players to stay fit and available. Chelsea had that with Cech, John Terry and Frank Lampard, whereas we were without Roy Keane, Rio Ferdinand and Ruud Van Nistelrooy at vital times.

Ruud suffered after his injuries, but I'm sure he'll come back even better for that. A little bit of adversity can make you a stronger person, and I think that will be true in his case. He is a strong character mentally, so he'll be OK.

Roy Keane is a different type of player now. When he first came to United it was as an attacking, goalscoring midfielder; now he sits in front of the back four, screening the defence, which is a job he could do for a few years yet. Claude Makelele does it brilliantly for Chelsea without getting out of his own half. Makelele's contribution tends to get overlooked, but he's the one who gives the others the freedom to play.

There has been a lot of talk about Keaney becoming manager of United one day, and I can see that happening somewhere down the line. He knows a lot about the game, he articulates that knowledge very vocally, he commands respect and can draw the best out of others. He's got all those qualities going for him, but you just never know who is going to make it and who isn't when they turn to management. What I would say is that Keaney has got all the credentials, and everyone says he is quite like the present manager in his attitudes and make-up, which I think is right.

On a personal level, family life just gets better all the time. We're moving in to a new house I'm having built, back in Worsley, in the summer of 2006, and we're really looking forward to that. We've been in the apartment in Manchester for two years, and it will be great for Libby to have a garden and a permanent home in the surroundings where I grew up. I'll definitely feel more comfortable there, with Mum just up the road and Stacey's mum not far away. I can't wait for the three of us to settle down and be happy in that house. Then hopefully there will be an addition or two to the family.

Professionally, it still means everything to me to play for Manchester United. The pride I have in playing for the world's greatest club, and their fans, has never diminished in any way down the years, and fortunately the feeling seems to be mutual. Whenever I'm walking the streets or in the pub the reaction is great. People come up to me and shake my hand and tell me how much they've enjoyed seeing me play. The thing I find most gratifying is that it's people of all ages. Young kids want to talk to me, lads of my age like to have a word, and old men are appreciative, too. I get most satisfaction from the older ones, especially ex-players. I was at Mossley, watching my brother play, and this old-timer came up to talk to me. He'd played for Mossley donkey's years ago. 'I was a left-winger,' he said, 'and I've followed your career with great interest. I rate you as the best left-winger in the world. I used to watch the Busby Babes and then Best, Law and Charlton, and you're right up there with all of them. Apart from that I like the way you have conducted yourself.' This old boy must have been at least seventy-five, and for him to take the time out to say things like that was lovely, very moving. He'd seen so many great players, so many great teams, and his opinions deserved respect and meant a lot to me.

I think people know what Manchester United mean to me, and that I wouldn't want to play anywhere else. Before the contract was sorted out, when I wasn't sure how keen the club were to keep me, I did have to think about what it would be like to play somewhere else, but I definitely didn't fancy it, and now I'm fully committed to finishing my career at United. The bottom line is that you've got to be happy, and I don't think I would have been happy going to any other club in England. If I had gone, it would have had to be abroad, but fortunately it's not a decision I've had to make. I don't ever intend to.